PRAISE FOR

RISE IN RECOVERY

"Addiction can be the gateway to a spiritual awakening if we tap and reveal the deep underlying spiritual hunger. In this way, Kimberley Berlin offers a new beginning, a trailhead on the road to spiritual recovery. Bravo to Berlin for knowing and supporting the possibility in all of us for spiritual growth and discovery!"

—Lisa Miller, PhD, Columbia University professor and author of *The Awakened Brain: The New Science of Spirituality and Our Quest for an Inspired Life*

"Addiction imprisons our spirit, and the sign of true healing is to live from greater wholeness and freedom. *Rise in Recovery: The Spiritual Path for Healing Addiction* is a beautiful and wise guide, offering the practices and teachings that serve an authentic path to recovery."

—Tara Brach, author of *Radical Acceptance* and *Trusting the Gold*

"*Rise in Recovery: The Spiritual Path for Healing Addiction* is a passionate, well-researched, and pragmatic exploration of the power of spiritual practices in healing the mind, body, and spirit from the torment of addictive processes. Yet, this is no traditional religious discourse on addiction recovery. Berlin interweaves her personal story with an extensive, diverse portrayal of various expressions of spirituality. From ancient Eastern scripture, yoga, meditation, and Internal Family Systems (IFS) psychotherapy to traditional Twelve Step practices, Berlin offers a thought-provoking invitation to reexamine the influence of 'spirit' upon the healing journey. Written with heartfelt compassion for clients and valuable insights for clinicians, *Rise in Recovery* is a compelling read for anyone interested in addictive process recovery."

—Cece Sykes, author of *Internal Family Systems Therapy for Addictions*

"*Rise In Recovery: The Spiritual Path for Healing Addiction* is an essential book for anyone engaged in or interested in learning about the process of recovering from addiction. Kimberley Berlin demystifies spirituality and demonstrates how it can be incorporated into anyone's life, regardless of religious or spiritual background, to help them grow more deeply and nourish the soul. This book will help to further recovery under the bedrock of a solid foundation based on practical spirituality."

—Dr. Anita Gadhia-Smith, author of *From Addiction to Recovery: A Therapist's Personal Journey* and *How to Heal Emotional Trauma: 7 Keys To Finding Freedom And Self-Worth*

"With great wisdom and inspiring passion, Kimberley La Farge Berlin invites us to reclaim our true nature and live the spiritual life that is most meaningful for our own unique journey. *Rise in Recovery: The Spiritual Path for Healing Addiction* is a welcomed voice in recovery literature. This wonderful book is rich throughout, with insightful information on the vital benefits of implementing a spiritual practice in one's recovery while also providing the reader with tangible, accessible, and inviting examples of how to do so.

"With her deep knowledge, understanding, and integration of IFS, the Twelve Steps, and other recovery programs, along with thousands of years of collective wisdom from numerous spiritual traditions from around the world, Kimberley bestows upon the reader countless paths with which to begin or renew a spiritual path of recovery."

—Christopher Ratte, LCSW, certified IFS psychotherapist, senior IFS trainer

"*Rise In Recovery: The Spiritual Path for Healing Addiction* author Kimberley La Farge Berlin has captivated audiences on my *Addiction and Recovery* shows and helped hundreds of people seeking a new path in their own journey from addiction. I myself have used many of the tools and coping skills I've learned from Kimberley in my own recovery. Her humanness and empathy shine bright against the stark science surrounding drug addiction and alcoholism as it takes its toll on America and its youth."Berlin's ability to share new freedom from the traumatic injury caused by addiction has benefitted hundreds of my viewers who listen as she shares her own experience, hope, and strength. *Rise In Recovery* sets a new standard in treatment, bringing hope to the hopeless, dreams instead of dread to the lost, and a new life for those who have nearly lost their own."

—Christopher LoDrago, host of *Addiction and Recovery* on Recovery Channel, YouTube

"This is an honest and comprehensively researched book on how spirituality is an important aspect of the path of recovery. Most of us shift toward recovery from the depths of despair, and in our struggle to be free of the misery of addiction, many of us have some kind of experience where a deeper meaning is revealed to us. Unexpectedly, we connect to our innate way of knowing. This becomes our religionless spirituality. Kimberley shares numerous research and objective evidence on such subjective and personal spiritual experiences. Her personal and professional path (neuroscience, psychotherapy, Internal Family Systems) brings her to an instinctive recognition that the source of healing is the Self. She offers beautiful guidance on the myriad ways we can connect to this spiritual Self through the natural world, daily meditation, prayer, body movement, and stillness.

"I wholeheartedly welcome this book as our country reels from the revelations of the pharmaceutical industry's culpability in the opioid crisis. Kimberley asks the all-important question, 'Why would we trust an industry that profited from such a devastating epidemic to turn around and then treat it with the same approach?' I appreciate that she embraces multiple perspectives and practices to guide us toward including spiritual practices. Her approach is so practical. She asks us, 'How would you change your current daily schedule to bring spiritual practices to your life?' and then reports that several studies show that a minimum of ten minutes of meditation is sufficient to change our mind and brain. So today, I will take those ten minutes, soften my belly, breathe, and settle into the healing space of sustainable calm."

—Durga Leela, founder of Yoga of Recovery, author of *Yoga of Recovery: Integrating Yoga and Ayurveda with Modern Recovery Tools for Addiction*

"Anchored in extensive research and personal reflection, *Rise in Recovery* is a profound roadmap for healing. A brilliant scholar and passionate therapist, Kimberley Berlin insists that lasting addiction recovery must be an integrative approach to changing habits and mindsets while focusing on a connection to inner knowing through deep spiritual practice. She offers this essential and practical resource for mental health practitioners, clients, and anyone whose loved one suffers from addiction."

—Ann Batchelder, author of *Craving Spring: A Mother's Quest, a Daughter's Depression, and the Greek Myth that Brought Them Together*

"In this groundbreaking exploration into the depths of addiction and the transformative power of spirituality, Ms. Berlin masterfully bridges the gap between ancient wisdom and modern neuroscience. This book is a beacon of hope, offering a new lens through which to view the journey of recovery, not just as a battle against a physical or neurological disorder but as a profound opportunity for spiritual awakening and renewal. I wholeheartedly recommend *Rise in Recovery: The Spiritual Path for Healing Addiction* to not only those navigating their own path out of addiction but also to practitioners, families, and anyone interested in the profound interplay between our spiritual and physical selves."

—Marianne Styler, MD, certified IFS therapist and consultant, ICF certified professional coach

"In *Rise in Recovery: The Spiritual Path for Healing Addiction*, Kimberley Berlin, LCSW, explains that trauma is often one of the root causes of addiction. Through real-life examples and summaries of available research, she then lays out why some form of spirituality that strengthens the inner self is a key component of recovery. Berlin posits that spiritual practice is not limited to a traditional understanding of 'religion' and that even breath work alone can qualify. Part 2 of the book then shows how to begin crafting one's own spiritual journey. This book is a useful tool for anyone who seeks to understand or overcome addiction."

—Jennifer E. Hassel, author of *Badass Grief: Changing Gears, Moving Forward*

"Kimberley La Farge Berlin shares a powerful and inspiring journey of resilience, redemption, and transformation. Through candid storytelling, she takes readers on a deeply personal exploration of addiction, trauma, and the search for healing. Berlin's honesty and vulnerability are striking, offering valuable insights into the complexities of addiction and recovery. Berlin masterfully weaves together ancient wisdom, contemporary research and science, and personal anecdotes to offer readers a comprehensive understanding of spirituality's role in fostering inner peace, resilience, and, again, healing. What a wonderful blending of heart and mind! Overall, *Rise in Recovery: The Spiritual Path for Healing Addiction* is a must-read that offers hope, guidance, and encouragement to anyone navigating the challenges of addiction and seeking a path to recovery."

—Mechelle Wingle, founder and owner of *The Wholeness Network*; Host of *The Wholeness Network Podcast*

"More than a guide to treating addiction, *Rise in Recovery: The Spiritual Path for Healing Addiction* offers a holistic approach to healing the soul, mind, and body from addiction through the rich, spiritual practices of multiple faiths and traditions, including meditation, prayer, mantras, and yoga. Kimberley also offers comprehensive resources to enhance any person's spiritual life, whether in recovery or not, to bring hope and gratitude into each day."

—Christine P. Corrigan, author of *Again: Surviving Cancer Twice with Love and Lists*

"This is a powerful and moving read . . . combining heartfelt personal experience, cutting-edge research, master clinical acumen, and practical tools for long-lasting recovery. I highly recommend this book to anyone suffering from the soul sickness of addiction and their loved ones who have been impacted."

—Adena Hope Bank, LCSW, LISAC, BCETS, CP, author of *Covert Emotional Incest; The Hidden Sexual Abuse, A Story of Hope and Healing*

"In *Rise in Recovery: The Spiritual Path for Healing Addiction*, author Kimberley Berlin provides a refreshing and transformational perspective on addiction and recovery. Not only does Berlin thoughtfully connect with readers using true stories that are sure to resonate, but she paves a new and profound pathway to living in peace. First is the comprehensive understanding of addiction, and then the spiritual journey to true healing. This is really a book about life and how our purpose is to know our best selves and beyond."

—Ryan Lindner, author of *The Half-Known Life: What Matters Most When You're Running Out of Time*

"Kimberley Berlin has captured the essence of what I call 'the experiential metaphysics of healing and transformation.' I'm always amazed when a writer captures so much of my own story of healing despite the very different events, places, and people. In reading her book, you may realize that we're not all that different, after all, nor are we all that far apart."*Rise in Recovery: The Spiritual Path for Healing Addiction* is an important contribution to the experiential science of addiction treatment and recovery. Kimberley's personal story of healing is combined with evidence-based research and abundant practical resources from a wide range of spiritual traditions. Whether you are struggling with an addiction yourself or in a relationship with someone who is, Kimberley's book will help you open doors to your own inner healing and growth."

—Vincent Terreri, MS, LPC, author of *Ginger Befriends Her Monster* and *Ginger Heals Her Monster,* illustrated books for families to understand and practice the Internal Family Systems model

"Kimberley L. Berlin, a level III integrated family psychotherapist, devoted a large part of her career and her heart to helping our veterans when they returned from war. The tragedy of war continues when our vets come home suffering from not only physical injuries but also traumatic, emotional, and mental injuries. This has become a significant national security problem, morally and practically, as recruitment has cratered and fentanyl deaths rapidly increase.

"In her groundbreaking book, *Rise in Recovery: The Spiritual Path for Healing Addiction,* Berlin shares her personal story, which informs her compassion, empathy, and experience. She offers a new approach to help secure a new beginning for those who cannot now see a way forward.

"The methods she discusses are miraculous for those who have lost faith in the existence of miracles. Her groundbreaking studies began when she was a member of the White House staff, continued through her work at the Department of Defense and US Health and Human Services, and continue today with this book, *Rise in Recovery: The Spiritual Path for Healing Addiction.* Our veterans, as well as others who have suffered trauma, would greatly benefit from the new approach and treatment Berlin has pioneered."

—Michael Ledeen is a former consultant to the National Security Council, a former special advisor to the Secretary of State and the Department of Defense, and a former scholar at CSIS, AEI, and FDD. He is the *New York Times* bestselling author of *Accomplice to Evil: Iran and the War Against the West*

Rise in Recovery: The Spiritual Path for Healing Addiction

by Kimberley La Farge Berlin, LCSW

© Copyright 2024 Kimberley La Farge Berlin, LCSW

ISBN 979-8-88824-298-8

All rights reserved. No part of this publication may be reproduced, stored in a retrieval system, or transmitted in any form or by any means—electronic, mechanical, photocopy, recording, or any other—except for brief quotations in printed reviews, without the prior written permission of the author.

Published by

3705 Shore Drive
Virginia Beach, VA 23455
800-435-4811
www.koehlerbooks.com

KIMBERLEY LA FARGE BERLIN, LCSW

RISE
IN RECOVERY

*The Spiritual Path for
Healing Addiction*

VIRGINIA BEACH
CAPE CHARLES

DEDICATION

To Don, the love of my life,
without you, I never would have come this far.

To Margaret because you "saw" this book
and believed I could do it.

TABLE OF CONTENTS

Foreword 1

Part One 3

    Introduction 5

    Chapter One: Understanding Addiction 9

    Chapter Two: One Story of Recovery 26

    Chapter Three: Foundations of Spirituality 41

    Chapter Four: Know Your Brain, Know Your Mind 53

    Chapter Five: The Grounding of Spiritual Practice 70

Part Two 91

    Chapter Six: Creating Spiritual Recovery 93

    Chapter Seven: Breath is Your Life (Pranayama) 112

    Chapter Eight: Meditation, Mindfulness
    & Contemplation 128

    Chapter Nine: Prayer & Mantra 143

    Chapter Ten: Body Recovery 167

    Chapter Eleven: Living the Spiritual Life 193

Acknowledgments 199

APPENDIX 1: Daily Spiritual Practices.. 201

APPENDIX 2: Mantras and their Translations (Unedited)........................ 205

APPENDIX 3: Prayers (Unedited) 221

APPENDIX 4: Resources... 235

BIBLIOGRAPHY.. 249

NOTES.. 261

FOREWORD

When it comes to mental health, we are living in a time of crisis. Addiction is one of the most detrimental and deadly public health issues we face today, and it is out of control. To heal individually and collectively, our understanding of addiction and how to recover from it must evolve.

With *Rise in Recovery: The Spiritual Path for Healing Addiction*, Kimberley Berlin has answered the call of the hour.

In the pages of this book, you will find a critical upgrade to contemporary perspectives on treating addiction. First, if we are to overcome addiction, we must understand that the mind, body, and spirit all work together as one unified system. There is no physical or mental solution for addiction without including the spiritual aspect of the human experience.

Berlin brings together science, psychology, spirituality, and mind-body practices. These ingredients form the basis for an effective solution to the formidable challenge of recovering from addiction in all its manifestations.

Rare is the Western-trained therapist who has recognized the spiritual dimension of health and healing and its necessity in the treatment of addiction. It is one thing to train in school as a therapist. It is quite another thing to have personally experienced the depths of addiction, to have survived it, and to turn those lessons into spiritual wisdom that can be passed on. Like a bodhisattva, Berlin has returned from those depths to share her hard-earned wisdom and to lighten the load of people who are struggling with mental health and addiction issues, which is to say . . . almost everybody.

This book is rendered even more powerful by its humanness.

I was riveted as I made my way through Berlin's personal story in chapter 2, which explains so much about the origin of her wisdom and depth of experience. By sharing her personal story of addiction so vulnerably, you can't help but feel close to her. She becomes someone you are rooting for. At the same time, she is a wisdom keeper who carries an important message for you. If in chapter 2, when you hear her story, you feel empathy and connection, by chapter 11, you realize this is someone who has elevated herself into wisdom, and you are being invited along.

One does not have to identify as an "addict" or even as a "person in recovery" to relate.

This book will hold value for anyone who struggles with patterns of belief and behavior that no longer serve them.

Each chapter includes a section called *Mindfulness Moment* with questions for reflection that bring the teachings home and focus the reader on their own direct experience. There are also three appendixes chock-full of transformational practices and resources that you should not miss.

If you take the time to adopt these evolutionary principles and practices into your life, this book will be a catalyst for your continued healing and transformation.

Kimberley Berlin has truly created something special. Enjoy it, and please pass it on.

With love and gratitude,

Tommy Rosen, best-selling author of *Recovery 2.0: Move Beyond Addiction and Upgrade Your Life.*

PART ONE

INTRODUCTION

For the past twenty years, I've counseled addicts and alcoholics and sought to guide them from self-loathing and degradation to a sober, rewarding, and stable life. I worked at inpatient and outpatient facilities, clinics, and group practices, where I learned what to do and what not to do. In 2014, I broke away from traditional approaches to addiction and opened a private practice that allows me to process healing in a way that I instinctively knew would restore clients to a life of health and joy.

For me, the many challenges of recovery are personal; I understand my client's confusion and pain because I, too, once sank into the morass of drugs and alcohol and struggled for years to find a path back to sanity. The work of numerous experts in the field has lit the pathway for my recovery and subsequent career. Their work has influenced my approach to psychotherapy and healing, making me a better person and, I hope, a better therapist.

My path of spirituality was born decades ago amid chaos and trauma. Something within me sought the solace of a church and, not long after, the peace that yoga and meditation bring. Despite days and nights of obliteration from drugs and alcohol, that "something" kept bringing me back to the cushion and the mat. Richard Schwartz, PhD, who developed Internal Family Systems (IFS), calls this the *Self*. It is a part of us that is intrinsically "pure joy and peace,"[1] from which all personal healing comes forth. That undefinable internal voice directed me to take hold of every spiritual tool from the East and the West and throw myself headlong into the teachings. What I didn't know at all, I began to appreciate. When I already thought I knew, I learned more. The spiritual path saved my life.

When I entered the field of addiction treatment as a therapist, I was determined to share this knowledge with my peers. It was met with great resistance because, at the time, the "medical model" predominated clinical thinking. I was often called on the carpet for my attempts, and one particular scolding resulted in a personal wake-up call (included in the chapter on "Body Recovery"). The prospect of breath techniques, yoga, or prayer as a tool for healing was too far out for the average clinic or center. A shift finally occurred when technology advanced in neuroscience to capture the effects of these practices on the brain in real time. At last, science was proving what the wisdom of world traditions has been saying since the dawn of humanity.

The confirmation that spiritual practices heal the brain began a sea change in how professionals in the mental health field approached addiction. Gabor Mate, Bessel van der Kolk, Rick Hanson, and Daniel Siegel, leaders in the mental health field, advocate the use of spiritual practices as a comprehensive approach to healing body, mind, and soul.

In 2014, *Recovery 2.0: Move Beyond Addiction and Upgrade Your Life* was published by Tommy Rosen. This seminal work outlined a new direction in the field of recovery and is masterful in its vision and message. Using the wisdom of ancient Indian scripture, the practices of Kundalini yoga, nutrition, and a healthy lifestyle in sobriety, Tommy broke new ground using spiritual practices to heal addiction. Through a series of "coincidences," I met Tommy in Costa Rica during his 2015 Thanksgiving Yoga and Recovery Retreat. From the moment I was introduced to him, I knew he was to become my teacher. I absorbed his knowledge like a sponge and have never looked back. His workshops, virtual teachings, and retreats worldwide have inspired my life and my practice as a therapist.

Years of training in IFS has given me an approach to psychotherapy that has helped me merge two seemingly different worlds: one of the spirit and the other of the psyche. Traditional mental health training tends to focus on thoughts, behaviors, and motivations; while valid, I have always maintained that it is the spiritual path that can genuinely change an individual. No other approach can. This is particularly true when dealing with alcoholism and substance abuse. IFS offers the best of both worlds: healing traumas and psychological wounds (known as burdens) and helping clients to connect to their authentic inner being, the seat of their consciousness, known as the Self.

This book is the culmination of my knowledge and my desire to pass it on to those who still suffer as I once did. It is for people who find themselves in the narrows of their lives, believing they have few or no options. And it is for those who feel alone in their suffering and have nowhere to turn.

My primary message is simple: *Nothing is permanent. Everything changes.*

To that end, what you are struggling with today will change tomorrow.

There is hope, and a better life is waiting for you.

All you need to do is take the first step toward freedom.

You will find yourself carried the rest of the way.

Of that, I am certain.

CHAPTER ONE
Understanding Addiction

"All the suffering, stress, and addiction comes from not realizing you already are what you are looking for."
—Jon Kabat-Zinn

"Addiction is any behavior you continue to do despite the fact that it brings negative consequences to your life."
—Tommy Rosen

"Addiction is giving up everything for one thing. Recovery is giving up one thing for everything."
—Source Unknown

My original training in the treatment of addiction was grounded in what is commonly referred to as "the medical model," which defines addiction as a *chronic* disease of the brain reward system. In time, I recognized that the medical model is only *one* part of a greater whole. My experience fostered the realization that my lifelong practice of yoga, breathing practices, meditation, and mantra was a significant portion of a spiritual approach to healing that could be incorporated into or used in tandem with the medical model.

Working with clients over the years, I discovered it was useless to tell them drugs alter the brain, or that their thinking had become distorted, or to attempt to guide them into an appropriate level of "motivation for change." I saw actual changes when I connected with them by gaining trust and giving them a safe space to vent, cry, and process difficult emotions. More often than not, that change was remarkable.

James[1] was a dedicated alcoholic, a gifted and talented artist, and a sexually traumatized gay man who came to me after a three-week stay at a treatment center. I looked at him and recognized both a kindred artistic spirit and the agony of addiction that he had lived with for almost forty years. Using the IFS model, we worked together to spur the traumatized parts of his inner world into releasing beliefs and emotional burdens he'd carried for decades.

We engaged in meditation, yoga, breathing techniques, and mantras. He became dedicated to these practices and employed them daily as he worked through the traumatic debris of his youth. Soon, his cravings for alcohol vanished.

James was promoted at his job, left an abusive relationship, and found a charming home he could call his own. He faced his enormous financial debts and began paying them off. In addition to regularly attending Twelve Step meetings, working the Twelve Steps with a sponsor, and engaging in weekly psychotherapy with me, he returned to his love of art and music. In a relatively short time, his paintings were included in gallery exhibits.

None of this was as easy as it sounds. It was tough. *Really* tough. But James understood the nature of his inner demons and told me often, "If I don't keep on this path, no matter how difficult, I'll end up going back there—and *there* is a place I never want to see again."

Science of Addiction

No drug or type of alcohol cares who you are, what you do, or what social strata you come from. It just wants you to drink more, do more

---

[1] *All names of clients have been changed, and in some instances, names reflect composites of several clients.*

drugs, and always want more. This is a relentless, soul-destroying, life-sucking process that will diminish you until you become someone you don't even recognize.

Bankers, plumbers, lawyers, cashiers, accountants, taxi drivers, CEOs, street cleaners, senators, police officers, congresspersons, sanitation engineers, US presidents, mothers, fathers, sisters, brothers, friends, young, old, Black, White, Hispanic, Asian, Native, short, tall, fat, thin, beautiful, ugly, famous, unknown, average, exceptional, educated, high school dropout—anyone can be an addict.

Addiction can take hold of anyone at any time. Whether you're playing Russian roulette with heroin or opening a second bottle of wine while dining at home alone, a tipping point eventually comes and turns the scales against you. For some, this occurs with the first "hit" or line; for others, it is the tenth year of use. But there is always that moment when a person becomes "hooked," whether they know it or not.

Substances such as alcohol, marijuana, opiates, or stimulants seize critical neurochemicals that feed the brain reward (the feel-good) system. Ironically, the pleasure initially engendered eventually wears off, and in its place comes endless suffering. In the Tibetan Buddhist tradition, a demon god known as the "hungry ghost" is driven by an intense emotional need to fill himself with anything that could appease his physical desires. But his mouth is tiny, and his belly is bloated and empty. No matter how much he tries to consume, he continues to starve. Gabor Mate describes, "This is the domain of addiction, where we constantly seek something outside ourselves to curb an insatiable yearning for relief or fulfillment."[2]

Our addicted brain takes us hostage by an uncontrollable force.

Most drugs (alcohol, marijuana, cocaine, heroin, etc.) target the brain's reward system. This is an essential factor in understanding addiction and recovery. When drugs enter the brain, they flood the circuits and cause dopamine and serotonin, the "feel-good" chemicals, to be activated at abnormal levels. This creates the "rush" of good feelings, producing euphoric sensations. Some drugs can generate up to *ten times* the amount of normal dopamine levels.

At a certain point, dopamine and serotonin levels reach a threshold. The natural dopamine production is compromised and can drop to abnormally low levels. The sensation to an individual is that of being "flatlined" with its accompanying depression, lack of energy, and inability to feel pleasure. This leads to needing to ingest more of the substance and raise the dopamine to levels where the individual once again feels "normal."

This vicious cycle forms the basis of what is referred to as "tolerance," where more is needed to produce the previous effects. But tolerance can also have a converse reaction in which less of the substance creates a more heightened effect. The reward system has become compromised, and the brain signals are so damaged that lower amounts of substances produce higher levels of neurochemicals. This phenomenon is often seen in persons in advanced stages of alcoholism or the phenomenon of Wernicke-Korsakoff syndrome— also known as wet brain. Small doses of alcohol create high levels of inebriation in what is a seriously damaged brain.

Over the past two decades, pain medications such as OxyContin or Oxycodone have been prescribed in historic amounts. An eye-opening book titled *Dreamland: The True Tale of America's Opiate Epidemic* by veteran investigative reporter Sam Quinones details how this epidemic developed into the out-of-control national and global epidemic it has become. Tolerance to opioids requires users to increase their intake to avoid getting "sick" from withdrawal symptoms, which is why so many individuals go from using an opioid-like Oxycodone to more potent substances like heroin and fentanyl to achieve the same effects.

When the delicate balance of the brain is disrupted by alcohol or drugs, our normal behaviors change. Perceptions alter—our sense of reality shifts. Denial supersedes self-honesty.

Rabbi Abraham J. Twerski, MD, a pioneer in addiction treatment and founder of Gateway Treatment Centers in Pennsylvania, notes that the distortion of thinking in the substance abuser is a combination of self-deception, denial, and contradictory logic. One example is the alcoholic who regularly makes a fool of themselves in public when drunk but refuses to go to a Twelve Step meeting because "I might meet someone I know, and I would be mortified!" Another often-used excuse is, "Those people are not like me." [3]

As the personalities of alcoholics and substance abusers change subtly and eventually overtly, they become unrecognizable individuals from whom they used to be. A loving, doting mother turns into a raging and emotionally abusive parent. A model employee becomes surly, shirking duties and calling in sick one too many times. A sister who once would go to the ends of the earth for her sibling becomes cruel, belittling, and hostile. Families despair, and loved ones end up at a loss as to what to do.

Recovery, which requires an uncompromising surrender, a fearless assessment of oneself, and healing of the causes and conditions, is the path that allows a person to return not only to the former version of themselves but to a higher version of their best self.

Approaches to Treatment

Moral failure, lack of willpower, nature, nurture, genetics, and environment have been noted as the causes of addiction. They go back centuries, beginning with the theory that a drinking problem is "the devil's work."

Historically, medicine has focused on alcohol and alcoholism despite drug use dating back to 5,600 BC. In 1780s America, alcoholism was referred to as an "odious disease" arising from the abuse of "ardent spirits."[4] Individuals suffering from alcoholism were regarded as insane and placed in asylums. When it came to treatment, there was little distinction between *dipsomania* (from the Greek "thirst frenzy") and schizophrenia, with accounts from the late 1700s through the 1800s describing the horrors of institutionalization.

From the late nineteenth century well into the twentieth, electroconvulsive therapy and frontal lobotomies were standard procedures. Administering morphine was thought to "vaccinate" against the cravings, and hydrotherapy and ice baths were used to shock the system. The pervading theory of the era was to destroy the desire for alcohol by ignoring what might have caused it in the first place. Addiction was perceived as a moral issue, a sin to be eradicated from a satanic hold on the soul.

In the early twentieth century, psychotherapy was also introduced as a pathway in treatment. Freud's contribution was the theory that addiction was not a primary disease but symptoms of a "neurotic conflict or underlying psychosis, or manifestations of a disordered personality."[5] Such behaviors resulted from hidden forces over which the individual had seemingly no control." Psychoanalytic perspectives also viewed alcoholism as "latent homosexuality," perversions, and maladaptive behavior.[6]

As we will see later, Carl G. Jung, an esteemed psychoanalyst and former student of Freud, would ultimately bring the concept of spirituality to the process of healing from addiction. A series of coincidences would pave the way for Jung to influence the formation of Alcoholics Anonymous unwittingly. Several decades later, Karl Menninger saw alcoholism not as a disease but as a "suicidal flight from disease, a disastrous attempt at self-cure of an unseen inner conflict."[7] Such insight was not mainstream thinking at the time; in fact, it was outrightly rejected. It would be decades before the understanding of inner conflict would be considered in treatment solutions.

The Birth of Alcoholics Anonymous

In 1935, a stockbroker named Bill Wilson was visiting Akron, Ohio, on a business trip. He had been sober for five months after years of repeated failures that included hospital visits, dry farms, and sanatoriums. He passed a bar in the hotel lobby, and even though the tinkling of glasses and elegant décor beckoned him, he stayed fast to his promise to himself and his wife, Lois (who had told him she would divorce him if he drank again), and headed for a phone booth. This was the era when humans were on the other end of the line, and in small towns like Akron, *everyone* knew everyone's business. Particularly the phone operators. Bill asked if any alcoholics in the town could use someone to talk to. He was directed to the town surgeon, who had struggled with alcohol his whole life. As he was known to do, Dr. Bob had tied one on the night before and was in bed nursing a hangover. Bill entered his bedroom and introduced himself. "Hello, Dr. Bob. I'm Bill, and I'm an alcoholic."

The two talked well into the night, sharing experiences and struggles with alcohol, their unexpected successes, and consistent failures. Bill had made and lost millions as a stockbroker, and Dr. Bob had jeopardized his medical career numerous times. But something happened during that meeting that would alter how addiction was thought of and treated for almost a century afterward. Two "drunks" feeling understood by each other, respected, and accepted. To this day, Alcoholics Anonymous uses this model as its foundation for all its meetings, which are safe places where one can share without recriminations or judgment and where the only requirement is "a desire to stop drinking."

From the mid-1930s to the late 1990s, treatment centers would engage patients using a Twelve Step approach as a basis for inclusivity and commonality. Staff were more than likely in recovery themselves; in many cases, it was a requirement for counselors. It was not unusual for staff members to have gone through the very treatment center they were now working in.

In the 1950s, a new paradigm emerged that created a means of educating and credentialing recovering persons to work in the field. This led to the next logical step: legitimizing the credentialed recovering alcoholic as a multidisciplinary treatment team member and teaching the new workforce to understand "boundaries" between a clinical interaction with patients and the more personal, off-hours engagement of a Twelve Step relationship.

What would become apparent in the modern evolution of addiction treatment is that alcohol and drugs are a sedative for emotions and a remedy for a desperate feeling of emptiness. Substances are used when we are bored, tired, or isolated. We reach for them because we feel less than or too much. We do it alone so no one can see our pain, or we join others so that our pain is invisible in the name of socializing.

Professionalization of Treatment

The history of addiction treatment in the twentieth and twenty-first centuries is complex and complicated. The professionalization of treatment facilities unwittingly created an environment where out-of-pocket expenses limited access to the wealthy. To level the playing field, insurance companies became partners in the fiscal dance between reimbursement and fraud. In the wake of the opioid pandemic, one treatment center after another was shut down when greed overrode the desire to "treat" and end suffering. This left an enormous gap in services, which, in the early 2020s, continues to deny access to treatment for millions of Americans.

Treatment approaches vary along a spectrum that ranges from "medication management," where clients are prescribed drugs to manage cravings, "harm reduction," where clean needles are distributed to offset the risks of HIV/Aids or HepC, "moderation management," where clients are taught how to drink "responsibly," and a myriad of every conceivable healing protocol in between. Often a one-size-fits-all approach is used, overlooking that a homogeneous model may, in fact, be leading to the relapse rates that continue to remain in the upper percentiles.

Trauma as an Underlying Cause

When the pain is too great, the path of least resistance is to escape. Whether that path is found through alcohol, drugs, food, cutting, shopping, or sex, to name but a few, the need is virtually the same: Numb the pain. Feel nothing. While there may be many sources, the primary source is often complex trauma.

Bessel van der Kolk, MD, is one of the groundbreaking researchers on trauma and the mind-body connection.[8] Since the 1970s, when he began researching veterans experiencing post-traumatic stress disorder, he has dedicated his professional life to studying how humans adapt to traumatic experiences. Using the most recent findings from neuroscience to attachment theories, van der Kolk has shared his findings on treatments that not only heal trauma but have long-lasting, if not permanent, effects.

His work has led to numerous breakthroughs in our approach to addiction treatment through a better understanding of trauma as an underlying cause of this disease. Trauma should be understood not as a single episode or event but as a series or combination of events that, particularly in childhood, can have lasting consequences on our physical and mental health. Van der Kolk has shown how trauma creates residence in our brains and bodies.

Addiction may have origins in childhood trauma, attachment disorder, abuse, or multiple painful experiences that can impact a person's emotional life and leave them wounded. When anxiety or painful experiences are eased by a substance such as alcohol or drugs, specific actions occur in the brain as unpleasant feelings are replaced either by that much-desired numbness or by a sense of pleasure, calm, and well-being.

This repeatedly happened when I was living the life of a drunk and an addict. An unpleasant thought or sensation would arise; it could be a memory of abuse from my past, something someone had said, or a sense of unease that I couldn't control or understand. Rather than confront it and process it, I would pour myself a drink, smoke a joint, or do a line, and if those "medications" weren't available, I would go on a significant sugar binge. But always, I avoided facing up to my feelings. And the more I did this, the backlog of unexamined thoughts, fears, and feelings weighed on me, making the next bout of drinking and drugging inevitable.

Van der Kolk's solution to healing trauma is nurturing trust and interpersonal connection, both of which are found in Twelve Step programs. For Van der Kolk, another path is to learn to "inhabit your body" through yoga or other forms of somatic experiences.

Gabor Mate, MD, is a veteran of addiction medicine. Working on the streets of Vancouver and in the Portland Clinic tending to the heroin, methamphetamine, and crack-use disordered, his career has spanned over thirty years. A leader in the field, Mate focuses on relieving the pain and suffering of addiction. Unlike his predecessors of the 1950s or even 1990s, his approach combines humanistic psychology with a spiritual orientation. He refers to his model of healing as "compassionate inquiry."

Mate returns to the theme of "chronic substance abuse . . . as an attempt to escape distress."[9] His interviews with hundreds of clients bring forth an emergent theme: the consequences of addiction are nothing compared to the fear of life that his clients have.

The self-medicating cycle includes the attempt to place at bay depression, suicidality, anxiety, and post-traumatic stress to eradicate the memories of extreme childhood physical, sexual, and emotional abuse. As Mate has often asked his audiences in countless presentations, "We shouldn't be asking 'Why the addiction' but 'Why the pain?'"[10]

Disease versus Multiplicity

Neuroscience and epidemiology have informed how we define addiction with a disease model and are as close to an accurate representation from a scientific standpoint as we have come. The brain is altered by excessive use of drugs or alcohol, and personalities change. Communities are ravaged by the conditions of addiction, from homelessness to crime, and human suffering goes unaddressed. Millions of Americans cannot access help; if they do, the length of treatment is dictated by an incomprehensible maze of insurance rules and regulations.

Treatment approaches tend to focus on "motivation" for change,[11] or cognitive behavioral therapy through which one can solve problems by understanding unhelpful ways of thinking, and an insistence that a patient "accept God" to recover, to name but a few. These approaches leave out a critical understanding of addiction that, at its core, includes profound internal pain that cries for help but is too great for it to be heard.

The silence can be deafening.

Almost forty years ago, Richard Schwartz, a family systems therapist, began working with clients who referred to aspects of themselves that were bulimic, addicted, and self-harming as "parts." He would come to find that these "parts" are in every one of us and have their own voice, memories, beliefs, and opinions. He refers to this as "multiplicity" and distinguishes it from "multiple personality disorder" (think *Sybil*) or schizophrenia. The IFS model forms an entirely different psychotherapeutic framework than any other.

This is a model of hope and transformation. Unlike the traditional approach that guides a client to ignore thoughts, negate emotions, or disregard the conversations in their heads, IFS helps a client to focus on precisely what is going on *inside*. Our culture has taught us to keep our sights on the outside world, which is, at best, transactional in nature—"Do this for me, and I'll do that for you" or "Give me this so I can *be* that." We are so embedded in seeking happiness outside of ourselves, which causes us to activate a craving brain that will never reach the desired heights it seeks. This is suffering at its core.

I began my journey with IFS as a client. Working with a highly skilled IFS therapist, I rapidly transformed much of my trauma, reactivity, and woundedness. Years of held pain seemingly melted in a relatively short amount of time. The more I worked on the model, the more vital another part of me became. That part was calm, quiet, and relaxed. It held great insights into situations as they were processed. Past insecurities evaporated as courage and a sense of competence arose from a place within that I never knew existed. After a year of my own work, I took my first IFS course.

The more I began to use IFS with my clients who were struggling with addiction, the more I became convinced that Schwartz had developed something lacking in the traditional treatment models—namely, a compassionate approach to healing ourselves.

- How often has remorse, guilt, or shame pervaded our minds while in an active state of using drugs or alcohol?
- How intense has the struggle been to quell the voices in our heads that insist we are wrong, evil, and immoral? Especially since society echoes, or perhaps even begins, the reverberation?
- How many times have we sworn to ourselves that we will not do this again, only to wake up in yet another haze of blurred memory after the first drink or drug?
- What would it be like not to have to struggle so desperately and be able to befriend the supposed monster inside us that seeks to destroy us?
- What would it be like for that relentless internal voice that screams "more" to resolve its internal pain, relax, and become an ally in our sobriety?

In my experience, IFS transforms more pain in less time than years of cognitive behavioral therapy when used as the foundation in addiction counseling. It is no coincidence that Schwartz was asked to train the staff at High Watch Treatment Center, Kent, Connecticut, which now uses this evidence-based model as a primary treatment approach. My greatest hope is that treatment centers across the country will incorporate IFS into their treatment models.

When I was working in both inpatient and outpatient treatment centers, I observed that "traditional" treatment approaches tended to reinforce patients' emotional burdens. By that, I mean there was a tendency to "blame the victim" by focusing on the consequences as opposed to the root causes. "Well, your blood alcohol level was twice the limit; what did you expect would happen?" "If you hadn't relapsed, maybe your wife wouldn't have left you." "You need to own up to your character defects, or we can't help you."

This was on the cusp of a trauma-informed era that had not yet fully taken hold. The result was to silence the internal struggle and suffering of the individual and focus on numbing them further with medication or following a cookie-cutter approach. Day in and day out, I watched clients grit their teeth or use sheer will to get through a program so they could beat their internal wounding into submission. Adding insult to injury, the mantra, "Relapse is part of recovery," undermined patients' success by setting them up for a destructive, self-fulfilling prophecy.

A New Era of Addiction Treatment

With post-treatment relapse rates hovering from 60 to 70 percent and little to no change in more than a century, one has to ask, why are we doing the same thing over and over and expecting different results?

There must be another, or better, way.

I believe there is.

In 1990, Jon Kabat-Zinn published his first book, *Full Catastrophe Living*, describing a program he created at the University of Massachusetts Medical Center called the Stress Reduction Clinic. In it, he asserted that mindfulness and the practice of mindful living reduced stress and created space for a more meaningful life. Examining patients' stress reactivity, which included high blood pressure, accelerated heart rate, migraines, back pain, heart disease, and cancer, to name a few, Kabat-Zinn developed a new approach to health known as behavioral medicine. Over 4,000 patients went through his eight-week program with remarkable results. Symptoms of illness were reduced, high blood pressure rates were lowered, and migraines diminished. Almost a decade later, emerging technology in neuroscience would show the before and after images of the brain resulting from using the techniques known as mindfulness-based stress reduction (MBSR). It would take another several years for scientists to begin publishing their data, with remarkable outcomes.

At the same time, several authors published books in the early 2000s that took the idea of MBSR one step further, particularly as it related to addiction. Thomas Bien, a clinical psychologist, introduced the idea of mindfulness for the recovery of addiction. Not only that, but he also suggested that the spiritual nature of mindfulness, rooted in Buddhism, was a pathway to healing. A few years later, Kevin Griffin published *One Breath at a Time* and brought the practice of Buddhism to the forefront of the Twelve Step approach for addiction.

It would not be an exaggeration to state that what followed was a flood of books on the market that expounded the virtues of using MBSR, Buddhism, and many Eastern practices for the benefit of overall health, as well as psychological well-being. It would not be until neuroscientists were able to validate many of the claims through their own research that mainstream medicine and science would begin to accept the accuracy of the data.

By 2018, authors such as Gabor Mate, Bessel van der Kolk, Andrew Newburg, Mark Waldman, Daniel Siegel, David Eagleman, and Rick Hanson placed their imprimatur on the field of mental health.

Amid this, Tommy Rosen published *Recovery 2.0*. Through him, at one of his retreats and as one of his students, I learned how Eastern practices could be brought into addiction treatment. I put myself through advanced training and study and embodied the knowledge to bring it into a psychotherapeutic domain.

Within the past decade, a trauma-informed approach has emerged that is beginning to influence how we perceive and treat alcohol and substance use disorders. Meditation and yoga classes are offered to inpatient residents on a more regular basis. However, one element continues to be absent—a spiritual connection and the inclusion of spiritual practices. To be all-inclusive, the baby has been thrown out with the bathwater. By excluding spirituality, we have minimized the opportunity to connect to an innate and sacred way of knowing.

What became apparent as I worked the IFS model with clients is that the part of us that has engaged in drinking or drugging to numb our pain is terrified of surrender. That addictive part known as our *firefighters* views surrender as annihilation. Yet, engaging our internal system in spiritual practices, using a Self-led model, our firefighters begin to let go. They relinquish the terror grip and inexorable hold on us. Where once they convinced us to use substances or addictive processes to soothe or numb our past or present trauma and pain, now these parts shift in their intention to protect us, by accepting the experience of connection to "something else." With each moment of insight, while connecting to the Self, the clutching loosens, and the bedeviling whispers to "use" disappear.

In the process of these enlightened moments, the part of us that Gabor Mate refers to as a hungry ghost, consuming ourselves and everything else in sight, begins to diminish in power and size. It is in the death of the addictive parts of ourselves that we find resurrection. Surrender becomes a transformation into the light. This is accomplished with an inordinate amount of self-compassion, self-forgiveness, and courage.

Mindfulness Moment

Alcohol

Are you currently drinking on a daily or almost daily basis?

Are you drinking more than two drinks at a time? Three? Four?

Are you able to stop after the first drink?

Do you have a strong urge to continue drinking?

Are you waking up feeling less than optimal after drinking the night before?

Are you noticing feeling irritable, anxious, or depressed?

When you reach for a drink, are you

Feeling overwhelmed?

Feeling angry?

Feeling depressed?

Feeling justified?

Not wanting to feel?

Marijuana

Are you currently smoking or vaping marijuana on a daily or almost daily basis?

Are you using edibles?

Are you noticing an increase in lethargy or lack of motivation?

Are you noticing any changes to your memory?

When you reach for marijuana or other drugs, are you

Feeling anxious?

Feeling bored?

Using it to sleep and/or relax?

As you think of these instances of use, what occurs to you?

What reflections do you have?

If you are newly sober, how could you use the past to guide you into the future?

If you are in recovery, how do you face your own resistance each day?

What do you consider to be possible in your life?

How resistant are you to the concept of spirituality?

How far are you willing to go to change your ideas about a higher power, the divine, or any other spiritual reference in order to remain sober?

CHAPTER TWO

One Story of Recovery

I've played in the fields of the rich and famous;
I've laid in the ditch with the fallen.
I stood up and made my own path into the Light - which
accepted me with open arms.

The field of addiction treatment is one of the few areas of mental health where a high percentage of practitioners are themselves in recovery. While there may be many therapists who are personally familiar with depression or traumatic childhoods, their lives have not been upended by the devastation of addiction. As I outlined in the previous chapter, from the 1930s to the 1950s, treatment center staff had inevitably attended the very treatment center they worked in. Their experience and recovery were paramount to understanding what their patients were going through. Bill W. understood what Dr. Bob was experiencing because he, too, had tried and failed to get sober until he had a spiritual awakening that changed his life forever.

There are many lessons I have learned throughout my recovery journey. One of them is that our experience, strength, and hope can help others on this path in a way that can forever alter their destiny. The other lesson is that despite the shared human feelings of shame, regret, and despair that can accompany addiction, each one of us has a unique story. This is mine.

My first drink was at the age of two. This surprises many people.

It shocks some and appalls others. But I grew up in the South of France, where giving children wine was a normal part of the culture.

That drink occurred on a warm summer afternoon, during which my father and our Italian landscaper planted Jerusalem Pines along the driveway that led up to the house. There was also other work: laying flagstones for a patio, structuring retaining walls, plastering, and painting. The house was a ruin that was the dream project of my parents, a young American couple seeking a new life overseas.

I ran freely around the cement bags, shovels, and piles of stone, and when it was time for lunch, Mr. Bertolino, a name I shall never forget, sliced some salami, pulled at a baguette, and broke off a piece. He slapped some cheese for a makeshift sandwich and poured me a glass of wine.

I sat under an almond tree, ensconced next to Mr. Bertolino's big frame, as the pungent smell of salami and red wine filtered to my nostrils and soft breezes wafted through the surrounding almond and fig trees, making rustling sounds that soothed. I felt safe. I could not have known then that I had ample reason to seek safety; though everything around me was bucolic and lush, life inside our house would become increasingly sullied by my parents' ugly fights, betrayals, and raging alcoholism.

My solace was found in nature. I got lost in the sound of the cicadas, the scent of lavender growing all around us, and the ever-changing blues of the ocean far below. I was fascinated by how nature unfolded: the sun moving through the sky, buds blossoming into flowers. I reveled in the beauty and order of that world. As I became more aware of the mayhem that characterized my parents' interactions, I came to believe, even at that early age, in the existence of some greater power that would protect me.

We moved to London when I was five years old. There was constant drama inside our home, which had been featured in magazines for its elegance. Instead, there was ugliness. Fights. Screaming. Police and blue lights. I hid inside the cupboard in my bedroom and created a fantasy world of fairies and sprites who wrapped me up in invisible cloaks of protection. There was additional comfort when my father read me bedtime stories or listened to my tales; I felt cherished and adored him.

London was a world of buildings, dangerous roads, belching buses, and rattling taxis. Gone were the languid days of wandering through fruit orchards or walking on endless beaches in the Mediterranean. Down the street from our house was St. Michael's Church, where I used to sit in the last pew among the top hats. Inside the church walls, I sought that lost sense of peace.

It was a strange thing for me to do. My father was an atheist, and my mother was a lapsed Catholic. Yet going to this church became a ritual I thoroughly enjoyed. When I heard the bells, I did not associate their ringing with a marking of time. Instead, they seemed to be calling, "Come here." So, I did. I would sneak down the stairs of our home, out the front door, and head straight for the enormous red double doors of the church entrance.

I remember the sense of belonging that enveloped me as I entered. As long as I remained there, I was safe, caressed by the dazzling colors of stained glass fracturing the light above me.

I did not understand one word the priests spoke, nor did I know the hymns that were sung. I knew only that there was "someone" very great above, and many times throughout my life, I would address whatever this greatness was. "Hello, it's me down here," I would say, "and I want You to know I'm thinking of You. I hope you are thinking of me, too."

However, on the day my mother discovered yet another of my father's love affairs, no power above or imaginary sprites could keep my mother from a quivering rage. She grabbed me and declared she would throw me off the fourth-floor balcony. Always jealous of the bond between my father and me, this was her attempt to gain my father's attention and threaten an act of twisted revenge. I don't recall who saved me, and my memory goes blank about much of what happened after that. But I remember that my father stormed out of the house and never returned.

Years later, when I finally saw him again, he had moved on with his new family and did not have time for a young girl who constantly sought his approval in her desperation for the solidity of a father figure. For decades afterward, I would twist myself into a dozen alternate realities to once again be a daughter worthy of his attention. Dancer, photojournalist, restaurateur, sailor, entrepreneur, valedictorian, doctoral candidate, and ultimately, presidential appointee to the White House. No matter my path or how hard I sought to excel, the love I yearned for was not forthcoming. I was chasing a fantasy. Or a ghost.

In New York City, my mother remarried, and I attended school, but nothing behind the doors changed. I became a sullen, withdrawn thirteen-year-old who would occasionally sneak a glass of wine or two when the adults were out of the house. Never too much to be noticed. Just enough to take the edge off the anxiety, fear, and constant self-doubt that plagued me.

Another divorce precipitated our move to Palo Alto in Northern California. Left to my own devices, I soon made friends with kids who smoked pot, skipped classes, and got into trouble. But as they say, "God had other plans."

One day, I took a different street home and passed a ballet studio. Ballet had been an essential part of my life in London, where I had studied with Dame Marie Rambert of the storied Ballet Rambert. I had been chosen to perform for a BBC television special, and there was much discussion about my future as a promising ballerina. Then came the move to New York, which ended my ballet lessons. As a result, I lost four or five critical years of training.

In Palo Alto, I knew I had to find a way to resume training. So, I walked up to the studio's front door, knocked, and was met by a petite woman who would become my teacher for the next two years. I took on some part-time jobs to pay for my lessons. This woman saw what Dame Marie had seen. Though she was hard on me, I knew her guidance was borne of faith that I could excel.

Shortly after discovering the dance studio, I was riding around the Stanford University campus on my bike and saw flyers for a free workshop. I had no clue what it was about, but the word "yoga" was prevalent, and something inside me *knew* I had to attend. In those first two hours of participating in yoga, breathing techniques, chanting, and meditation, I felt one thing: I had come "home" to myself. From that day forward, I practiced yoga and meditation, learned the words of Sanskrit mantras, and read Hindu texts. For the rest of my life, those practices and the spiritual teachings accompanying them would provide salvation on many occasions.

I applied to Ballet Rambert's summer school program when I was sixteen. I was accepted, but housing and costs were problematic. It was decided that I would stay at my half brother's flat in Notting Hill Gate, six blocks from the ballet school, and get a part-time job.

By then, I was struggling with five to seven pounds that would not come off. One of the teachers was relentless in her criticism and told me that if I didn't lose the weight, I wouldn't make it through the program. She told me to talk to the school doctor. I made an appointment and was prescribed "vitamins" to help curb my food intake and increase my energy levels. These little aqua pills magically bestowed self-confidence and boundless energy to meet the demands of a rigorous dance schedule. And they weren't vitamins; they were amphetamines.

One night, I sat in my half brother's living room, where some of his friends had gathered. Someone passed around a joint. I did not realize it was hashish nor that it was opiated. This was all the rage in Europe during the late '60s. Opium mixed with hashish was brought back from India, Pakistan, and Afghanistan by hippies seeking "enlightenment." I could not have known then that my half brother was a drug dealer who would eventually be arrested in one of Britain's largest LSD drug busts. It was in this world of darkness that I had unwittingly been placed.

The combination of an amphetamine high during the day and an opium nod at night took its toll, but I was young, resilient, and, even when stoned, focused solely on dance and yoga.

Soon, I was developing a proper understanding of classical ballet's techniques and artistry, and my body was responding to the "vitamins." The pesky pounds were falling off, my legs became long, lean, and muscular, and the puppy fat on my abdomen gave way to a honed core. Even the bleeding toes from pointe shoes indicated I was becoming a ballet dancer.

My body changes were noticed by my teachers and half brother. He began to make suggestive comments about my appearance, which embarrassed me. I had always been known as the "ugly duckling" in the family—with jokes about being a "Heffalump" or horsey-like. I became more self-conscious than when I had carried those extra pounds. One of the many regular houseguests who availed themselves of the extra couches in the living room and comprised a stream of new faces every week made it patently clear what he thought of this "new me." It made my skin crawl with fear. He was one of the few who stayed long-term.

One weekend, my half brother and his girlfriend went out for the day to drop LSD in the British countryside with the houseguest and friends and were not expected back until late that night. I was sound asleep in my bed in the back bedroom when I was awakened by the weight of a body on mine. It took seconds to realize who it was. I froze at the sight of the leering face in the semi-dark. The house guests' physical strength overpowered me, and once again, my mind went blank.

This event would be repeated throughout the summer. I was too terrified to say anything to anyone, too shocked by what was happening, and shamed by the thought that his behavior was caused by something I had done.

Goaded by anxiety and relentless self-loathing, I drank more wine every night. I bought myself a bottle of gin, which I kept in my room and mixed with lemonade, to drink whenever a particular sensation came over me. A tingling would start in my chest, followed by a sense of intense pressure around my ribs. It felt as if my interior was caving in. At the same time, I had the sensation that a band around the inside of my head, vice-like, was trying to explode outward. I called it the "in-outs" due to the physical experience of simultaneous expansion and contraction. Years later, I would learn that this is a common trauma-related response created by the dysregulation of our nervous system. It is the brain's way of trying to make sense of something that is beyond comprehension. Alcohol calmed these sensations and became a daily habit.

I returned to the US a better dancer and a traumatized sixteen-year-old who could not process what had happened. I still told no one. I merely retreated deeper into myself. Expressing myself was torture, and my unprocessed emotions often exploded into angry outbursts.

Two years later, I was accepted into the prestigious dance department at the Juilliard School of Music in New York City, where we were trained by the best modern and classical teachers. I excelled and was invited to audition for the Martha Graham Dance Company. But my insecurity was overwhelming, and I blew off the audition, getting drunk instead. By then, I was meeting well-known dancers who invited me out in the evenings to Regine's or Studio 54, where I danced to pulsating disco music, snorted inordinate amounts of cocaine, and guzzled champagne until the early hours of the morning. Legs like jelly, I stumbled to the sidewalks to hail a cab, often falling before hitting the back seat. Friends began to tire of my "clumsiness." On several occasions, total strangers picked me up off the ground.

I attended master classes with many greats and did well there but always choked at auditions. Filled with dread and fear, I would lock myself in my apartment and drink. I left Juilliard before getting kicked out for drunkenness and then spent almost a year floating around, trying to land somewhere—but I always got in my own way.

I began an endless cycle of "geographical cures," packing up and moving somewhere until my drunkenness and unacceptable behavior exhausted everyone, including me. Careers changed with the addresses. Colorado: solar housing and environmental concerns. Paris: photojournalist. Florida: sailing and charter yacht work throughout the Caribbean. But the drinking continued. I maintained a daily routine of keeping my "levels" steady from noon to bedtime. Alcohol was the only thing that kept those "in-outs" at bay.

The sailing business took me almost worldwide, but a ferocious hurricane permanently scared me out of the waters, and I bought a restaurant in southern Spain. It was a new beginning, filled with promise. The restaurant was quite successful for nearly two years. Then came the Gulf War, which shut down tourist businesses on the Costa del Sol. That hit me hard. I was one of the hundreds of tourist-dependent entities that crashed into bankruptcy. I lost my restaurant and my home. Luckily, a friend let me stay at an empty ramshackle property in Morocco on the edge of the Sahara near a fishing village called Essaouira. I was grateful for the haven.

I made money by translating business documents from French to English. I lived simply and spent much time on the house's roof, gazing into the distance. I set up cushions, a mat, and Moroccan rugs to create an open-air sanctuary overlooking the Sahara. I meditated daily and would go through my yoga routine while a setting sun cast an orange glow on thick shrubs and argan trees. When the stars came out, I sipped wine from my friend's well-stocked cellar, depleting it nightly, gazed at the heavens, and often fell asleep before watching the sun rise.

I returned to the States and landed in Florida, where my mother lived. I experienced several episodes of going off the tracks in an alcoholic haze, which led me to enroll at a local college outside of Fort Lauderdale to get a degree that would support a career. I wasn't sure what my major would be, but on my way to the registrar's office, I went down the wrong hallway and found myself in the front office of the School of Social Work. I had no idea what social work was, but after reading the pamphlets and course materials, I thought this could be a perfect fit.

That moment began a journey that has remained stable for more than thirty years. I controlled my drinking to get good grades and graduated with a bachelor of social work, magna cum laude, in 1993.

The master of social work (MSW) was the next logical step. In the fall of 1994, I enrolled at Florida International University, bankrolling it with scholarships, grants, and money amassed from working as a secretary for a year.

I lived in a beautiful little cottage that bordered a soccer field. The beach was a short bike ride away, and the handsome international photographer I was dating lived just across town. The MSW is a clinical training program, offering community organizing and public policy tracks. I discovered a passion for public policy and the about-to-be-passed welfare reform law. As I thought myself too old, at thirty-nine, to spend an additional three years in clinical internships and residency, focusing on policy made more sense to me. Nights were spent writing papers, studying, and drinking.

I never drank to excess around anyone else. I had put embarrassing public falls and blackouts behind me. I made deals with myself. No drinking before noon, even on weekends. No drinking before classes. I drank alone in the safety of my own home. My level of denial about my drinking was beyond delusional. It was a secret I had hidden from the photographer and everyone else. After all, I wasn't an alcoholic. I just drank—a lot.

One night, he called to say he was coming by for a quick visit. I hurriedly gathered several empty bottles and dumped them into my neighbor's garbage can. It occurred to me that this wasn't quite "normal," but I ignored the alarm bells clanging in my mind. I was on my second liter of wine and answered the door, looking disheveled. I was caught unawares. Drunk. I gripped the edge of the door to keep from swaying. He scanned me up and down. He looked into my eyes. I stared back, but I saw what he saw: a drunken woman. He left without entering. I tried to walk him to his car but stumbled and had to grab the walkway's gate to keep from falling. His last glance was filled with pity.

As I watched his car turn the corner, I felt like bits of myself were falling away in an agonized crumbling. I cried. Waves of desperate sadness were mixed with the horrid recognition of what I had become. I stumbled toward the soccer field a few feet from my house. I knelt, hunched over, as a kaleidoscope of my life experiences unfolded in my mind: lost opportunities, failed relationships, children never to be had, careers never realized. The grass became soaked with tears occasioned by the pain of decades.

I abdicated everything I had stubbornly believed about myself, relinquishing the self-serving storylines I indulged in for years. The truth was all too obvious: I was an alcoholic. With that recognition, I sensed a calming presence, an unnamable energy that suffused my being. Two days later, on November 27, 1994, I gave up alcohol and embraced a new way of life.

I did not have the benefit of a treatment center, but I did have the grace of living in an area where Twelve Step meetings were attended by the most generous individuals I would ever know. Between classes and working, I went to every meeting I could within a twenty-five-mile radius. Having never woken up before noon on a Sunday, I was suddenly willing to show up on the beach at 7:30 a.m. to help set up an 8 a.m. meeting. I folded chairs after Friday night meetings and cleaned ashtrays.

I listened to the prayers and speakers with the ardor of one hell-bent on being saved. I read the Big Book and every unopened or barely-read self-help book on my shelves. I found a sponsor who taught me the steps and why they are so important. When my class schedule conflicted with my Twelve Step schedule, I started a meeting with several others in downtown Fort Lauderdale. To this day, "Downtown Dry Dock" meets every day at 5:30 p.m.

I began with my daily yoga routine, meditated for at least thirty minutes, and read spiritual material. I took a yoga class every Friday at a local community center. I listened to tapes by Jon Kabat-Zinn and Thich Nhat Han. I read Steven Levine, M. Scott Peck, and Mark Epstein. I returned to *A Course in Miracles* someone in recovery had introduced me to years before.

I made use of what yoga had taught me: drinking water with lemon slices first thing in the morning is an ancient yogic practice to cleanse the body; yogic breathing techniques are known to repair the endocranial and vagal systems and help with cravings; breath and meditation are, according to Kabat-Zinn, the baseline for mindfulness and body healing.

I eschewed dating and focused solely on my recovery and academic studies. I celebrated the first year of sobriety in awe at how much had changed in my life. I was about to graduate with my MSW as summa cum laude, earning a 4.0 grade point average.

The University of Southern California accepted me for a PhD in social work, emphasizing public policy. Still, I struggled with statistics and a program that, while exceptional, turned out to have nothing to do with my intended career track. I almost bailed in my second year. But cutting and running had been my style for too much of my life, and I had a dogged determination to see something to a successful end. So, I stuck it out at USC.

My dissertation chairperson was controlling and arrogant. My fear of her authority resulted in following her recommendation of two years of research, only to be told, before my oral defense of the dissertation, that she did not think the work was relevant and to redo the research. In my fourth year of the doctoral program, I withdrew from USC.

I was never as close to relapsing as I was then. But the Twelve Step program and my spiritual practices had given me the strength and tools to press on. I called a friend who said she knew of some think tanks in Washington, DC, that could use my expertise. I decided to explore my options, and, as she was out of town, she set me up to meet with her boss, a "curmudgeon," she said, whose "bark was worse than his bite" and who might be of help to me.

According to the American Oxford Dictionary, a curmudgeon is "a bad-tempered person, especially an old one." I pictured a frowning older man with a cane and bow tie and assumed that this was the fellow I would be meeting at the Tivoli Bakery at 2:15 p.m. on January 27, 2000.

Only one person was seated at a table in the bakery, and he was neither old nor wearing a bow tie. He was my age and very handsome. I asked if he was Mr. Berlin. When he asked, "Kimberley?" it was with a look I shall never forget because the same look was on my face.

Oh, my God, I thought, *it's him*. In a nanosecond, I realized I had just met the man with whom I would spend the rest of my life. In another split second, I realized I was never meant to have finished the PhD. All the moments and events of my life culminated in the Tivoli Bakery. As his hand reached out to shake mine, I was convinced, without reservation, that there are no "coincidences" in God's world.

After many months of blissful, romantic courting, we were married in 2001. Our love story includes the alteration of our careers, as I assumed a post in the Bush administration as a presidential appointee specializing in welfare reform, and he became involved in the intelligence community. It includes purchasing land in Leesburg, Virginia, to build our dream house. It also consists of my battle with cancer and subsequent victory.

When I returned to work post-surgery and cancer treatment, I was promoted to a higher position in the Department of Defense. I had landed as far from my original goal of establishing myself in social work as I could have possibly gotten. During a knowledge management (KM) conference, I looked around at my colleagues, discussing various information technology solutions for disseminating information. This worthy concern had nothing to do with my schooling, passion, or purpose. I needed to return to social work and contribute whatever I could to the pressing matter of addiction.

And so, at fifty-three, I embarked on literally hundreds of hours of training to reach a professional status that I had thought myself too old to pursue a decade earlier.

It took eighteen months in night school to amass the required state credits and licensure qualifications to become a certified substance abuse counselor, 3,000 hours of supervised residency to be eligible for the licensed clinical social worker state examination, followed by another year for the National Board Certification as a master addiction counselor.

During the residencies and low-paying jobs, I learned through experience what worked and what didn't. Lessons come in many forms, none more profound than watching counselors treat clients harshly or engage in rigid policies and procedures that only serve to alienate them. Compassion was often seen as a weakness, and discussions about spirituality or neuroscience were frowned upon. I was almost fired for talking to inpatients at a hospital about how drugs and alcohol affected the brain; I was chastised by a supervisor when I offered to teach meditation to clients in one-on-one sessions. When I provided Narcotics Anonymous (NA) meetings at a methadone clinic where I was the director, I was reported to headquarters and told in the harshest terms that NA had no place in medically assisted treatment. I was then fired on the spot.

In 2014, I took a leap of faith and started my private practice. I created my model using the neuroscience of addiction as a foundation and mindfulness meditation as a tool for anxiety, depression, and post-acute withdrawal symptoms. I shared up-to-date information with clients on the nature of addiction and the healing process, including various resources ranging from neuroscience to nutrition.

I introduced clients to yoga and breathing techniques. A comprehensive bibliography of suggested readings was available in the waiting room. I read voraciously about the neuroscience of spirituality and attended countless seminars and workshops on meditation techniques, mantras, and sound healing. Eventually, I became a certified yoga teacher in the hatha and Kundalini traditions. I hosted weekend workshops for clients and the community and promoted the idea of spiritual healing for addiction.

Over the years, spirituality has formed the basis of my approach to treating addiction in all its forms. My discovery of IFS confirmed what I had long recognized instinctively as the source of healing: the Self.

Colleagues suggested that I share the knowledge I'd gleaned from years of research, countless hours studying the ancient writings of the Vedas, Upanishads, Dhammapada, the Bible, and the Torah, and decades of meditation practice that included ten-day silent mountaintop retreats at informational conferences.

When clients refused to go to a Twelve Step meeting, I brought it to them. When clients told me that they were atheists, I would teach them about the spirituality and solace to be found in the natural world through simple things like long walks in the woods, forest bathing, kayaking, camping, beach trips, river rafting, zip-lining, tree climbing, swaying in a hammock, gardening, or just plain looking at the stars. All of these, I explained, are connectors to a spiritual Self.

The darkness that ruled me during my active addiction melted into a light. While insecurity and that familiar sense of unworthiness still have their way from time to time, they have been tamed by daily meditation, prayer, body movement, and stillness. The trauma of my childhood and adolescence can never "go away," but today, I am free from the effects of that trauma and the way it translated into a constant, driving force to be numbed and soothed by any anesthetic I could get my hands on.

The journey God chose for me was one of many twists and turns, a labyrinth of learning opportunities, a tapestry woven by multiple threads of experience. It has been a journey in which I've come to understand that nothing is permanent and that the relief of my pain and suffering could only come from my dedication to daily spiritual practices. Any wisdom I have gained is a direct result of my experience and the many teachers who have guided me along this path.

    I could not have imagined in my wildest dreams that the suffering I endured as a drug addict and alcoholic would lead me to practices that would define and ensure my future happiness. Nor could I have imagined spending the rest of my life sharing what I have learned to guide others to happiness of their own. Above all, I could never have envisioned a life of service, serenity, faith, hope, and trust in a higher power that has never let me down.

CHAPTER THREE

Foundations of Spirituality

"All problems are psychological, but all solutions are spiritual."

—Thomas Hora, MD

"I could see peace instead of this."

—A Course in Miracles

What is Spirituality?

There are moments in our lives when something leaves us in absolute awe—a spectacular sunset or sunrise, reaching the summit of a mountain peak, a quiet moment during which stillness is interrupted by a hummingbird flying close by, a performance of music or dance that makes our hearts soar, the expanse of a night sky unobscured by city lights, where we can see the Milky Way, the eyes of a loved one when they ask us to marry them, the birth of a child.

Our awareness extends and connects outside ourselves, bringing us into focus with something so much bigger and grander than ourselves. The day-to-day minutiae of our lives—from endless emails to twenty-four seven news cycles—retreats into insignificance.

A stillness descends upon us, and from it arises an awakening within, where our being is calm and centered. Suddenly, we feel connected to an energy that seems infinite and indefinable.

The ancient scriptures of the Vedas call it "Ātman," a Sanskrit word that means inner Self, spirit, or soul. In Hindu philosophy, especially in the Vedanta school of Hinduism, Ātman is defined as "the true Self of an individual beyond identification with phenomena, the essence of an individual."[12]

Zen Buddhism refers to this inner experience as the "Tao," or the flow of the universe. The knowing of the Tao is not a mere concept but internalized through direct experience.

In IFS, we call this the *Self*, which Schwartz defines as our true "being-ness" and inner essence. He describes it as "pure joy and peace, and from that place, you can manifest clusters of wonderful leadership and healing qualities and a sense of spiritual connectedness."[13]

When the Self-energy arises within us, it is experienced as one of opening, expanding, and filling us with brilliance, a shimmering light. Some say the air seems lighter, and some have reported that the sense of calm they discover is like being bathed in love.

In my experience, new energy within my internal system is generated when the barriers and burdens to the Self are removed. That energy makes me more open to my experience of being—and to others. That "something else" is unfathomable. A portal opens to the divine.

Call the divine whatever you will—God, Jesus, Allah, Buddha, Vishnu, Krishna, Yahweh, Siva, the cosmos, the infinite, Mother Nature, the generator, good orderly direction, the all-knowing, the all-that-is. When divinity flows into us, we become a vessel of peace.

Perhaps it is the "peace that passes all understanding," as spoken of in Philippians.[14]

Perhaps it is "Shalom," derived from the names of God, the Hebrew word for completion or wholeness.[15]

Perhaps it is Om, the cosmic vibration underlying all existence that subsumes everything within the "one Self."[16]

Spiritual Process

The process of spiritual discovery is not found by delving into our past but by becoming acquainted and comfortable with our present. When we are alert to the present moment, we reduce the chatter of our inner thoughts that can so easily distract us from what is real.

In the present moment, the "now" is where we see the truth of our minds and discover our Self. We shift from the ego's conversation, inevitably focused on the negative, to a different dialogue that sounds softer and expresses itself in compassionate tones.

Some call this *creative insight*, and some call this *connection*. It has also been referred to as a spiritual dialogue. This concept predominates the writings of the Vedas and Upanishads written circa 1500 BCE, the Tanakh or holy scripture of Judaism written from 1200 BCE to 100 BCE, the Yoga Sutras written between 500 and 400 BCE, and the Dhammapada or writings of the Buddha in the first century BCE.

Concept of Spirituality

Spirituality is a broad concept. The Oxford English Dictionary defines spirituality as "relating to or affecting the human spirit or soul as opposed to material or physical things."[17] Other definitions range from "a sense of connection to something bigger than our smaller version of ourselves"[18] to "an inner process of connectedness with the sacred."[19] Spirituality involves a search for meaning and can infuse us with curiosity, creativity, and connection.

People may describe a spiritual experience as "sacred" or "transcendent" or simply a deep sense of aliveness and interconnectedness. There is an authenticity in the heart, an immense listening at the being's center. Some call it "God whispers," and others the "still voice within."

It is a quality of life concerned with higher thought, which may lead us to a higher purpose. It involves a relationship to our *spirit* or *soul* that can offer transcendence to an awakened state. The root is "spirit," which means "animating or vital principle in man and animals." In Latin, *spiritus* means "soul" and "courage, vigor, and breath," and is related to *spirare*, to breathe.[20] In Greek, it is *pneuma* which is variously translated as "soul," "psyche," or "spirit."

Spirituality is better thought of as a boundaryless dimension of human experience. There are no rules or regulations in a spiritual search; while there are many options for direction, there is no "one way" to achieve transcendence. Unlike the often referred to "dogma" of religion, with *dos* and *don'ts*, regulations and restrictions, or insistence on beliefs, spirituality is "religionless."

This does not mean one cannot be religious *and* spiritual, but being spiritual does not require a religious orientation. Perhaps this aspect of spirituality, once understood, appeals to atheists and agnostics alike.

Spirituality has been written about by illustrious and influential authors such as Meister Eckhart, William James, Victor E. Frankl, Thomas Merton, Carl Jung, and the Dalai Lama, to name but a few. Great teachers of all persuasions have offered guidance and wisdom to help students move toward the sought-after experience of going beyond the limited range of their minds to a more expanded knowledge of the Self. It is perhaps why movements such as the "New Age" of the twenty-first century bring together so many individuals with a like purpose. It is also one reason we are experiencing another era of renewed interest in spirituality for health, wellness, mental health, relationships, and community.

The Big Book Clarification on Religion

In the foreword to the second edition, *The Big Book* clearly states that Alcoholics Anonymous is *not* a religious organization and welcomes all faiths.[21] To allow anyone to engage in relief from the suffering of alcohol abuse, Bill Wilson and Dr. Bob were very careful to state:

> *Alcoholics Anonymous is not a religious organization. Neither does A.A. take any particular medical point of view, though we cooperate widely with the men of medicine as well as with the men of religion.*
>
> *Alcohol being no respecter of persons, we are an accurate cross-section of America, and in distant lands, the same democratic evening-up process is now going on. By religious affiliation, we include Catholics, Protestants, Jews, Hindus, and a sprinkling of Muslims and Buddhists.*[22]

My experience with Twelve Step programs has cut a broad swath in understanding what this fellowship is all about. When I first entered the rooms of Twelve Step meetings in the mid-1980s, a woman came up to me after my first meeting and told me she would be my sponsor. She said that the only way I could get sober was to accept Jesus into my heart. When I informed her that I was of the "Eastern" persuasion, namely a Buddhist, she declared in no uncertain terms, "Well, you are going to have to get on your knees and beg God to remove that devil from your heart!" That declaration ended my participation and any effort at sobriety for another seven tortuous years.

Why Spirituality for Recovery?

I would come to find out that religion has absolutely no place in the Twelve Step program or, for the most part, in recovery. That is not to say that one cannot benefit if one is religious. What is important is the de-bunking of the myth that has stopped so many from engaging in a viable and long-term approach to recovery. Not the *only* one—a *viable* one. As Tommy Rosen states, ". . . there are many paths to recovery . . . just choose one."

Higher Power Has Many Meanings

I heard a story about higher power at a Twelve Step meeting in Los Angeles in 1997 that left a profound impression on me.

A woman was celebrating something like thirty years of continuous sobriety and told her story. I don't remember her name or even which meeting it was, although I believe it was either Rodeo Drive or Santa Monica—and I may have some of the details wrong, but this celebrant will forever be seared into my memory as one of the most important inspirations in my recovery.

When this woman got sober, she lived in the High Desert of Southern California, surrounded by an expansive horizon bordered by mountains in the distance. Her home was a one-story adobe house, with barely anything growing in the front yard except for a cactus called a saguaro. The thing had never grown an inch in the years she lived there, never changed, and never bloomed as it should have at least once a year. It remained in that barren state for almost ten years.

The woman explained that she was a die-hard atheist and resisted Twelve Step meetings for years, preferring to suffer with her alcoholism than go to "one of those Bible-thumping meetings." One thing led to another, and she found herself in the rooms of Twelve Step meeting. As she described it, she was kicking and screaming the whole way. She was told to find a "higher power" and struggled since she didn't believe in God or anything close to it. Her sponsor told her to use the group as her higher power. The woman resisted. Her sponsor suggested, "Just use anything that isn't you."

Every morning, she had coffee in front of her house, where she would watch the sunrise. One morning, she was looking at the cactus out front and announced, "Oh shit—you be my higher power then!" Every day after that, she would talk to the cactus, ask it to relieve her of her desire to drink, and treat it like others in the rooms treated their "God." Despite its ugliness, she described a growing affection for the plant. Mornings were spent in the form of "communion," where she would recount her joys, sorrows, challenges, and triumphs. She described spending much time just staring at it without any particular expectation of outcome.

The day came when she reached her one-year mark of sobriety. She was excited about the celebration planned at the Twelve Step clubhouse that night. She was proud of her accomplishment and anticipated the thrill of holding her one-year medallion in her hand, commemorating a year of hard work, dogged determination, and many talks with a cactus.

She stepped outside her house just as the sun rose, coffee cup in hand. Sitting down on the stoop to begin her daily dialogue, she looked at the saguaro. In full color and on every part of its exterior were radiant flower blooms. She was stunned and in awe. In ten years, it hadn't "done" anything—and there, on the day of her first anniversary, it had given her the greatest gift of all. Like her, it had bloomed.

She closed by saying, "It was right then and there, in between crying and laughing, with tears rolling down my face, that I knew, in my heart of hearts, that there was a God. Not like *your* god or *their* god, but *my* God."

Spiritual Awakening

This doesn't mean that a spiritual awakening is required for recovery or that successful recovery depends on a spiritual awakening. Many do recover by "sheer will" or other approaches that have become popular in the latter part of the twentieth and early twenty-first centuries.

In his correspondence with Bill Wilson, one of the founders of Alcoholics Anonymous, Carl Jung reiterated that people who had succumbed to hopeless alcoholism had only one hope, and that was for a "spiritual or religious experience, a genuine conversion." But what Carl Jung proposed was something totally unacceptable in his era, and for which he expressed concern, fearing he would be castigated or thrown out of his profession. While he used strictly religious terminology (devils and angels), he concluded that "mental alcoholism is a spiritual disease" that requires the individual to relinquish resistance and, in the words of Corbet and Stein, accept the "wakeup call from the Self to a greater consciousness."[23] His most famous admonition was *Spiritus Contra Spiritum,* referring to the need to use spirituality to fight the power of spirits or alcohol.

I have worked with many clients who refuse to go to Twelve Step meetings for multiple reasons. These range from a general resistance to the notion that they are not "like those people" to a belief that it is a religious cult. Some are adamant in their adherence to atheism, and then there are those who are equally married to agnosticism. For every client I have worked with, my goal has been to help them find a spiritual path that speaks to them—the life of their soul. While they may never have stepped into the rooms of a Twelve Step meeting— it has been the groundwork of Jung, Bill Wilson, and many others that inspired them to get and stay sober in the long run. Within the discovery of their "higher power," they could surrender, accept, and transcend their addiction.

Many have reported having a spiritual awakening that opened their hearts to a "connection" they had never felt before. Many have also reported feeling distinct compassion for themselves and others. Above all, they have described "something that shifted" within that gave rise to a distinct and visceral change—a change in how they perceived, experienced, and interacted with the world around them. And many became willing to go to a Twelve Step meeting and engage in a structured recovery program as their "contempt prior to investigation" transformed into acceptance, willingness, and an open-minded heart.[24]

The Spiritual Brain

The next chapter on neuroscience delves into how spiritual practices affect our brains. Recent research by one of the top psychospiritual academics in the country offers one of the first definitive conclusions about spirituality *and* the brain. Lisa Miller, author of *The Awakened Brain: The New Science of Spirituality and our Quest for an Inspired Life*, weaves her personal experience with the rigors of her research at Columbia University with jaw-dropping conclusions.

Investigating the relationship between "personal spirituality and various markers of mental health"[25] on adolescents, Miller found that teens with "strong personal spirituality" are less likely to experience clinical depression by 35 to 75 percent. This is an astounding figure, primarily when held up against other mental health interventions, including medication or clinical approaches that do not come close to these "prevention rates."[26] Further, Miller notes that when adolescents have a strong spiritual connection, they are 40 to 80 percent *less likely* to engage in the abuse of alcohol and drugs or to become dependent regardless of social functioning.[27]

Miller reported that she found "strong personal spirituality was the *only* variable inversely associated with suicide,"[28] which means that an individual who possesses a solid spiritual internal life (a ten on a scale of one to ten where ten is the highest) would have the opposite value regarding contemplation of suicide (e.g., one on a scale of one to ten where one is the lowest).

Miller's research also examines the correlation between spirituality and synchronicity, a concept developed by Carl Jung and later studied in quantum physics. The association between healing and spirituality came into focus as she theorized that, contrary to long-standing psychological thought, we do not heal when we impose a positive meaning on our lives, but rather, "we shift toward health when somehow, and usually through struggle, a bigger meaning is *revealed* to us."[29]

The more we pay attention to our spiritual awareness, practice, and engagement, the more synchronicity unfolds in our lives, reinforcing a spiritual connection between ourselves and the rest of humanity. Relationship and connectedness, having a solid feeling of belonging and having a place in life, as well as affinity with those around us, not only offers "the peace that passeth all understanding"[30] but also endows us with an illuminated awareness of our existence.

These healing and uplifting concepts are just beginning to be accepted in the traditional world of psychotherapy. They have started to creep into the language of addiction treatment partly due to a better understanding of how fellowships such as Alcoholics Anonymous afford the perfect opportunity for spiritual engagement. Dr. Miller's conclusion is groundbreaking:

> *What if the condition we pathologize and diagnose as depression is sometimes actually a spiritual hunger—a normal and genetically derived part of human development that is unhealthy to muffle or deny?*[31]

If we replace "depression" with "addiction," we arrive at the same conclusion—using archaic pathology does not heal. Engagement in spiritual awareness and practices can. Thus, mental health practitioners are beginning to acknowledge the power of spirituality as a primary purpose of the human condition.

A significant next step is understanding how spirituality can heal our brains, treating conditions ranging from alcoholism, drug addiction, trauma, anxiety, and depression, to name a few. How fascinating that today's science is not only proving what ancient writings had instructed but also giving us deeper insight into the *how* and the *why*.

Mindfulness Moment

Can you remember a time in your life when you felt completely at peace?

Has there ever been a time when you felt connected to everything around you?

Was there a time when you felt like part of the elements of nature or the cosmos or both?

What made those moments different from "ordinary" life?

Would it be conceivable to live more moments like this in your day-to-day life?

If you do not believe in "God," do you have a concept of a higher power?

Do you consider yourself to be spiritual? Or religious? Neither? Or both?

How do you define that for yourself?

If you are resistant to the idea of participating in a Twelve Step program, what are your concerns?

Are you willing to put these aside to see if there is another way of looking at it?

Would it be possible to consider going to a meeting, or two, and seeing what it really is like?

> If not—are you willing to look at other sources of recovery, such as Recover 2.0, Dharma Recovery, Smart Recovery, Secular Organizations for Sobriety (SOS), or Women for Sobriety?

CHAPTER FOUR

Know Your Brain, Know Your Mind

"The good thing about science is that it's true whether or not you believe in it."
—Neil deGrasse Tyson

". . . we have to recognize that we are spiritual beings with souls existing in a spiritual world as well as material beings with bodies and brains existing in a material world."
—John Eccles

"Our hopes, dreams, aspirations, fears, comic instincts, great ideas, fetishes, senses of humor, and desires all emerge from this strange organ—and when the brain changes, so do we."
—David Eagleman

Neuroscience is a complex discipline focused on the brain, its circuitry, neurons, and the chemical compounds that support human life. It might seem to have little to do with spirituality or recovery. But I have come to understand that we must grasp how the brain works and how it can work *for* or *against* us. When we are dependent on or abusing substances regularly, we have an unseen coconspirator: our brain. Understanding how our brain operates in an addictive or recovering state allows us to support its health and, by extension, our mental and physical well-being.

On an unforgettable night in 1981, when I used drugs from an unknown source, I experienced what could only be described as a living hell. What should have been a twenty-or-so-minute cocaine high, with residual energy lasting an hour or so, ended up being eight hours of walls melting and body dysmorphia that sent me onto my knees begging for someone, anyone, to help.

I didn't dare dial 911. To do so would have landed me in jail for buying and using an illegal substance. Instead, I prayed. Mightily. During the last few hours, my mind felt like it was mired in poison. That scared me more than anything because if I had one thing working in my favor up to that point, it was my intellectual capacity. The idea that whatever substance I had taken could destroy my mental functioning terrified me.

The next day, hungover, frightened, and disoriented, I vowed never to do drugs again. And I didn't. For me, there would be no more cocaine, amphetamines, barbiturates, or hallucinogens. I was literally scared straight.

If I had known at age twenty-five what damage drugs and alcohol could do to my brain, I probably would never have had another drink, much less another joint, and could have spared myself another fourteen years of self-destruction. Even so, when I did quit alcohol years later, my brain had suffered significant damage, which would take almost a decade to heal.

What I've come to understand and marvel at is the incomprehensible complexity of this organ: its parts, functions, connections, chemicals, hormones, and astounding ability to heal from damage. I began to learn more about what my brain had endured when I had a SPECT scan conducted through the Amen Clinics several years ago. It was a fascinating process, which showed that many parts of my brain showed significant damage due to alcoholism, cocaine and marijuana addiction, and emotional trauma. During the evaluation, it became clear that the regeneration of critical areas of my brain had occurred through my persistent practice of meditation, breath- and bodywork, and nutrition.

As a cancer patient, I had undergone a rigorous course of chemotherapy. The effects of massive doses pumped into my body showed up distinctly in the brain scans. Visibly damaged areas from addiction and trauma showed up as "brain injury."

Specifically, the areas where my memory is stored, known as the hippocampus, showed impairment. Before treatment, I was a walking Rolodex. I could hold multiple ideas, tasks, and thoughts in my mind, a skill I was known for when I worked as a White House appointee. Within four to six weeks of the chemotherapy, it became challenging to communicate simple words such as "car keys" or "dry cleaning." I resorted to using hand signals or miming to convey what I needed or when words were utterly lost to me. To this day, I continue to experience "chemo brain"—permanent damage to the hippocampus and other areas associated with memory, spatial visual acuity, and emotional regulation, such as anxiety or depression.

The more I learned about the brain, the more I threw myself into the study of it with a passion second only to my love of spiritual practices. After learning the fundamentals, I read more extensively and discovered authors delving into a new branch of this science, calling it "neurospirituality" and "neurotheology."[2] As an evolving field, it continues to break new ground with more fascinating discoveries.

Brain Imaging

Breakthroughs in the early 2000s in the technological development of scanning equipment enabled the field of brain sciences to understand further the form, function, and complexity of integrated circuitry

---

[2] Authors Daniel Siegel, Andrew Newburg, Mario Beauregard, Daniel Goleman, and Bonnie Badenoch, are but a few of the groundbreaking theorists engaged in "neurobiology," "neurospirituality," and most recently, "neurotheology."

that endows humans with a capacity for mental processing. Over the past two decades, it has rapidly advanced, allowing us to see critical brain areas in real time. MRI, fMRI, SPECT, and PET[3] scans have become the standard for imaging, resulting in extraordinary progress in understanding how this remarkable organ works.

In the past twenty to thirty years, these scans have assisted the medical and research fields to assess multiple conditions of the brain, such as anxiety, depression, trauma, and neurological disorders, to determine what types of treatment result in positive outcomes. This is particularly true for addiction, where brain images of individuals who have abused alcohol, marijuana, methamphetamine, opioids, or heroin, to name a few, afford an enlightening glimpse into a three-dimensional world.

Daniel Amen, MD, is a double board-certified psychiatrist regarded as one of the foremost experts on utilizing brain imaging science to inform clinical psychiatry. Amen's work helped to educate the National Football League about the risks of inadequate helmets to players' brains. His "brain bank" consists of over 65,000 SPECT scans reflecting conditions ranging from ADHD, traumatic brain injury (TBI), and post-traumatic stress disorder (PTSD) to substance use disorders. Amen's admonition to addiction treatment specialists is to consider the fact that "Psychiatrists are the only medical specialists that never look at the organ they treat."[32] Understanding the effects of substances on the brain can be accessed on the Amen Clinics scan library, where pictures tell a dramatic story: https://www.amenclinics.com/spect-gallery/addictions/.

In 2007, NIDA launched a comprehensive publication entitled *Drugs, Brains, and Behavior: The Science of Addiction*. In its fifth edition, this critical work broke new ground in our understanding of drug and alcohol interactions in the brain. Further, it explained how the reactivity of drugs causes individuals to continue using until

---

[3] Magnetic resonance imaging; functional magnetic resonance imaging; single-photon emission computed tomography; positron emission tomography.

the breaking point, which can range from finally hitting bottom to succumbing to overdose and death. Culling from an extensive library of brain scan images, professionals and laypeople alike could begin to understand the complexity of neural activity, the impact of neurochemistry, and critical areas associated with our reward center that are affected by addiction. According to Dr. Nora Volkow, director of NIDA, demystifying the interaction of our biology and brain mechanisms has helped "shed light on the shadows of powerful myths and misconceptions about the nature of addiction."[33] Of primary note is the emphasis on addiction as a "disease of the brain," specifically of the reward center.

Structure of the Brain

The math is stunning when it comes to assessing what is inside your skull. There are 1.1 trillion cells in the average brain, with over 100 billion neurons receiving 5,000 connections or synapses to each neuron. This calculates to five hundred trillion points or contacts within your brain. Each neuron fires between five to fifty times per second, transmitting neurochemical information that regulates every process, from the movement of a finger to the complex computation of Einstein's formula for the theory of relativity. Each signal is transported through the body by your central nervous system, including complex messages that regulate your stress responses. If these were bulbs connected like Christmas lights, they would stretch the distance from Earth to Neptune and back 1,000 times!

Your brain enjoys states of functionality that range from awareness of your surroundings to sight, sound, touch, emotion, danger, temperature, and feelings. These are calculated to be 10 to the one-millionth power (or $10^{1,000,000}$), which your brain creates by firing neurons at any given moment. Multiple states exist in multiple moments. In each of these, neurons make lasting connections to each other. Brain and mind are inextricably linked, with the mind using the brain to make the mind. "Mind is what the brain does."[34]

There are multiple areas of the brain that engage in different functions that make up our reality and personality. For the purposes of appreciating the neuroscience of addiction and spiritual healing, let's focus on the two most important: the brain reward and limbic systems.

The limbic system assigns meaning to things you see as they happen, which is why two people perceiving one event will see it differently. The classic example of this is asking ten people what they saw at the site of an accident and receiving ten different versions. From the perspective of addiction, the limbic system coordinates pleasant experiences (sights and smells) with pleasant memories. Finally, this area monitors danger and engages in the judgment of good/bad, pleasant/unpleasant, and safe/scary. This is important from a two-pronged perspective: a pleasurable experience will be embedded in your memory and remain a point of reference in the future. A negative experience will not only be embedded in your memory and be a point of reference, but your system will seek a way out of the discomfort or unpleasantness associated with it.

Coursing through every part of your brain is a complexity of liquids transported from one place to the next through electrical impulses. These are known as *neurochemicals* and carry intricate messages to your neurons. They are then transmitted to receptor sites that receive the information and process it to the next neuron. All this happens in a millisecond, with over 100 billion neurons firing and transmitting throughout your brain.

Thoughts, perceptions, ideas, understanding, judgments, opinions, reactions, feelings, emotions—the entire domain of your internal experience results directly from these intricate network interactions.

In a perfect world, your brain is in a relative state of equanimity: composed, balanced, even-tempered, and mentally alert, with body, mind, and spirit in harmony. But we do not live in a perfect world, and even those who are ultra-mindful of health and self-care are still subject to stressors beyond our control that affect our neurological system.

Imagine, then, what can ensue when you pollute your brain with mind-altering substances that alter your consciousness and can even change the person you are. Alcohol, drugs, nicotine, caffeine, and, yes, even sugar all contribute to a miasma of damage to your delicate brain system. While sugar does not alter your consciousness, it does affect many brain functions, which we will explore later.

In her unique and revealing book, *Never Enough: The Neuroscience and Experience of Addiction*, Judith Grisel lays out three laws of psychopharmacology:

(a.) All drugs act by changing the rate of what is already going on;
(b.) All drugs have side effects, and
(c.) The brain adapts to all drugs that affect it by counteracting the drug's effects.[35]

Whether you ingest an aspirin or drop a hit of acid, in addition to the effect of the substance on the brain, there is a *bidirectional* relationship in which the brain responds *to* the substance. The capacity of your brain to adapt to mind-altering substances leads it to compensate for the associated changes you experience.[36]

The prime example of this is *tolerance* for a substance. When your brain becomes accustomed to a certain level of alcohol or drugs, it adjusts. The effects begin to diminish despite identical amounts consumed. We become accustomed to drinking a glass of wine with dinner, and one night we tell ourselves, "One more glass of wine won't hurt." Then we find ourselves thinking, *Go ahead and finish the bottle; there's only a little left*, or *Take another hit; you're not quite there yet*. Your brain has become used to amounts and levels. One glass is no longer pleasurable; two are better. The more we use, the more our brain demands an increase in the substance to achieve a previously experienced level.

The first time a drug is used, it gets registered in the brain system as a unique event. For instance, the immediate effect of cocaine is an intense pleasure and a sense of invincibility. From the moment of ingestion, the pleasurable experience is recorded in the brain reward center with increased levels of dopamine. This creates a desire to repeat the behavior because the brain is hit with such intense pleasure upon ingestion but rapidly descends to even lower levels of dopamine and serotonin once the initial effects wear off. Yet the repeated behavior is in vain. The well-known adage, "chasing the dragon," is a perfect description because no matter how often any substance is used, the original, exhilarating experience can *never* be replicated.

Dopamine plays one of the essential roles in this process. This feel-good chemical informs your being of pleasure and dictates your motor control; any disruption to your dopamine levels can wreak havoc on how you function and feel. Substances ranging from alcohol to marijuana, cocaine to methamphetamine, and MDMA to LSD all adversely affect dopamine levels. When pushed through the neurons at ever higher rates, natural dopamine production is reduced because the receptor sites become compromised. They are flooded by the substances, resulting in significantly reduced natural regulation.

This process keeps driving us to use a substance merely to achieve a sense of normalcy. We experience increased anxiety and depression because dopamine levels are compromised; in seeking balance, the brain signals for more of what will make it feel better. More substances create more imbalance, which creates more demand. This vicious cycle can shift an individual from use to abuse to addiction in a very short amount of time.

Reduced dopamine levels can seriously compromise an individual's emotional and mental functioning. Equally, reduced dopamine levels in the brain are also associated with mental health challenges such as depression, panic or anxiety disorders, schizophrenia, bipolar disorder, and obsessive-compulsive disorder (OCD).

Suppose you experienced trauma or repeated adverse events while growing up, heard a constant stream of criticism aimed at you, or were belittled by siblings, schoolmates, or family members. Your brain will have stored those memories in your limbic system, where pleasant and unpleasant experiences are embedded. It will seek out activities that will numb the pain or soothe emotional repercussions. This can range from excessive shopping to obsessive online gaming, from self-harm to self-punishment.

Your brain will tell you to soothe yourself with alcohol or drugs. Or, in the case of extreme trauma, it will demand that the memories are wiped out entirely. That can happen as part of a protective process or because we have used catastrophic drugs that take us out entirely, like fentanyl, opioids, or heroin. In the depths of our minds, we know that what we are doing is destructive:

- We wake up hungover and swear we won't drink that day. Hours later, we stop at a bar or buy a bottle on the way home.
- We get into fights with loved ones; they are "nagging" us about our drug or alcohol use.
- We resent others for minor slights.
- We become increasingly irresponsible.
- We swear we will change.
- We lose our families, our homes.
- We keep using to make the pain and shame go away.

There is only one way to stop this vicious cycle, and that is to *stop*. While the body and brain experience withdrawal, which, I admit, is highly unpleasant, stopping is the initial step in recovery. Alcohol withdrawal should be monitored closely as it has been known to cause strokes or heart attacks. Once the initial detoxification process has been achieved, staying stopped depends upon the *path* of recovery.

I always give my clients this adage to help them maintain the intention to quit alcohol and/or substances:

"Today, you don't drink or drug. No matter what.
If someone dies, you don't drink or drug.
If you lose your job, you don't drink or drug.
Now, you can drink or drug tomorrow. Just not today.
But when you wake up in the morning, what day is it?
It's today.
And today, you don't drink or drug.
You can only drink or drug tomorrow."

Healing the Brain

It takes considerable time for your brain to heal from addiction. The standard twenty-eight to thirty days at a treatment center is only the beginning. While clients do feel an enormous shift after inpatient treatment, their healing has a long way to go. Estimates of time range from eighteen to twenty-four months and up to five years.[37]

Ninety days of abstinence allow dopamine levels to *begin* to return to normal levels. The average time for significant brain areas, including the reward system, lobes, and neurons, to restabilize is fourteen months.[38] However, this does not mean your brain returns to its original state. It is only restabilizing. What substances you used, how much, and for how long will determine the length of time for healing. It also depends on whether you are on a steady diet of cigarettes, coffee, and sugar or if you are willing to address your nutrition, health, and well-being for the long term.

Post-acute withdrawal symptoms (PAWS) are a group of physical, mental, and emotional conditions resulting from damage to the central nervous system (CNS). It is caused by the after-effects of alcohol and drug abuse when a person faces the initial stress of coping with life without addictive chemicals. PAWS can present serious obstacles for an early recovering person in more ways than one. Symptoms include sleep disorders and changes in thought processes, problems with memory function, reactive emotional responses, increased sensitivity to stress, and lack of physical coordination. Old injuries can suddenly become the focus of new pain. Roller-coaster rides of emotions can take someone through extreme highs and lows, all in one day. Energy can fluctuate between a forty-yard dash of cleaning every closet and drawer in the house to being immobilized on the couch with glazed eyes looking at the TV.

Not understanding or managing PAWS in the early months or years of recovery can lead to relapse. Therefore, it is vital to be aware of and recognize these symptoms so that comprehensive healing of the mind, body, and spirit can take place. Attention to nutrition, reducing caffeine intake, resting and engaging in healthy sleep patterns, exercising the body, and hydrating with water and juice all help to offset the adverse effects of PAWS.

Over the past several decades, psychopharmacology has increasingly come to the forefront for treating addiction or reducing the risk of relapse. Medication management, or prescribing drugs that inhibit cravings, has become more popular as illegal drugs have become more potent (think opioid and fentanyl crises) and, by extension, more challenging to treat. Other approaches include administering vaccines that ultimately render a particular drug impotent in an individual's system. But drugs replacing drugs is highly controversial and the source of endless arguments among addiction specialists. One has to ask, in light of the pharmaceutical industry's culpability in the opioid crisis, why would we trust an industry that profited from such a devastating epidemic to turn around and then treat it with the same approach?

Neuroplasticity

One of the primary miracles of the brain is that it can heal itself. This is referred to as *neuroplasticity*, which is the ability of the brain to "modify, change, and adapt both structure and function"[39] through growth and reorganization and compensate for injury and disease by forming new neural connections to respond to changing conditions. Neuroplasticity happens in numerous ways, ranging from reshaping neural networks and changing existing levels of neurochemicals to creating new neurons (*neurogenesis*).[40] While nerve cells that have died can never be resuscitated, new circuits and connections can be, and are, created.[41]

While most neuroplastic activity occurs early in life, recent studies show that elements involved in neuroplasticity can occur throughout a lifespan and are not solely associated with human growth and development. When an individual commits to altering their negative way of thinking and acting, they can alter brain chemistry and function.[42] This is good news for any of us who have struggled with alcohol or drug use disorder and want to give ourselves a second chance in our lives. This is a significant message of hope.

New pathways can be formed in the brain by repetition. This was first discovered in 1949 by Donald Hebb, PhD, who coined the phrase "neurons that fire together, wire together." Through his work, we have come to understand that what we focus on will strengthen neural pathways. This is why meditation, journaling, breathwork, prayer, chanting, mantra, affirmations, and so many other practices benefit neuroplasticity.

But there are two sides to every coin. It turns out that this capacity takes place whether we are focused on positive or negative thoughts or behaviors. Repeating negative thoughts or beliefs strengthens that particular pathway in our brain. Telling ourselves over and over that we are worthless is like a set of mega push-ups for our mental diet. However, we can choose what we ingest to feed the muscles of the mind. As Richard J. Davidson has pointed out, mindless pursuits such as spending "long hours ingesting what's on the screen of our digital devices" can diminish our mental sharpness. Our neurons do not discriminate the content of the diet; it is up to us what we choose to ingest.

As information flows through us via sensory channels, our

nervous system changes. Rick Hanson, PhD, emphasizes that your brain is constantly looking for danger to initiate a fight-flight response. This originated when we roamed the savannas or defended ourselves from saber-toothed tigers. As a result, we are conditioned by our evolutionary process to seek out trouble. Referred to as "negativity bias," it involves your attention consistently focusing on what could go wrong. This occurs because your mind is imprinted by any negative experience, so much so that you focus more on criticism than on words of praise. Your brain is wired to seek out experiences that cause pain or fear to avoid similar experiences. However, by doing so, your mind tends to incline toward a continuum of negative thinking.

My own experience with negativity bias took years to address. Raised in a toxic and emotionally traumatic environment, I spent decades thinking the worst of myself and what might happen to me. To say that I lived in a constant state of anxiety would be an understatement. The thing that I found to settle this state of being at an early age was alcohol. Later, I would turn to drugs to do the same thing. But when I quit, I felt shell-shocked by the raw experience of a mental process that seemed to be revving at 100 miles per hour in a negative rant. Returning to my memories of yoga as a young girl, I found classes and attended them regularly. I set up an altar in my bedroom and began a morning practice that included journaling, making a gratitude list, reading spiritual material, and meditation. The whirring in my brain became a very low hum in a short time. Years later, I noticed that it was no longer there.

Rick Hanson has written extensively on the ability of the brain to be retrained from this automatic negative response to one of intentional engagement of positivity, calm, and happiness. Neuroplasticity forms the core of how positivity can become the default of our brain responses.

Learning new skills, experiencing positive events, and creating pleasurable moments in our lives help to make new neural connections in our brains. This leads to the development of new synapses that can combat memory challenges, anxiety, and depression.[43] Practicing and repeating positive behaviors strengthens these brain parts, supporting positivity in our minds.

By *not* repeating negative behaviors, such as using mind-altering substances or defaulting to negativity bias, synapses previously involved in addiction or pessimism become weaker. The negative "inputs" are replaced by positives, which alter the structure of the brain system. As a result, new circuitry strengthens our ability to overcome anxiety, depression, and the negative patterns that contributed to the original substance abuse. Using the brain's inherent capacity to heal and function without addictive substances increases the effectiveness of psychotherapy, hard-wires new behaviors and coping skills, and increases resiliency. There are many practical ways to encourage and engage in forming new synapses, as we will see in part II of this book.

Hundreds of research articles have been written on the brain's healing capacity through meditation. As I've mentioned, meditation was one of the things that helped me disengage from negativity bias to a calmer state of being. But one body of science is codifying this process: research on employing spiritual practices to change the structure and function of the brain positively is now referred to as "neurospirituality." And it has examined what happens when we engage in meditation, prayer, mantra, chanting, and breathing exercises, to name a few, regardless of any religious orientation. These studies continue to expand the body of knowledge and point to remarkable wisdom expounded over 3,000 years ago.

Healing the Brain—Spiritual Practices

When you remove damaging substances, your brain will begin to reorganize itself. However, eliminating alcohol or drugs does not guarantee effective neuroplasticity or healing of your brain. Through longitudinal studies and repeated brain scans of subjects, neuroscientists are now finding that specific activities engage the brain in particular ways.

Groundbreaking research conducted by Andrew Newberg, MD, and Mark Robert Waldman focuses on the effects of prayer, daily spiritual rituals, hymns, and meditation across multiple religious and spiritual domains. The results were shared in two books, *How God Changes Your Brain* and *How Enlightenment Changes Your Brain*. Other works by Rick Hanson, PhD, such as *Neurodharma* and *Resilience,* and Daniel Seigel, MD's work *Aware,* all speak to the power of spiritual practices for healing the brain and make vital contributions to this expanding body of knowledge.

I have found it particularly compelling that, to date, there is very little research of comparable rigor and validity in which addicted individuals are subjected to brain scans to mark a baseline and then scanned again after becoming engaged in spiritual practices. This would be a massively expensive endeavor that would take significant time, staffing, and resources. However, NIDA and many universities have engaged in research on a much smaller scale. Brain scans by Amen Clinics show before and after imaging of addicted persons with compelling results. This is encouraging for the future of addiction research and for impacting much-needed treatment.

For decades, we have discussed the importance of "social support" in a recovering person's life. In the past five to seven years, this has come to mean a connection to a faith-based network, whether church, temple, or group. Taking it one step further, spiritual *practices* have come to mean more than attending church services or participating in Bible study, although these can be central to faith-based recovery. More and more, we are seeing how a personal relationship with a higher power informs activities outside of the religious framework and engages recovering persons who, in the past, may never have had a belief, much less faith.

In the mid-1960s, hippies, scholars, and seekers traveled to India, resulting in a wave of Eastern knowledge returning to the

US. Over half a century later, that influence remains. Meditation, breathwork, prayer, selfless service, positivity, compassion, kindness, concentration, physical yoga, spiritual study, mantra recitation, chanting, and personal devotion, including becoming a monk or nun, have informed what *spirituality* means. In the 2020s, we are seeing younger generations turning to faith-based teachings, whether Judeo-Christian or Eastern.

Neurobiology of Spirituality

In 1997, Dr. Kenneth Kendler of Virginia Commonwealth University published a multi-measure genetic-epidemiologic study on religion, psychopathology, and substance use. In this publication, he examined the extent to which spirituality is associated with genetic or environmental factors. His findings showed that people could be spiritual without being religious and religious without being spiritual.[44] He discovered that high levels of personal devotion mirror low levels of depression and that a personal relationship with a higher power carries a "protective" benefit, whether one was raised in a religious environment or not. He found that a sense of spirituality in one's life decreases the risk of alcoholism and nicotine dependence.[45]

Kendler's assertion that spirituality is an innate human ability was the first of its kind. His findings revealed that spirituality is not just an abstract concept or a belief but a quality that each individual is "born with the capacity to experience"[46] as a birthright.

While researchers all agree that spiritual experiences are subjective or strictly personal in nature, we now have objective evidence. Through brain scanning techniques, we see that these experiences have specific effects on various brain regions. When we experience a closer relationship with the divine, it turns out that our brain responds in many positive ways that we are just beginning to understand. Brain scanning of the twenty-first century corroborates what ancient texts have claimed since 5,000 BCE.

Mario Beauregard and Denyse O'Leary brought forth compelling evidence in *The Spiritual Brain* that supports the neurotheological work of Newburg and others. They conducted extensive studies with Carmelite nuns to observe brain patterns during prayer, meditation, contemplation, and mystical experiences. They found that these encounters happen because the nuns connected with an *objectively real spiritual force that exists independently from the individuals who have the experience"* (emphasis added).[47]

This is an astounding hypothesis, particularly since, for centuries, the world of science has denied any possibility of a supreme or cosmic force, energy, deity, or, dare I say, God—otherwise known as the "absolute." But the oral and written traditions of the Vedas, Sutras, Torah, Dhammapada, and Bible have all said virtually the same thing for thousands of years:

Be still and know God.

This is the way of transformation; this is the path of healing.

CHAPTER FIVE

The Grounding of Spiritual Practice

"There is no joy in the finite; there is only joy in the infinite."

—The Chandogya Upanishad, VII, 23.1

"Let all your deeds be for the sake of heaven."

—Ethics of the Fathers, 2:17

*"Direct your eye right inward, and you'll find
A thousand regions in your mind
Yet undiscovered. Travel them and be
Expert is home-cosmography."*

—Thoreau, *Walden*

There is much wisdom in the world, but none as compelling as that handed down to us over 5,000 years ago in ancient Vedic scripture. It seems that our ancestors knew more about the nature of being than most modern philosophers. For that reason, if you are recovering from addiction or trying to maintain sobriety, there is much to be gleaned from these wise and insightful teachings.

Ancient wisdom is as relevant today as it was thousands of years ago. It has taken us millennia to unlock the sagacity found in religious and spiritual texts and apply them as a pathway to end personal and collective suffering. This is particularly true for those of us who are, or want to be, in recovery from addiction.

Centuries ago, sages in the East believed that we possess layers of consciousness that can move us through progressive states from ignorance and suffering toward a knowledge of the Self. These layers reveal themselves at various stages of our lives, beginning with early childhood, into teens, young adults, and then adults. Understanding these phases and how to harness the positive qualities and release the negative ones underscores the process that leads us to arrive at a state of pure or near-pure consciousness.

When we reflect on the average teenager's "rebellious" stage and young adults' "know-it-all" stage, we can appreciate how experience becomes our best teacher. As a teen, we can quickly become caught up in the use of alcohol and drugs to be part of the "in" crowd, and for many, this is just a passing phase. But as those of us who have walked the narrows of our lives know only too well, that stage can become a way of life. The journey back to the Self becomes the spiritual path of healing in recovery.

As we learned in chapter 2, spirituality is a concept outside of prescribed religious cannons that is timeless, boundaryless, and the essence of who we are at our core. But it is one thing to have a spiritual orientation as part of our human experience; it is another to engage in spiritual practices in our lives. According to ancient scriptures, the journey to self-knowing leads us to the highest state our mind can achieve; traveling that pathway brings us to a personal knowledge of the divine.

Explorers of consciousness have sought answers to timeless questions:

- *What is our purpose?*
- *Why are we here?*
- *How can we end the suffering that seems inherent in our human condition?*

- *How can we achieve a state that will lift us above the mundane?*
- *How can we find happiness?*
- *How can we discover joy?*
- *How do we achieve a higher consciousness?*
- *What is it that we have to do?*
- *How do we have to do it?*

As humans, we err; we falter, fight, take, and lay bare. But it is also true that we have the highest potential in the animal kingdom, with the capacity for good and the extraordinary. We can also point to great acts of creativity, courage, and compassion for all the wars, destruction, and savagery that humankind has engaged in. Our potential for greatness inspires us to do better and *be* better. So, when we find ourselves in the perilous narrows of our lives, challenged with despair and suffering, trying to attain sobriety or maintain it, we need to turn to proven roadmaps that can lead us back to balance and help us to thrive once again.

The answers to our human dilemma have not been found in traditional science because there is a mechanistic denial of a higher power, the presence of "something else," energy, force, or reality outside of ourselves. Nor have answers been found in religions whose dogma requires that we adhere to strict guidelines, beliefs, and behaviors. Neither are answers to be discovered in sects and cults that can narrow worldviews with restrictive assumptions.

But ancient wisdom tells us that the answers we seek—and need—come from something else that resides both *outside* and *within us*. And that is a vital message for anyone seeking to reinforce their sobriety or suffering from the ravages of addiction.

Spiritual Practice

The first lesson I learned in my recovery came as I knelt in the grass that night in 1994. I had to relinquish the misperceptions of myself and surrender to the truth. For too long, I believed others had caused me harm, which required that I anesthetize myself from remembering. For too long, I believed I was a victim.

The truth was that I was a hopeless, hapless alcoholic who could not stop drinking. The pain of this realization, breaking open a locked, wounded, and cynical heart, was more than I thought I could bear. The tears I shed felt endless. As sobs racked my body, I thought I would fall off the planet and end up in a dark abyss from which there would be no return.

Instead, after what seemed like hours clutching the soccer field grass, hunched over and alone, when the last sob had left my body, I suddenly felt relief. Something began to wash over me. I had let go of decades of suffering, and my healing began by admitting to myself and something above me that I was an alcoholic. While the hard work was ahead of me, I was starting the process of putting years of shame, guilt, and wretchedness behind me.

So began my first lesson in spiritual practice: *surrender*. Relinquishing my ideas and concepts of who I thought I was, the stories I made about my life, my tragedies, and my successes. Letting go of the denial. Releasing the defenses.

The next lesson I learned in recovery was consistency. Doing something every day whether I wanted to or not. No more excuses. I went to meetings every day. I made my bed every day. I made a commitment to engage in my spiritual practices every day.

Meditation was not a foreign concept to me. Over the years, I practiced the techniques of Tibetan Buddhism and Indian schools of yoga and studied with well-known teachers. Despite that, my practice was erratic at best and could barely be called disciplined. I sat on a cushion when I was desperate or despairing. My prayers were often of the "foxhole" variety and studded with urgent requests to be rescued from a bad situation, usually of my own making. I rarely said "thank you" when I was spared. Looking back, I can see that I so often was.

The Big Book says, "The spiritual life is not a theory. *We have to live it.*"[48] When I first heard these words in a meeting, they struck me like an arrow in the center of my forehead. Here was an instruction that had otherwise eluded me. Despite years of study and on-again-off-again stretches of practice, I realized I had not *lived* my spiritual life. I had treated it like a theory with the result that it had provided virtually no long-term benefit or change.

The day after my last drink, I shifted from theorizing to living the teachings I knew so well but had not fully taken into my heart. I committed to being disciplined about my practice and creating a daily schedule that included numerous approaches. And I stuck with it. Twenty-nine years later, I still practice daily to maintain my spiritual condition.

Mindfulness

One of the first things I did was to systematically go back through every book I owned by an author who took inspiration from ancient wisdom. There were quite a few that had never even been cracked open. I started with Jon Kabat-Zinn's *Wherever You Go, There You Are* and absorbed every word and instruction he offered. In the first paragraph of the introduction, he points out, "Whatever has happened to you, it has already happened"; a first instruction speaks of the need to "pause in our experience long enough to let the present moment sink in." This meant taking enough time in my day to appreciate what was happening as it happened.

One of his insights particularly impressed me:

> *"Mindfulness requires effort and discipline for the simple reason that the forces that work against our being mindful, namely, our habitual unawareness and automaticity are exceedingly tenacious. They are so strong and so much out of our consciousness that an inner commitment and a certain kind of work are*

necessary just to keep up our attempts to capture our moments in awareness and sustain mindfulness. But it is an intrinsically satisfying work because it puts us in touch with many aspects of our lives that are habitually overlooked and lost to us."[49]

Zinn instructs us to engage in non-doing, stopping what we are doing, focusing our attention on our breath, rising early to implement our practice, and giving ourselves to the discipline of concentration and mindfulness, which, he assures us, will invoke qualities of "elevation, massiveness, majesty, un-movingness" only when we practice, practice, practice, and practice again.

After a lifetime of seeking and achieving perfection in dance and so many other endeavors, it struck me that the word "perfection" is never mentioned in Zinn's or anyone else's teachings. Practice is so much more inviting. And more achievable.

In the program of Alcoholics Anonymous, the precept of "progress, not perfection" is a mantra that permits us to move through our lived experience with a new acceptance of how things are *meant* to unfold—instead of our idea of how something *should* unfold.

When we allow ourselves to become aligned in the natural order that is around us, we are automatically helped by an unseen force to let go of our impatience, unrealistic expectations, or ideas of being perfect.

Awareness of Breath

From Thich Nhat Han's *Peace Is Every Step*, I relearned breathing techniques. His instruction was so simple that it was almost laughable:

"Breathing in, I know that I am breathing in;
Breathing out, I know that I am breathing out."

Despite its over-simplicity, I engaged in conscious breathing every day, repeating these words to myself repeatedly. No matter what I was doing—folding laundry, making the bed, driving, or standing in line at the grocery store—those two sentences were always at the forefront of my mind. The more I practiced the breathing techniques, the more my conscious mind shifted toward a greater calm and clarity with each day.

Once I had consumed my existing library, I used the public library and other resources to access meditation, mindfulness, and spirituality materials. I would discover that an entire body of science had begun to emerge involving research into the neuroscience of these practices.

I was in the second semester of my master's degree, surviving post-acute withdrawal symptoms and absorbing the materials in my spare time as if my life depended on it. I pursued a daily meditation practice and applied the techniques given in the various scriptures. Little did I know at the time that researchers at Harvard, Stanford, and UCLA were studying the power of these teachings on the brain, mainly as it related to depression and anxiety. These ancient teachings showed that when used, the brain's neural pathways were altered and facilitated healing. While I focused on "breathing in and breathing out," I was helping my brain to reset. While I spent time with my eyes closed and focusing on "this moment," I was guiding neurons in various areas of my brain to rewire and create new patterns. The result eventually shifted my attitude, perceptions, and perspectives.

Knowing Our Minds

Meditation, engaged by sitting in silence, is the key to becoming the master of our minds. The instructions from virtually every spiritual source give the practitioner a method and a means to rise above personal limitations and experience a heightened awareness of reality as if roused from a deep sleep. For me, it was waking from the nightmare of addiction—the false belief that by using drugs or drinking myself into a stupor every night, I would relieve myself of the emotional pain that had held me in a vice grip for decades. When I focused on my breath, stilled my mind's chatter, and engaged in deep concentration, there were moments when I forgot that my body even existed.

If we sit still long enough, we can begin to notice how our mind works. First, this thought intrudes, then another. "Don't forget to call about the reservation for dinner," "Better make sure the tank is full before that long drive," "Oh, remember that beautiful coastal drive a few summers ago?" "Why didn't we do that again?" "We're way too busy these days, doing too much," "Why can't we get back to taking time off?" "Just never enough time!" "When are things going to change?" "I don't know if I can keep up this pace, and I'm not getting younger!" "Damn, that lady was mean about the older gentleman taking too much time at the checkout," "I really should have said something," and "Why don't I speak up more often?" "You always think of things too late," "You're always late," "You're not organized enough," and "You really are a failure."

The litany continues in an endless spiral until we realize that we have gone down a rabbit hole of thinking. These thoughts can take the form of sudden, consuming, destructive ruminations, dwelling on catastrophes that have yet to occur, or magnifying and replaying events that have already happened. We can be catapulted into the future by fantasies or ricocheted into the past by regret.

In meditation practice, something snaps us out of our reverie, and we can label the activity as "thinking" and return to the breath. We come back to the present moment and refocus on this moment, right here and right now. It takes time and practice, but once we begin to recognize these mental patterns, we can begin to alter the frequency and intensity and increase our acceptance that this is what the mind does. Training it to come back to the breath is just that, training.

Ethics and Values

The Eastern scriptures assert that harmful compulsions, such as addiction, can be transformed through a committed spiritual practice. Later, the writings of the Torah, Bible, and Twelve Steps all reflect the same general instructions. In yoga, they are known as the Yamas and Niyamas. In Christianity and Judaism, they are known as the Ten Commandments. They all offer instructions that, if we adhere to them, are virtually guaranteed to change the course of our lives.

These consist of

- *Surrender to a higher being,*
- *Honesty in all our affairs,*
- *Confession of our wrongdoings,*
- *Nonviolence and non-harming,*
- *Using our speech wisely,*
- *Refraining from greed,*
- *Selfless acts,*
- *Engaging in gratitude.*

This seems like an overwhelming list of behavioral changes, but we are not expected to achieve them all at once! We take it one day at a time.

When we engage in "rigorous honesty," we end the game of lying to ourselves and others. This is a very big deal. The nature of addiction is to keep us trapped in an illusion. We have created so many stories in our minds that we no longer know what is really true. Getting honest about our past and present frees us. We no longer have to worry about hiding. We no longer have to worry about what we said to whom and when. We no longer have to cover any tracks.

Confession is endemic to every spiritual and religious school in history. Whether Buddhist or Catholic, Baha 'I or Islam, Judaic or Hindu, confession should be seen as sharing our burdens with someone else. Like rigorous honesty, admitting our wrongs gives us an opportunity to clean the slate. Sharing it with someone else means we don't have to do it alone. We can't erase what we have done, but we can take responsibility for not repeating our mistakes.

Non-harming means just that. We don't hurt others. Respecting the sanctity of life—human and animal—is our responsibility as stewards of this planet. There is and has been way too much division, rancor, violence, and hatred in our world. It's up to us, individually, to stop the default of our negative thoughts—and change our minds. Literally and figuratively.

Non-harming includes using our speech wisely. Words really can hurt. We should never be responsible for throwing the "first arrow" that the Buddha speaks to. The first arrow carries the pain and hits us hard when it lands. The second arrow, our reaction to the pain, is what can cause suffering. Would you want to be the source of that kind of hardship in someone else's life?

Greed is all around us in so many forms. For many, more is not enough. It goes beyond acquiring the newest gadget or toy, shiny bauble, or latest fad. Forget FOMO (fear of missing out). Greed is, at its core, an attempt to fill a bottomless hole inside us. Nothing seems to satisfy the insatiable hunger. Like the hungry ghost of Asian Buddhism, there is a suffering of the appetite. At the same time, greed prohibits us from being generous. We are so afraid of losing what we own—money, belongings, things—that we guard ourselves from giving what is truly important: compassion, kindness, love, empathy, appreciation, and understanding.

Selfless acts are the opposite of greed. Giving others our time, connection, listening, and attending are precious gifts from one human to another. In the well-known book *Random Acts of Kindness* and the foundation of the same name, Rabbi Harold Kushner points out how one tiny act can offer incredible transformation—to the giver and the receiver.

A few years ago, I suggested to a client that she engage in random acts of kindness to offset an almost obsessive focus on negative beliefs she had about herself and others. June was convinced she was worthless, a failure, and doomed to a life of complete loneliness. As we uncovered the source of these ideas, we also discovered there was a wealth of wanting to give inside her. But the part of her that carried the negative beliefs would not let go of its grip. So we created a plan for a different journey. Each day, June was to focus, intentionally, on an act of compassion that she could offer to another human being. She began by letting someone at the grocery store go in front of her, then helped an elderly neighbor move the garbage cans to the street. There were dozens of examples that she cited where, telling her fear that everything was going to be okay, she was able to connect with strangers and neighbors who thanked her and expressed their gratitude. Over the course of several months, the litany of negative beliefs began to dissolve into an acceptance that, in fact, she was an important part of a much greater whole.

Selfless acts, honesty, nonviolence, gratitude, and using our speech wisely help us to loosen the binds of self-seeking. We live without fear or looking over our shoulders by doing the next right thing, no matter the personal consequences. We no longer have to wait for the other shoe to drop.

Spiritual Practices in Buddhism

The beauty of Buddha's message is that suffering is acknowledged as a reality. There is no sugarcoating that sickness, handicap, disease, or pain are real. He then tells us that there is a cause for suffering. That cause is our mind, thinking, and perceptions, the thinking that tells us we don't have a problem with alcohol or drugs when it is eminently clear that we do.

The Buddha calls the cause "craving," "clinging," and "desire." He explains that when we are experiencing something we do not like or want to be changed, the feeling of being trapped becomes exaggerated, and we experience our thoughts as torture. How often did we reach for a drink or a drug to stop uncomfortable feelings and sensations? How often did we use alcohol or drugs to assuage jealousy, anger, resentment, or trauma? But no matter how much we tried to drink or drug the pain away, the experience returned, sometimes more vigorous than ever. We could never escape the suffering if we were still clinging to the desire to be released from it.

As I worked through the causes of my own addiction, it became apparent that I had used drugs and alcohol to numb painful and uncomfortable thoughts, emotions, and physical sensations. I buried so much of what made me unhappy or uneasy, yet those things festered in the darkness of my subconscious. After engaging in a committed spiritual practice, the fog cleared, and I saw how my need and desire to escape had created the path to addiction. I had replaced one form of suffering with another.

But when we change our minds, which includes altering our perspectives in our thought and belief patterns, we can begin to end our own suffering. Taking the First Step ("We admitted we were powerless over alcohol—that our lives had become unmanageable."), we can relinquish our attempts at controlling outside forces and clinging to beliefs that no longer serve us. From there, we can begin to see how much of our suffering is self-made.

Spiritual Practices in Christianity and Judaism

For anyone in recovery or hoping to find a path to sobriety, there is much to be gleaned from the teachings of Jesus Christ and his disciples. These teachings are grounded in love, respect, compassion for one another, and self-awareness. Jesus taught the importance of giving, not judging others, not stealing, and not hoarding wealth. He emphasized the importance of prayer and the golden rule, "Do unto others as you would have them do unto you."

One of the most powerful messages of the New Testament is that "The Kingdom of Heaven is Within." This mirrors the teachings in the Upanishads of the Vedas and the Dhammapada of the Buddha. It reminds us not to seek peace or happiness *outside* of ourselves. Jesus taught that the divine is within—that our relationship to God is personal, and our connection to God is in our hearts.

In the Twelve Steps, steps two and three echo this sentiment by guiding us to seek help through belief in a power greater than ourselves and turning our will and lives over to God's care as we understand God. Throughout the steps, we are guided to engage in a personal relationship with a higher power to help us relinquish behaviors that no longer serve us, heal relationships we have harmed, and continue daily to examine our thoughts, words, and deeds in order that they be aligned with divine energy. The suggestion to engage in prayer and meditation to improve our conscious contact with our higher power provides a path that can lead us to find the Kingdom of Heaven *within.*

In the Judaic writings of the Torah, we find instructions for an "all-encompassing moral compass."[50] It is said that the Torah is like a love letter, offering meaning and nuances as expressions of love to the reader. According to many rabbis, spiritual maladies can be remedied by absorbing the guidance of the five books of Moses.[51]

There is an inspiring alignment between Torah and the Twelve Steps in that both offer lifelong pathways that carry us forward one hour, one day, or one week at a time. As a guide to living, with clear instructions from the Ten Commandments, we learn that prayer, contemplation, surrender, and humility are the foundations that help us cleanse ourselves of actions that no longer serve us. *Finding Recovery and Yourself in Torah* by Rabbi Mark Borovitz is a shining example of a modern-day writer who uses the Torah in conjunction with the Twelve Steps. Throughout this daily reader, instructions, suggestions, and reminders are given to abide by the teachings, and in so doing, we are helped to "return, repair, and respond." Return to your true Self and God; repair your past misdeeds and respond to what is asked of you by others and God.

Nature as a Spiritual Practice

Over the years, I have worked with many atheists and agnostics who express an initial and sometimes vociferous resistance to engaging in any spiritual practice such as meditation, prayer, chant, or study of "scriptures." But I believe it is essential for these clients to begin with simple practices like breathing techniques, so I begin by teaching them how to breathe and use particular techniques that can take even the most despairing individuals from the darkness of trauma, anxiety, depression, and addiction to the peace and calm of the light. I assure my clients that today's rigorous neuroscience supports all these practices and that there is no requirement for a belief in anything, *per se*. More often than not, clients become willing to bypass their initial resistance and begin their journey to healing.

Jack came to me at age twenty-eight after a decade of severe polysubstance dependence and alcoholism. Highly intelligent and creative, with a sharp wit and an impeccable ability to debate, he walked into my office a broken young man. Drugs and alcohol had led him to a complete breakdown, landing him in a psychiatric ward. Anxiety-ridden and depressed, with random panic attacks and acute self-loathing, Jack had been raised a Catholic but lived the life of an atheist. He refused to consider Alcoholics Anonymous or any other fellowship because of "the God thing." Instead of forcing him toward that pathway, I began by teaching him breathing techniques in addition to our engagement in psychotherapeutic work. I instructed him to follow his breath for one, three, and five minutes at a time without mentioning "meditation" or "contemplation." After several months, he reported engaging in these techniques daily on his own and enjoying the benefits, which included lessening his anxiety, the absence of previous panic attacks, and better sleeping cycles. He had lost weight, begun working out, and was eating more healthily, and his overall demeanor was significantly positive. He had not had a drink in almost 120 days and no drugs in nearly 160 days.

During one session, Jack commented that he had been walking down the street when it suddenly struck him that he had never felt this good before and that the feeling could be described as "happiness, or even joy." He added, "It was almost as if something else was a part of me, something holding me up or surrounding me." When we explored this further, Jack quietly reflected, "Could this be what you refer to as the universal energy, the divine? Not 'God' in the religious sense, but the *something else* that moves the earth, nature, the cosmos?"

I nodded in agreement that he was experiencing the effects of ancient wisdom in practice that had brought him to the point of personal transformation from within.

A year later, Jack altered his life path by returning to school to pursue a degree, leaving a dead-end job at a bar, and having a significant relationship with a young woman. Today, he talks about his willingness to accept something greater than himself, guiding him in his daily decisions and activities. He doesn't call it "God," but he is unequivocal that "whatever this is," it embodies the best of his Catholic upbringing with a new perception of the importance of consistent spiritual practice. If he slacks off for a day or two, he "feels the negative effect almost immediately," but when he "sticks with it day in and day out," he feels centered, calm, and focused.

None of the techniques I taught Jack or any other client are necessarily referenced to a particular religion. I use the wisdom of scriptures of those who are faith-based to engage in support, strength, and hope. For those not aligned with any particular religion but accepting the concept of a higher power, the ancient practices become a guidepost for healing.

Mindfulness Moment

> What are your values, and how do you live them in your life?
>
> As you review the list of core spiritual values, how many can you say you adhere to?
>
> How many would you like to become more mindful of?
>
> List ten things that you are grateful for.
>
> How often do you say, "Thank you"?
>
> When was the last time you engaged in an act of kindness or compassion?

Summary of Part 1

As we have seen, addiction is not a moral failing. It is a relentless, soul-destroying disease that alters the structure and function of our brains, resulting in changed behaviors and perceptions. Ultimately, it brings us to our knees, unable to recognize who we have become.

My addiction and alcoholism have made me familiar with the internal messaging we give ourselves: negative self-talk, guilt-tripping, self-condemnation, and self-shaming. We rarely feel good about ourselves, often filling our minds and hearts with agonizing self-loathing. We seek what is outside of ourselves to feed a "hole" within us that can never be filled. As Gabor Mate admonishes us, we shouldn't ask, "Why the addiction?" We should ask, "Why the pain?"[52] As Dr. Bruce Perry aptly points out, we should not ask, "What is the matter with you?" We should ask, "What happened to you?"[53]

The chapters you've read serve to affirm a life-saving truth: a new era in the treatment of addiction is upon us. Noted experts call for the treatment community to view these addictions differently and with a different eye toward healing. They argue for removing stigma, recognizing trauma as one of the root causes of addiction, and understanding the power and benefits of spirituality as one of the primary pathways to recovery.

By differentiating between religion and spirituality, we can engage in a more meaningful way with the divine, which can be defined as a power greater than ourselves, an energy that we can connect to from within, and an entity that can guide us in our lives toward internal peace, compassion for others, and self-love.

The healing path in recovery from addiction begins with surrender, an admission that we need help. From that moment on, we are carried by a force far more extensive than we can imagine. Call it universal love, the divine, higher power, nature, or god. Define it as whatever feels comfortable to you personally. Know that once experienced, it will never leave you.

The spiritual process places us squarely in the *now* and allows us to connect with our Self-energy. While spirituality is a broad concept with many definitions, it is not only a boundaryless dimension of the human experience but also a transcendent one. Each of us comes to know our higher power and derives meaning from that relationship. Our spiritual awakening gives us a chance to connect to our hearts and a feeling we never had before.

Science has caught up with over 5,000 years of ancient wisdom. We must understand the workings of our brain—this remarkable and delicate organ. Only then can we appreciate how much damage has been caused by drugs and alcohol. Knowing the parts of the brain that are affected helps us to incorporate spiritual practices that support neuroplasticity, the brain's ability to heal itself. We can begin to use the techniques with an enhanced understanding of the positive changes available to us.

The wisdom of the ancients cannot be encapsulated in a short chapter. But we can, at the least, begin to understand what so many wisdom traditions and religions called for in their quest to improve the human condition. Basic tenets repeat themselves throughout history and bring us to the current day, where we can avail ourselves of centuries of knowledge to help us on our path to healing.

Part II of this book presents the how-to of spiritual practices to help heal addiction. We will explore techniques, tools, and methods to enhance your recovery path. You will learn the power of creating a spiritual space that you can come to each day. You'll learn critical breathing and meditation techniques and how they impact the neural connections in your brain and stimulate healing. You'll learn how mantras and chants can strengthen your memory. Body recovery, such as hatha yoga, Kundalini, and Gaga movement, are all different choices that support healing the body from trauma.

Whether you are currently in recovery, want to end the vicious cycle of addiction and live a sober life, have a family member who is struggling, or work with clients who are seeking relief from their suffering, part II of *Rise in Recovery* holds the key to opening the doors of transformation for you. It is where the work begins and flourishes.

FOUR NOBLE TRUTHS[54]

I. There is suffering: Birth, decay, death, sorrow, lamentation, pain, grief, and despair are all suffering.

II. There is an origin of suffering: Craving, which gives rise to lust, desire, pleasure, and temporal happiness.

III. There is a way to extinguish suffering: the complete fading away and extinction of craving, forsaking, and giving up, the liberation and detachment of it.

IV. The way is through the Noble Eightfold Path.

THE NOBLE EIGHTFOLD PATH[55]

1. Right understanding	Samma-ditthi
2. Right Mindedness	Samma-sankappa
3. Right Speech	Samma-vaca
4. Right Action	Samma-kammanta
5. Right Living	Samma-ajiva
6. Right Effort	Samma-vayama
7. Right Attentiveness	Samma-sati
8. Right Concentration	Samma-samadhi

YAMAS [56]

Ahimsa	Non-harming, nonviolence in thought, word, and deed
Satya	Truthfulness
Asteya	Non-stealing
Brahmacharya	Right use of energy
Aparigraha	Non-greed

NIYAMAS [57]

Saucha	Cleanliness
Santosha	Contentment
Tapas	Discipline
Svadhvaya	Study of the self and texts
Isvara	Surrender to a higher being

THE TEN COMMANDMENTS: [58]

I am the Lord thy God...

1. *Thou shalt have no other gods before me.*

2. *That shalt not make for yourself a sculptured image, any likeness of what is in the heavens above...*

3. *You shall not swear falsely by the name of the Lord your God...*

4. *Remember the sabbath day and keep it holy.*

5. *Honor your father and your mother that you long endure..*

6. *You shall not murder.*

7. *You shall not commit adultery.*

8. *You shall not steal.*

9. *You shall not bear false witness against your neighbor.*

10. *You shall not covet your neighbor's house: you shall not covet your neighbor's wife, ..*

PART TWO

CHAPTER SIX
Creating Spiritual Recovery

*"Have patience in all things, but chiefly
have patience with yourself.
Do not lose courage in considering your own
imperfections, but instantly set about remedying
them—every day begin the task anew."*

—Saint Francis de Sales

*"Of all-that-is wonderful in the human being,
our most glorious asset is the capacity to change ourselves."*

—Eknath Easwaran

Our brains rewire and heal, our bodies repair, and the spirit is renewed when we relinquish the numbing substances we've used to mask emotional pain or trauma. But this is just the beginning. Without a spiritual recovery that restores our hearts and souls, we never entirely change our thoughts, beliefs, or relationships with others and the world around us. Instead, we remain in the state of "dry drunk," a condition in which we no longer drink or use drugs but still think and act as if we were. Inevitably, this leads to relapse or leaves us just as miserable as when we were using.

There is no one formula to achieve spiritual recovery, no one-size-fits-all practice. There are many paths to choose from, and each eventually leads to the same destination: a life of profound personal change, compassion, acceptance, gratitude, joy, and serenity.

The challenge for many is choosing which path will work best for them. And, once a course is selected, we may be challenged to uphold the daily commitment that is required of us. Just as New Year's Eve resolutions seem destined to fail, our promise to engage in a renewed way of life can end before it is even given a chance. The prospect of disappointment is just too great. We may rationalize our way out of pursuing a pathway to health and happiness by telling ourselves that, like the diets we tried and failed, this is just another "thing" that will result in another failure. These thoughts may be, in part, precisely what held us back from getting sober in the first place. But what if there is another way?

For those who have tried it, the spiritual path in recovery has proven to be life-changing. Taking that first step can seem daunting, but with a few simple guidelines, you can begin crafting your own journey. You will experience a new calm, centeredness, contentment, happiness, and even joy in a short amount of time.

The spiritual path asks us to do things differently. To approach life with a different perspective. To regard our past through a different lens. It offers an opportunity to connect differently with ourselves and others without fear, reticence, blame, guilt, shame, or regret. The spiritual path allows us to give ourselves the vital gift of self-love. Because so many of us have never felt we were worthy of love and have had abiding contempt for ourselves, the concept of self-love can seem foreign or terrifying. Yet eventually, if we are to recover fully, we must make a conscious decision to give this option a chance.

After all—what's the *best* that could happen?

Years ago, I devised a four-step approach to creating a daily spiritual practice that helped me break through my resistance and rationalizations. I had not engaged in anything consistently in decades. Drugs and alcohol had consumed my life to such an extent that my spiritual path crumbled into bits and pieces of half-read books and halfhearted attempts at getting back on track.

On the third day of my sobriety in 1994, something propelled me to take some new actions. I remember the day vividly. It was November, and the worst of the Florida summer heat was behind us. The sky was a radiant blue, with cool offshore breezes wafting through the windows. I cleaned my small cottage from stem to stern as if to cleanse every nook and cranny from the damaging residue of my final days of drinking. With dishes washed, floors scrubbed, counters polished, bathroom sanitized, fresh sheets on the bed, pillows plumped, my possessions organized, and clothing hung properly in the closet, I sat down on the front steps of the cottage and took a break. It was then that a still and clear phrase arose in my conscious mind, repeating, "Polish the Buddha, set up an altar, light a candle, begin again."

The phrase became more and more insistent. I got up from the steps, went inside, and cleared a space in my living room to accommodate an old, disintegrating yoga mat and a cushion from my couch. I lit a candle and said,

"May I begin again.
May I meet myself here today and every day.
Amen."

I closed my eyes for ten interminable minutes. Culling from long-lost memories of teachings, readings, and experiences, I pulled forth the Tibetan mantra "Om mani padme hum" and began repeating it. When my mind wandered, I sought to engage it with something else: my breath. When distracted again, I repeated, "Here, here, here," until ten minutes was finally up. At the time, those ten minutes felt like a hundred hours of torture. But I had declared an oath to myself to begin again. This was not a declaration for someone else or an external reason or rationale. This was for *me*.

That commitment led to a daily practice that has rarely been interrupted, enjoying stretches of hundreds of days of consistency many times over. From that first day, I began to sculpt a connection for myself that would be something I *wanted* to do, something I looked forward to. The concept of mental discipline was welcome, unlike my years as a dancer, where so much physical pain accompanied a daily routine. As I became dedicated to my practice, I soon felt devotion and strength; I could not imagine my life without it.

Commitment

A commitment requires making a solemn promise to take action.[59] It differs significantly from our easily broken promises on January 1 to go to the gym every day and lose ten pounds. A commitment calls for a firm decision that takes precedence over everything else. Put another way, it is a vow, which means we adhere to it and don't make excuses, break our promise, or let ourselves down.

The challenge of a commitment is *seeing it through*. This is tricky for those of us coming out of years of active addiction, during which we became accustomed to neglecting so much of what is vital in our lives. We have ceased to water the garden of our soul, leaving it to dry out—arid, forgotten, and bare. But gardens can be very forgiving. We must pull out weeds, turn over the earth, plant some fresh seeds and water, and watch our efforts flourish.

I use a garden analogy because when we plant seeds, they don't just sprout up overnight and give us a head of lettuce or a beautiful bunch of sunflowers. They require daily maintenance by tending to fledgling plants, watching them become seedlings, transplanting them, and giving them permanent homes to bloom in year after year. So it is with the business of our spiritual recovery. We just need to take that first step, make the commitment, and show up every day to "begin the task anew," a helpful phrase crafted by Saint Francis de Sales.[60]

Discipline

I discovered early on that telling myself I would get up at 4 a.m. every day to do two hours of meditation, prayer, and yoga was simply not doable. It wasn't realistic to expect that of myself when I also had to go to work, school, and home to study. My days were long, and raising unattainable expectations was a surefire way to fail. So, I decided to approach my discipline of commitment differently.

I first examined my schedule to see how I could sustain a daily practice. Getting up at 6 a.m. to engage in twenty minutes of meditation and prayer, followed by another twenty minutes of yoga, was far more reasonable. The first day after my "spring clean" in November, I set the alarm for 6 a.m., an unheard-of time for me to awaken. But without the fog from two liters of wine dulling my brain, I rose with less grudging resistance than I had in years. I sat on my cushion, took a deep breath, lit the candle, and repeated the words that had come to me the day before.

"May I begin again.
May I meet myself here today and every day.
Amen."

Closing my eyes, I followed my breath. Repeatedly, I brought my attention to it. My mind wandered; it ran amok, made lists, chattered about the past, and projected into the future. Each time I realized it had taken itself for a stroll, I brought my attention back to focus on inhaling and exhaling. For ten minutes that, once again, felt like hours, I hung in there. Finally, I opened my eyes and engaged in "prayer," which was reading spiritual material that would inspire me and keep me on this healing path. I took notes from these readings in a brand-new journal bought for this purpose and used a new pen whose ink didn't smear. After another ten minutes, I got up; keeping "doable" in mind, I performed three rounds of sun salutations on my mat. None of this was easy. It took effort, and some days I had to push myself to get out of bed and get on the cushion. This was new behavior, and I was creating new habits in my life and new neural connections.

Throughout the day, I reminded myself to bring my attention back to my breath. If I started to get anxious about a class assignment or money being in short supply, I recited the Serenity Prayer frequently. I attended a meeting of Alcoholics Anonymous every single day. Instead of drinking myself into a stupor in the evenings, I went to bed at a reasonable time and wrote out five things that I was grateful for. I would read until I fell asleep, which was an entirely new behavior for me.

Rinse, repeat. I would wake up the next day and perform the same action as the day before. While the daytime schedule might have been different, the morning and evening routines never wavered.

After about six weeks, I realized that the ten-minute meditation was less about my mind going off in a hundred directions and more about being able to stay focused on my breath for one or two minutes at a time. I realized I was making progress. I went from three to five sun salutations. The material I was reading each morning was becoming understandable. I was absorbing the words and seeing how they could be implemented in my own life.

When I celebrated my first year of sobriety, I got up at 5:45 a.m. to do fifteen minutes of meditation and ten rounds of sun salutations. My evening routine expanded to include another ten minutes of meditation before bed.

With my daily commitment to my sobriety and spiritual recovery, the discipline I engaged in began transforming into something else. My perception of this personal promise to myself began to alter. I came across a passage by Jon Kabat-Zinn that discusses mindfulness practice as committing "fully in each moment to being present. There is no 'performance.' There is just this moment."[61] I slowly began to acknowledge that this discipline had begun to take on a new dimension: dedication.

There are many ways to engage in spiritual practice. My method worked for me, but I am not saying you should do what I did. As we will see shortly, there are numerous approaches to a daily discipline where we take the time to connect with ourselves, commune with our higher power, and steady our minds.

Dedication

The New Shorter Oxford English Dictionary defines dedication as "single-mindedly loyal and conscientious." Books and monuments are dedicated, and humans can dedicate themselves to a particular cause or purpose. When we become dedicated to something, we find a more profound reason that propels us to sacrifice certain aspects of our lives to achieve and maintain our goals. This includes resisting the desire to hit the snooze button for "five more minutes" or "just this once."

After several years, my spiritual recovery practice went from getting up at 6 a.m. to getting up at 5 a.m. and looking forward to twenty- or thirty-minute meditation practice followed by another twenty to thirty minutes of prayer and yoga. I had over an hour to do what had become a routine that gave me something I had not had in decades: self-respect. I was living up to my promise. For the first time in a long time, I had given up excuses and was embodying the Twelve Step moniker of "suiting up and showing up." Not only for myself but for others.

While my practice has focused on different techniques, shifted in sequences, and added materials outside my comfort zone, it has remained steadfast for the past twenty-eight years. Every morning, in one way or another, whether at home, on an airplane, in a hotel, or visiting friends and family, I get up well before anyone else, place myself somewhere quiet, and engage in meditation, contemplation, prayer, and self-renewal.

Dedication involves planning. If I am traveling, I make sure that I schedule my morning routine despite time changes. I once woke up at 2 a.m. in a foreign country with my internal clock telling me it was time to practice. I got up quietly so as not to wake my husband, got dressed, tiptoed out, and walked a few empty blocks until I came upon a temple. The doors were closed; no one was in sight, and everything was wrapped in total silence. I made myself comfortable on the steps and settled into a profound meditation. Without realizing it, I sat for almost three hours in complete stillness. The sunrise touched the horizon, and I remained seated, looking around me, absorbed in the blessing of being in a remarkable place, sober and connected to self and the divine. How different this experience was from being in Morocco decades before, homeless, hungover, and having no purpose in my life!

If my practice sounds extensive, it has grown over the years from a time when ten minutes felt like hours to where hours feel like minutes. Not everyone will want to engage in this kind of rigor. But as so many researchers have made clear, based on the evidence, ten minutes a day is sufficient to change your mind and change your brain.

What I have come to learn over time is that I would never have envisioned myself being involved in such an in-depth spiritual program. Each person experiences something different. For each program created by our tastes and style, once started, the commitment and discipline take on a momentum that leads to results that far exceed our initial expectations.

The amount of time you spend on your spiritual practice is a personal decision. If you work a stressful job with high demands, distractions, and a twenty-four-seven mindset, you may tell yourself that it's impossible to get into spiritual practice. Allowing yourself to *change your mind* about that belief means the difference between changing the quality of your life and your recovery or being stuck in a rut heading toward burnout. Ask yourself, honestly, *How much time do I waste watching stupid TV or scrolling on TikTok or Facebook?* Ask yourself if it would be possible to get up twenty minutes earlier every day for the gift of silence, breathing, and calm. What lengths did you go to when you were drinking or using drugs? How much time did you waste chasing your high? You have an opportunity to do things differently. You can engage in behaviors that will change your life and begin to appreciate the precious minutes of connection.

Perhaps you are a mother, wife, and businesswoman, and you somehow juggle all those responsibilities and pack it into one day. Or you are a husband, father, and businessman with enormous work responsibilities. Where on earth are you going to find the fifteen or twenty minutes a day to sit quietly, breathe, meditate, or do yoga? Begin by asking yourself how much time you spent drinking the night before and recovering from the hangover the next day. How much physical, emotional, and psychic energy was spent drinking so that you were adequately numbed out, sleeping terribly because your brain was saturated in alcohol, and then waking up with either a raging headache or your entire brain feeling like it was in a fog? I can assure you that after several days of not drinking, you will begin to sleep better, you will wake up more refreshed, and your evenings will suddenly have more hours in them. Somewhere in all of that exists the fifteen or twenty minutes to sit quietly, close your eyes, focus on your breath, read an inspirational passage, and jot down some notes about your insights.

They say that dedication is not for the fainthearted. I believe that may be true, but I also know that you can't *begin* by being dedicated to something. Dedication is an evolving journey of many steps, resulting in an eventual awareness that life is so much different than it was before. Once we arrive there, we realize we have gone further than we ever imagined because we have been steadfast.

When roadblocks inevitably arise in life, our dedication to spiritual recovery must double down. Challenges, upsets, illness, and unforeseen crises can derail us, but only if we let them. Setting our daily intention to begin anew offers us the opportunity to greet each day as a unique one. It helps us remain centered, focused, and aligned with our recovery. Our dedication becomes our salvation.

Devotion

There are hundreds of examples of illuminated beings who exemplify spiritual devotion. The Dalai Lama, Mother Theresa, Mahatma Gandhi, Bishop Desmond Tutu, Martin Luther King Jr., St. Francis, St. Theresa, Thomas Merton . . . the list is long. From eradicating Apartheid in South Africa to healing the untouchables ravaged by leprosy in India to altering the trajectory of equal rights in America, these men and women have shown us how to better the lives of others and ourselves.

We can bring devotion to our realm in ways that change our lives and the lives of our family members, friends, and even our community. We can "transcend our limited identity and limited self-interest" and take on a "God's-eye perspective," as so beautifully stated by Bishop Desmond Tutu.[62] When we place ourselves in the light and see through the eyes of the light, we transform our relationship with everyone we meet. We move away from the self-centered "me, my, mine" to a relational "we, our, ours."

When astronauts ventured into outer space and witnessed Earth floating in an endless expanse, their awareness of life for humans on our planet was forever altered. Selfish interests, wars, terrorism, poverty, and hunger took on a new meaning. This is referred to as "the overview effect" and is a reminder that life here on this planet is very precious, and so much of what the human race is concerned about, such as who is right and who is wrong, having more "likes" on social media than someone else, or being the first to own the latest gadget is, in fact, meaningless. There is something so much greater than those concerns.

Creating a Sacred Space

Our devotion can be reflected by creating a space in our homes where we can spend quality time in our spiritual endeavors. This is a place of grounding. It becomes our "true north"—a fixed point where we can go to be centered and connect to our Self and Higher Power.

Creating a place for yourself to engage in your daily practice is not necessary; it's essential. When we designate an area in our living domain to be the seat of our spirituality, we are claiming an energetic space and preparing to imbue it with our commitment, discipline, dedication, and devotion.

Going out and buying expensive Balinese teak altars or fancily decorated Japanese chests is unnecessary. Of course, if you want to and can afford to, by all means, do. But over the years, I have found that creating a simple altar or spiritual space is inexpensive, easy, and meaningful. You can take a piece of wood, place it on two bricks or orange crates, and cover the wood or the whole thing in a piece of colored fabric, and you have an altar. Another option is to lay a small rug in the corner of a room as a space designation. Place a cushion that you will sit on in the middle, and you have just created a meditation space. A small chest or trunk found at a consignment store or Goodwill can be repainted and serve as storage and as your altar.

Creative options know no bounds. What is essential is to make something that you will treasure and treat with a certain reverence. No matter how simple or ornate, when we recognize that our altar is the spiritual bookmarker for our daily practice, we welcome the time to be there every day.

Anything can be placed on an altar. Statues, photographs, or pieces of art. These are very personal items that speak to our self-energy. Candles and incense are lovely staples as they can be used as an invitation to our daily practice. Or perhaps a rosary or mala beads laid out can be the reminder that your practice is waiting for you.

Nondenominational altars support a myriad of items from nature. Stones found in a river or brook, feathers found on the beach or in the woods, shells, crystals, and driftwood can all serve as items that will draw you to your practice each day. Or perhaps just a journal and an inspirational book are all you need. In the Japanese Zen tradition, there is very little on the altar's surface, signifying simplicity and the importance of emptying the noise from our internal and external world.

I have had many altars in many residences, and each one has been a call to my daily meeting with my Self and my higher power. Some have been ornate, and some embody simplicity. I have also made altars in my natural surroundings where I sit and engage in a calm, centered connection with the trees, brooks, birds, and various animal residents of the outdoors.

We can create any space anywhere, whether a corner of a room or the entire space. When we designate an area that we decide will be imbued with the sacred, add personal items that are meaningful to us, and care for that space daily, we remind ourselves that we are here for a much higher purpose. The altar is a physical manifestation of our spiritual transformation.

Daily Practices

Sakyong Mipham, son of Chogyam Trungpa Rinpoche, lineage holder of the Shambhala Tradition, has repeatedly stated that if we engage in daily practice, two things must be in place: a comfortable seat and a reasonable amount of time. In a retreat I attended years ago, he said, "If you are not comfortable in your seat, you will not go to it. It has to invite you, and you must feel that you could stay there all day because it is pleasant and easy."[63] Why, he added, would you want to come to a cushion or a meditation seat that is hard, uncomfortable, and makes you feel that you just want to leave it? He then admonished us to "be reasonable about the time you will commit to your practice. If it is ten minutes, make it the best ten minutes you can. Don't expect yourself to practice for an hour when you only have ten minutes! Then you disappoint yourself!"[64]

Whether you plan to use your spiritual space to meditate, pray, journal, read, or practice bodywork, it must be comfortable. Otherwise, part of you will resist being there, and the whole exercise becomes self-defeating. I once purchased a cushion from a high-end yoga and meditation store, loving the fabric's color and being enticed by the austerity of the design. When I got home, eager to try it out, I sat down and ended up fidgeting, trying to get comfortable; my hips and legs were unsupported, and my back began to ache from the strain. If this happened after less than two or three minutes, what would it be like after an hour? I returned the item and found something that better supported my body and was comfortable. I learned a valuable lesson in the process.

Daily practice means just that. You engage in something each day and become disciplined about doing so. Tommy Rosen points out that the "root of the word discipline—*disciple*—means 'student of' or 'follower of.'"[65] When we adopt a student's mind, we become willing to learn. When we allow ourselves to be a student, we will, after much practice, realize the true sense of joy that comes from single-pointed intention, attention, commitment, and dedication. As Shunryu Suzuki pointed out in *Zen Mind, Beginners Mind*, "If your mind is empty, it is always ready for anything, it is open to everything. In the beginner's mind there are many possibilities, but in the expert's mind there are few." [66]

Remaining teachable and open to learning new ways of seeing, doing, thinking, or being can mean the difference between a dry recovery that engages only in abstinence or one that is filled with positive change, renewal, and a great sense of happiness and well-being.

Agnostic or Atheist Spiritual Recovery

Many clients who come to recovery are not religious, and many do not believe in the idea of a "traditional" God. For many, the very word *god* creates resistance. I have made it my life's work as an addiction therapist to accommodate agnostic or atheist clients by reframing what it means to have a "spiritual connection." As discussed in chapter 2, spirituality is religionless; there is no dogma or absolutes in a spiritual perspective. Spirituality is more about connection, compassion, and stillness within us that is welcomed and embraced.

You do not have to believe in God to have spiritual recovery. As we learned in an earlier chapter, a cactus can be a higher power. The most basic place to start for an atheist or agnostic is with nature. There is no question that the realm of the oceans, earth, and heavens can be awe-inspiring. Watching the waves roll in and out on a beach is a meditation. So is walking on a beach and feeling the grains of sand under your feet. Watching gulls, egrets, or pelicans fly over the waves and flitter along the shore can connect us to "other." As the saying in Twelve Step meetings goes, pick a higher power, anything; just make sure it's not *you*.

Living in a city does not preclude a connection to nature. I've lived in metropolitan areas such as New York City, London, Miami, and Los Angeles, and I have always been able to find nature. Central Park, Hyde Park, Griffith Park. Any major city in the world has a place where we can go to seek peace from the perpetual noise. The suburbs may be a clustered housing outpost of a city center. Still, some of their assets are walking and running paths built into developments that facilitate the enjoyment of the outdoors. Whether walking the dog or the baby stroller, connecting to fresh air, the elements of rain, sun, snow, and everything in between—the outdoors helps our health and spiritual well-being.

One client of mine, whom I will call Samuel, could not abide by the idea of participating in any activity close to what he perceived as religious. This included meditation, reading inspirational writings, and the like. When asked what he longed to do on his own, away from anyone else, his reply was to run or ride his bike through the miles and miles of trails near his home. Having spent years focused on drinking or getting over the effects of daily drinking in the form of wicked hangovers, his passion for physical activity had long gone by the wayside. Together, we created a daily schedule in which he could commit to running, biking, or walking and mentally reviewing a list of things he was grateful for.

Over the course of several months, Samuel reported on his daily routine; his descriptions began to take on a different timbre than when he first began. He reflected on his experience of peace while riding a trail as the sun rose, saying, "I don't know how to describe it. I feel so connected to the sky as it begins to lighten and the trees and plants along the trail as they catch the sun's rays—hearing the birds waking up—it's a vastly different experience than I have ever had in my life. I guess others would call it being in touch with God. I'm just going to say something special happens to me when I'm out there. I like it, and it feels good, so I want to keep doing it." Several months later, Samuel asked me if I would teach him to meditate and what nondenominational, inspirational books I might recommend.

Samuel was like many who do not embrace the idea that God still embraces nature's power. And what better place to find God than in the natural world? Even if we don't use the word "God," we can connect with something greater than ourselves, which is the basis for spiritual recovery in its simplest form.

In atheist or agnostic spiritual recovery, we can still choose to come to our sacred space and meditate, breathe, engage in yoga or other bodywork, read inspirational materials that speak to us, journal, and center ourselves.

Christian Spiritual Recovery

I have had many Christian clients of varying denominations, from Catholic to Baptist and Episcopalian to Nondenominational. Some attend church regularly, and some lapsed a long time ago. Some are devout. Some are noncommittal.

For those who have lapsed, I found it helpful to engage in a conversation about what took place in their lives that caused their faith to take a back seat. For some, it is the belief that "I can't be forgiven for my addiction." For others, "I felt God turned his back on me when I fell into the abyss of drugs." When I ask what they loved about their faith, I usually hear, "the message of love" or "the feeling of acceptance during services." When I ask them the last time they prayed, they will usually tell me, "I haven't prayed in ages, and then it was just the kind of prayers to get me out of trouble."

It is hard for anyone to begin again. But start again . . . we must.

Starting our day connecting with God as we understand God, be it Jesus or the Holy Spirit, we feed our brain with hope and potential. I always suggest that before getting out of bed each morning, we thank God for the day ahead:

> *"Thank you, God, for this day, its beauty, and its possibility. May I remain sober today."*
> *"Oh, Divine, may this day be fulfilled in Your will. Please keep me from any substances today."*
> *"Our Father, may You guide me today toward healing. Help me to stay clean today."*

I may suggest that you sit with literature from the Bible or influencers in your faith with a cup of coffee or tea. Perhaps the 23rd Psalm resonates or the Beatitudes (Mathew 5:1-12). Or maybe the Prayer of St. Francis of Assisi, the Prayer of St. Ignatius, the Lord's Prayer, or the Hail Mary.

The writings of Thomas Merton may be appealing, as are the writings of St. Augustine, C.S. Lewis, or Mother Theresa. Many authors have written commentaries on Christian thought. My favorite is Eknath Easwaran, who wrote several books of essays on St. Paul, St. Augustine, Mother Theresa, and Thomas A. Kempis. Whatever the choice, spend five to ten minutes reading a passage and making notes about what resonated and what was brought into focus for you.

Breathing techniques can be used throughout the day to connect to God. Saying "thank you" as a prayer or grateful thought is a beautiful way to acknowledge that you are being given gifts daily.

Night allows us to engage in contemplative practices taught in this tradition. Reviewing the day and all that we are grateful for helps us to make an honest assessment of our actions, reactions, and the gifts freely given to us. Every twenty-four hours allows us to connect meaningfully with our chosen faith. Attending church regularly or becoming a member of a sober community will enable us to leave our sense of isolation behind, bringing us closer to others seeking recovery and a sober life. As participants, we engage in the miracle of healing; eventually, we can help others do the same.

Judaic Spiritual Recovery

Over the past several years, I have embarked on a study of the Judaic traditions, ideals, writings, and teachings. I am by no means an expert, but I have benefited, as a student, from some of the most learned scholars. While I am not Jewish, I nonetheless engage daily in readings from Rabbi Abraham J. Twersky, MD, whose book *Living Each Day* contains scripture from the Torah, commentary from noted rabbinical wise men, and suggestions on how to live each day ethically.

Jewish traditions hold many rites and rituals connecting us to spiritual life with little effort. If you were raised in a Jewish household and observed the Sabbath but lost your connection along the way, why not use this day as a reminder to detach from the outside world? Unplug, turn off your cell phone, and spend some time reflecting, reading, and reconnecting.

In some Judaic traditions, prayers are recited before taking water, food, or other sustenance into the body. There are prayers upon waking, throughout the day, and ending the day to sleep. You can say one prayer or many. As you will see in the chapter on prayer and mantra, this is a way to connect, become centered and calm, and raise your compassionate awareness of yourself and those around you.

You can attend Shabbat at your local synagogue or observe it as part of the conclusion of the work week. You can choose to keep kosher or be more mindful of your food. You can sign up for daily wisdom emails from several online resources (https://reformjudaism.org/; https://www.myjewishlearning.com/; https://www.chabad.org).

Whether you are comfortable with Conservative, Reform, or Orthodox Judaism, you can return to your roots and embrace the spiritual gifts of this tradition. Focusing on *yetzer tov*, or the instinct to do good, will keep you closer to *neshama*, your soul.

Above all, dedicating yourself to daily spiritual practices will lead you to a new relationship with yourself and your *Self*. You will know a "new freedom and a new happiness" because you will work through a commitment grounded in discipline, which will become a dedication in your life, leading to devotion. There may be bumpy days; there may even be less than stellar practice sessions. That is called life. But knowing that you met yourself on the mat, cushion, or chair, in front of an altar, lighting a candle, is the difference between saying to yourself, "Good job," or "I've let myself down, again." The former will take you further on the recovery path to healing; the latter will only undermine your confidence and self-esteem. Telling ourselves that we've done poorly can be disheartening and discouraging. Pushing ourselves that extra inch to get out of bed and be involved in spiritual recovery will take us to places of joy and happiness we never imagined.

As they say in Twelve Step programs, *"Don't stop before the miracle happens."*

Mindfulness Moment

What are you grateful for today?

What do you have today that you didn't have a year ago? Five years ago?

What intentional act of compassion could you give to someone, including yourself, today?

What are you willing to relinquish today to make your life better tomorrow?

How would you change your current daily schedule to bring spiritual practices to your life?

What are the distractions that you would be willing to relinquish to enhance your recovery?

CHAPTER SEVEN

Breath is Your Life (Pranayama)

"Breath is the bridge which connects life to consciousness, which unites your body to your thoughts. Whenever your mind becomes scattered, use your breath as the means to take hold of your mind again."

—Thich Nhat Hanh

"Then the Lord God formed a man from the dust of the ground and breathed into his nostrils the breath of life, and the man became a living being."

—Genesis 2, verse 7

"Awareness of breath is the beginning and end of the road to enlightenment."

—Brown & Gerarg

Our first inhalation is at our birth. We come into this world and gasp for breath. Our lungs empty the amniotic fluid, and we bring oxygen into our system. From that moment on, we spend the rest of our lives breathing. Breath is the source of life and begins on the inhale. At our death, we exhale. Everything in between is our existence.

In the past several decades, the importance of our breath on physical and mental health has entered mainstream medicine in a meaningful way. Research into yogic breathing techniques, known as *pranayama*, highlights the benefits of ancient techniques applied to modern science. More books are being published on the subject; the research community is beginning to embrace breath-focused therapies for physical and psychological treatments. Articles are emerging on topics like using breath for pain management, improved immune responses after COVID-19, insomnia, and anxiety.

Pranayama is translated to "control of life energy" (*prana=life energy, yama=control*). Ancient scriptures emphasized the importance of harnessing our breath for the fullness of our well-being and psyches. The *Yoga Sutras of Patanjali* devotes several chapters to explaining and describing the use and benefits of pranayama, defining it as ". . . the cosmic force without which nothing moves or functions. As gasoline, it moves the motorcar. As electricity, it radiates light through a bulb. Even our thoughts are moved by prana."[67]

Our breath impacts so much more than just bringing oxygen into our lungs. It affects our nervous and cardiovascular systems, regulates blood health, and impacts our mental health. Controlled breathing enhances our ability to relax, which is why so many forms of meditation focus on the breath. Our breathing slows and deepens when we are in a relaxed state and increases and becomes shallower when agitated or feeling panicky. Stress responses of the body are directly linked to the breath.

The sympathetic nervous system is our "flight-fight-freeze" response to danger, a perceived threat, or attack and can activate instantly. If you've been spooked by something, you know that your heart starts to race, and you may feel flushed or have the sensation of itchy skin.

The cascade of two major stress hormones—adrenaline and cortisol—hitting your system in seconds, can last anywhere from twenty minutes to over an hour. The sympathetic response may be helpful if you are in actual danger—your body will be able to run faster and act more quickly. But this is not a condition to live in permanently. If you suffer from panic attacks, anxiety, or PTSD, your body is in a constant state of hypervigilance. Since it cannot maintain this indefinitely, the brain signals that it needs something to soothe and calm. Some easier things to reach for are alcohol, video games, and shopping. Other items include drugs, gambling, and sex. While many of these may slow down the sympathetic response, it becomes an unhealthy process that quickly leads to more problems, specifically addiction.

Where Is the Breath in Our Body?

Virtually every client I have worked with believes that their breath takes place in their upper chest between the breastbone and the clavicle. They are usually surprised that their lungs extend further down to the base of their ribcage. The breath begins at the bottom and moves upward. When we take a puff from our upper lungs, we bring almost 50 percent less oxygen into our system than we need. When I work with clients on breathing techniques, I first show them an image of the anatomical structure of the lungs.

Your lungs are encased by the rib cage and positioned from the front of the torso to the backbone. The right lung is larger than the left, which shares anatomical space with the heart. The upper lungs contain the bronchia, which are tubular branches that divide into smaller components leading to the air sacs. An infection in this area leads to bronchitis or bronchial pneumonia. The upper lung is only a portion of the whole, not where breath begins. [68]

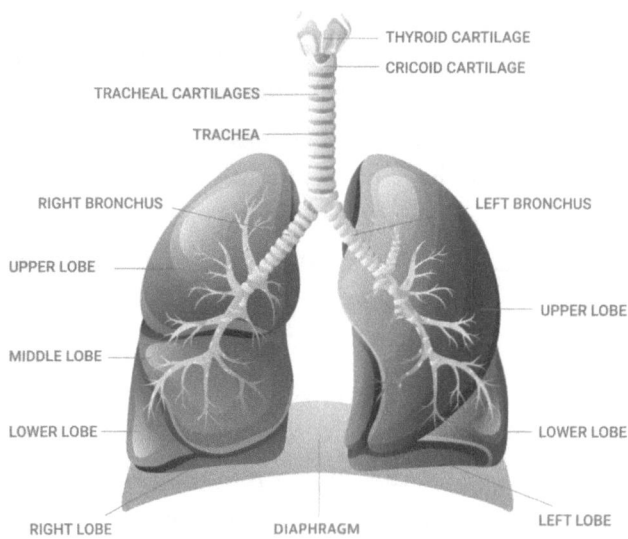

Figure 1 Lungs Diagram [69]

The diaphragm sits below the lungs and acts like a pump to help the lungs expand and contract. When we engage the diaphragm muscle, we support the lungs to bring air in or push it out. It may seem counterintuitive initially, but more air can come into the lungs when the diaphragm is in the contracted position (flattened). When the diaphragm is in an expanded place (opened), the air is pushed out of the lungs.

To engage the diaphragm muscles, the first thing we must do is soften the abdomen. Having rigid abdominal muscles prohibits the movement of the diaphragm and reduces the amount of potential oxygen intake. When you soften your belly, you can move the diaphragm with greater ease and have more control over your breath.

The Inhale

The first step of an inhale is to bring air into the nostrils, *not* through the mouth. Mouth breathing is a very detrimental habit leading to numerous illnesses and chronic conditions. When you breathe through your mouth, you increase your pulse and blood pressure; your body loses up to 40 percent more water as a direct result of mouth breathing. Structurally, when we breathe through the mouth, the soft tissue in the back of our mouth becomes loose and tilts inward, which narrows the airways, making breathing more difficult. Breathing through the nose strengthens the tissues and expands the airways, making breathing easier.

The inhale comes from a softened belly, which expands as you begin to bring oxygen into your nostrils, allowing the diaphragm to collapse and the lungs to expand. The lungs include the "thoracic" lung and the back of the ribs. When you bring air into your lungs, you will feel this part of your body open, and more air can enter your system. Oxygen is then brought up to the upper part of your lung (the bronchi) and further up to the vessels under your collarbone.

It's a smooth movement that is not strained, forced, or pushed. The inhale is all about expansion.

The more we think of the inhale as opening and expanding, the easier it is to bring oxygen into our system. When this method of inhaling becomes part of our daily breath routine, our lungs begin to expand and can take in even more air. Stories of pearl divers who go underwater without equipment and stay down for up to seven minutes at a time are an example of how lung capacity can be naturally enhanced.

A seventy-year research project known as the Framingham Study examined over 5,000 subjects for twenty years and determined that longevity was not correlated to heart, diet, or daily exercise. The direct correlation was lung capacity.[70] Medical science is finding that as we age, we can reverse the natural decline of our lung capacity by exercising and using breathing techniques to keep the lungs malleable. In doing so, we can maintain a healthy heart condition and immune system.

The Exhale

One of the basic tenets of breathing is that you need to breathe out properly before you can breathe in. The mechanics of an outbreath has to do with moving used oxygen, which becomes carbon dioxide in the blood to be expelled by your lungs. As much as every cell in our body needs oxygen to exist, it also needs to have a way to transport the used oxygen waste out of the body.

The exhale is a more passive activity than the inhale. Being mindful of how we exhale will help us to eliminate waste more effectively. In conscious breathing exercises, we use the abdomen to help the diaphragm push additional gaseous debris out of the body. The instruction is simply to pull the navel toward the spine at the end of an exhale. When you gently contract the abdominal muscles in this way, a significant amount of additional air can be expelled.

Other waste products leave the body through the exhale, helping to eliminate impurities from cells in the physical structure and the brain.[71] Receptors in the brain that control breathing monitor chemical compounds to increase or decrease oxygen in the body. When we are more active, our breathing rate increases to take in more oxygen. When we are less active, our breathing rates slow down. But additional effects impact our mental health and can remarkably support our recovery from substances.

Intentional Breathing

"Slow down and take a breath!" This advice heard worldwide in almost every yoga studio, stress management class, or meditation workshop is the basic instruction for intentional breathing. Also known as "mindful breath," this technique dates back thousands of years and can trace to Vedic writings, which formed the basis of yoga as we know it today.

Neuro- and pulmonary science can point to particular brain centers activated when we focus on the length, depth, and quality of our breathing. Intentional breathing stimulates the vagus nerve that travels from our brain to our abdomen, controlling the sympathetic nervous system, the fight-flight-freeze response to potential danger. The vagus nerve uses a brain chemical that initiates a relaxation response and activates our parasympathetic nervous system, our calming, resting state.

When we become anxious or stressed, almost every part of our body tenses: abdomen, shoulders, neck, jaw, chest; we might be trying to meet a deadline, dealing with too many emails, stuck in traffic, running late for an appointment, or feeling as if we are under siege from an overwhelming number of responsibilities. All these moments add to significant stress responses and can lead to many unhelpful behaviors to alleviate the pressure. Breath awareness and intentional breathing can change your brain's stress response and calm your entire system in minutes.

Paying attention to your breath is as simple as saying, "Breathe!" The moment you do this, you are bringing your focus on the inhale, which creates a chain reaction in your body and mind. Your brain networks respond positively when you focus on your breath, particularly those that regulate moment-to-moment awareness and body connection.[72] From the first inhale of intentional breathing, you activate the parasympathetic system, which includes generating acetylcholine. This critical neurotransmitter helps to slow the heart rate and dilate blood vessels. Dopamine and GABA are essential neurochemicals that help calm and regulate anxiety responses.

Breathing Techniques

Unlike our ancestors, the twenty-first century human has become habituated to operating from a place of daily stress. Instead of facing saber-toothed tigers, we are subject to constant demands for our attention—technology, twenty-four-seven news cycles, and required instant responses without any opportunity to be reflective. For many, our work life has transitioned to a virtual space like Zoom, where we are at once comfortable with not having to deal with traffic on a daily basis but are now more isolated than ever in our homes. Our brains have not been able to adapt to the very technology it has created, which has caused an unprecedented level of anxiety in our culture. It's the tip of the iceberg, as we have also faced global strife, economic uncertainty, and a virus that stopped the world in its tracks for over two years.

It's easy to say, "unplug," but the damage from decades of these levels of stressors has resulted in the most significant spike in mental health crises ever recorded. This, in turn, has correlated to the sharpest rise in substance abuse and dependence ever seen in our country.[73] For those of us in early or sustained recovery, these challenges have taken a toll. But there is a way to begin the healing process for the body and mind, and it is through daily breathing techniques.

Thich Nhat Hanh, beloved Vietnamese monk and author of *Peace Is Every Step*, gives the most basic and powerful instruction that I have ever encountered:

> "*As you breathe in, say to yourself,*
> '*Breathing in, I know that I am breathing in.*'
> *As you breathe out, say,*
> '*Breathing out, I know that I am breathing out.*'
> *Just that.*"[74]

He explains that we don't have to recite the whole sentence but instead just say the words "in" and "out" as a cue. This technique has remarkable effects as it brings body, mind, and spirit together, allowing us to access the antidotes to stress.

A dear friend of mine who is not only a sage soul but in long-term recovery told me that she was experiencing insomnia. She related that instead of fretting about not going or staying asleep, she began to use the meditation techniques she teaches students, namely, to repeat over and over in our mind, "Breathing in, breathing out." The benefit, she said, was not only calming her mind into a relaxed, meditative state, but she inevitably fell into a deep and peaceful sleep.

As she related this, I thought of my sleepless nights and decided to try this for myself. I was amazed by the instant calm it produced and how I fell into a restful sleep within ten to twenty minutes. This has become my mainstay, and I use the technique *before* going to sleep and find that if I do wake up in the middle of the night, it is much easier to get back to sleep by repeating the self-instruction.

Breath techniques range from extremely simple to requiring much practice to master. Different methods can range from the yoga tradition, such as hatha or Kundalini, which employs more vigorous styles. I encourage you to experiment with all of them as they will bring you a benefit, even if they may be challenging.

Counting Breaths

The most basic breath technique is to count while inhaling and exhaling. Beginning with empty lungs, expanding the abdomen, and using the diaphragm to bring oxygen into your thoracic and then upper lungs, count to four while doing so. At the top of your breath, hold for two counts. Then count to six for your exhale. The exhale should always be longer than the inhale. With a *4-2-6* count, your breath should feel relaxed, not strained. Remember to always pull in your navel at the end of your exhale to ensure all the carbon dioxide has been released from your respiratory system.

If this breath count feels easy, you can increase the count slightly to expand the benefits. Begin with a six count for the inhale, hold at the top of the breath for four counts, and then exhale for eight counts. The *6-4-8* breath count allows more oxygen into your system and more carbon dioxide expelled. The immediate benefit of this technique is the rapid generation of dopamine, serotonin, and norepinephrine.

Another counting technique is to inhale in a protracted, slow manner through the nose, counting from one to ten. Hold your breath for ten counts when you reach the top of the inhale. Then slowly exhale through your nose, counting from one to ten. When you have reached the bottom of the exhale, hold your breath and count from one to ten. Then inhale again and repeat the entire process. Counting backward from ten to one will enhance your concentration while you use this technique.

Nadi Shadona or Alternate Nostril Breathing

In regular breathing through the nose, we are bringing oxygen into both nostrils. An excellent technique to balance our system fully is to alternate our breath from one nostril to the other and back again. This is called *nadi shadona*. Nadi, in Sanskrit, is the energy channels in our body that are believed to carry our life force. The yogic philosophy of health asserts that these passages, known as *ida, pingala,* and *shushumna*, help to balance our subtle (*ida*), active (*pingala*), and spinal (*shushumna*) energies. When the nadi are blocked or not functioning correctly, we experience less vitality, stamina, and overall health. The breath moves energy through the nadi and helps to cleanse and restore any imbalances in these pathways.

I instruct clients to perform the alternate nostril breath technique first thing in the morning to set a balanced tone for their body, mind, and spirit for the rest of the day. The instruction is relatively simple and requires the practitioner to give a minimum of five to seven minutes to receive the full benefit of this breath exercise. If that is too much time, I suggest ten "rounds" (see below.)

You begin by placing the index and middle finger of your right hand on the "third eye" of your forehead. You will feel a slight indentation in your forehead bone between the eyebrows and about an inch above the bridge of the nose. The Ajna chakra, which corresponds directly to the pineal gland, is named for its pine cone shape. It is located deep in the middle of the brain and regulates the production of melatonin and our circadian rhythms or internal clock.

Your right thumb will regulate your right nostril, and your ring finger will regulate your left nostril. The left nostril controls the *ida*, the calming and relaxing channel of your body and brain. The right nostril contains the *pingala*, activating and stimulating your body for alertness and your brain for motivation and executive thinking.

Figure 2 Nadi Shodhana

With your eyes closed and sitting in a "noble" posture, close off your right nostril with your right thumb and begin breathing into your left nostril. This should be a long, slow inhale, using a count of six.

When you have reached the top of the inhale, close your left nostril with your right ring finger and open your right nostril to exhale. The exhale should be long and slow, using a count of eight. When the exhale has come to its natural end, inhale through the right nostril for a count of six, and then block off the right nostril with the right ring finger, open the left nostril, and exhale on a count of eight. This constitutes one "round," where you have inhaled and exhaled with each nostril. You can do ten rounds each morning or set your timer for five to seven minutes.

From a neuroscientific perspective, nadi shadona has many unique benefits. In addition to bringing equal amounts of oxygen to both hemispheres of the brain, the practice supports verbal and learning memory and regulation of the hypothalamus and pituitary glands.[75] Positive moods are enhanced due to the stimulation of dopamine, with cortisol significantly reduced, resulting in evidence that anxiety, panic attacks, and PTSD symptoms are alleviated.[76] Researchers have found that balanced breathing, such as alternate nostril breath, increases cognitive function.[77]

Ujjayi Breath or Ocean Breath

If you've ever taken a yoga class, you will have heard the term "ujjayi breath." This technique is used primarily during the exhale, usually while performing sun salutations. If you do not do yoga, no worries— this breath can be used anytime, anywhere.

First, take an inhale through your nose. As you exhale, constrict the back of your throat, or, to be precise, the "glottis" will make a "whooshing" sound as you release the air from your lungs. Ujjayi breath is also known as ocean breath because that sound created by pushing the air through your constricted throat can sometimes sound like the waves hitting the shore.

Once you have completed the exhale, inhale again and repeat the exhale with the constricted throat. It is strongly suggested to use regular counts for ujaya, such as inhale six and exhale six, inhale eight and exhale eight, or inhale ten and exhale ten. Do what is comfortable for you, and as the technique becomes more accessible, you can increase the count.

Research has found that ujjayi is beneficial for hypothyroidism, due to stimulating muscles around the thyroid gland and surrounding throat organs, and cancer patients receiving chemotherapy.[78] The benefits include releasing tension throughout the body, improving concentration, and regulating our system's heating and cooling mechanisms.[79] Other authoritative sources relate that ujjayi breath helps insomnia and lowers blood pressure.[80]

Sitali Breath or Cooling Breath

Sometimes we want to energize our system and increase energy or focus. But most times, we want to calm and cool it. Sitali breath is one of the few pranayama techniques that employ an open mouth for the inhale. It is recognized as a powerful cooling technique for bringing "unfiltered air into the lungs," which cools our internal system.[81] Research has also correlated the sitali technique to positive outcomes for increased body heat due to menopause, panic attacks, and even hot summer days.[82] According to Swami Saradananda, this breathing exercise is also very effective for "cooling anger."[83]

If you are type A or find yourself getting easily frustrated, energy-cooling exercises are highly recommended. The traditional yogic texts claim that pranayama reduces chronic physical problems, from skin rashes to stomach ulcers, hyperactivity, and "even bee stings."[84] The texts also assert that this technique assists in releasing digestive energy due to the ability of the breath to unblock the fourth and sixth vertebrae. Most importantly, this breath is used to detoxify the system; you will recognize a bitter taste on your tongue when first practicing. This indicates that your body is excreting toxins from your system, but with consistent practice, it is said that "a sweet taste will appear."

The technique involves making your mouth into an "O" shape and curling your tongue so that the sides touch or almost touch each other. Slowly inhale through the open mouth, bringing the air across the tongue and into your lungs. When you have fully expanded your lungs, hold your breath for a comfortable count (four, six, eight, or ten, as is your preference).

If curling your tongue is not possible, bring your teeth together, place your tongue against the back of your teeth, and inhale with a hissing sound. Unfiltered air will enter through your teeth and cheeks and cool in the same manner as the curled tongue sitali. The hissing breath is also known as "sitkari."

Kundalini Breathing Practices

Like the pranayama exercises given here, an enormous body of literature exists on Kundalini breathing practices. Of note is a well-known exercise called *Breath of Fire*, which, it is said, can raise our conscious minds to a state of enlightenment or nirvana. I have not benefited from such a claim, but I have experienced increased energy, focus, and stamina after continuous practice. This is not an "easy" practice primarily because of the coordination of the diaphragm and abdominal muscles and the emphasis on the exhale through the nose. Once you get the hang of it, however, Breath of Fire is highly recommended for increasing circulation throughout the body and strengthening the nervous system. The detoxifying principle of Breath of Fire makes it an essential element of Kundalini yoga.

We learned in conscious breathing to extend our abdomen outward on the inhale, which allows the diaphragm to contract, opening the lungs to increase oxygen intake. In Breath of Fire, the inhale is quick and short, emphasizing the exhale and pulling the navel inward toward the spine. A rhythmical pulsing beat is obtained, usually about two to three breaths per second.

Sitting in a noble posture, it is essential to have a straight spine, a soft abdomen, and relaxed arms. (In a more advanced technique, the arms are raised above the head at a sixty-degree angle). Inhaling through the nose quickly, the emphasis is on the exhale and pulling the navel inward toward the spine forcefully. This rapid breath technique utilizes only the abdominal muscles; every other muscle in the body should be intentionally relaxed.

If you are a beginner, go slowly to get a sense of muscle movement and coordination of the abdomen, diaphragm, and lungs. With practice, this breath technique will give you many benefits for years to come. I recommend watching a YouTube video with Kia Miller for in-depth teaching, which she demonstrates beautifully.[85]

Benefits of Daily Practice

When working with clients who are either trying to discontinue their use of substances, are recently sober, or are even in long-term sobriety, I first discuss the importance of breath and breath techniques. Modern research has used advanced measurement techniques and analyzed massive data sets on the effects of specialized breathing techniques on neurological, pulmonary, and circulatory systems. The results are remarkable. As the title of James Nestor's book so aptly describes it, breath has become a "new science to a lost art."

Attending to our vital life force, known as *prana*, we also listen to our minds, bodies, and souls. Breath is our sustenance, and the more we become aware of our daily, if not moment-by-moment, inhalation and exhalation, the more we increase and strengthen our resistance to stress, anxiety, and weakened immune systems. We can assuage cravings in early sobriety by using breathing techniques and regulating and balancing our nervous systems with continued practice. If the sages and scientists are correct, we can live longer by breathing better.

Mindfulness Moment

Are you a mouth breather or a nose breather?

Do you suffer from allergies, a deviated septum, or asthma? If so, what treatments have you sought? Traditional? Eastern? What have been the results?

Have you considered an acupuncturist?

Have you considered alternative methods of treatment?

Are you willing to try the simple intentional breath practice for just five minutes a day?

If you already practice breathing techniques, what have you considered to increase your practice to a more advanced level?

CHAPTER EIGHT
Meditation, Mindfulness & Contemplation

"There is no greater magic than meditation. To transform the negative into the positive. To transform darkness into light—that is the miracle of meditation."
—Bhagwan Rajneesh

"Meditation is a way for nourishing and blossoming the divinity within you."
—Amit Ray

"The resting place of the mind is the heart. The only thing the mind hears all day is clanging bells and noise and argument, and all it wants is quietude. The only place the mind will ever find peace is inside the silence of the heart. That's where you need to go."
—Elizabeth Gilbert

Meditation

Time and again, a new client will tell me, "I can't meditate. I've tried, but it's just impossible." Every time I lecture or teach a meditation class, I hear the same refrains: "It doesn't work," "I can't do it," "It's just not an option for me," and one of my favorites, "I can't get my thoughts to stop."

The misperceptions about meditation are as plentiful as the techniques and approaches to it. Twenty years ago, the practice was regarded as slightly fringe, but today, it is sewn into the very fabric of our society. Articles are published in popular media, hailing mindfulness as the answer to many of the ills that beset us, particularly stress. So many apps can be downloaded for mindfulness and meditation practices that it's hard to know which one to access. (See resources.)

Research on meditation has skyrocketed. In the 1990s, approximately twenty-five papers were published yearly. In 2013, over 100 articles were published, and in 2016, over 400 articles were published.[86] In 2020, an astounding 2,808 research articles were published on mindfulness and meditation.[87] Books written on the topic have created an explosion in the publishing industry. In the year 2000, only a handful of books were produced, but by 2022, there are literally hundreds of books available.

Meditation versus Contemplation

Meditation and contemplation are often interchangeable in society's vernacular. However, they are distinctly different. Contemplation can be described as a train of thought, particularly one that is spiritual or religious. Meditation, however, is training the mind to "rest in a particular focus that leads to a connection to the source of consciousness itself."[88]

Understanding this difference helps bring clarity to our spiritual goals and practice.

Contemplation is deep, reflective thought. In world religions, practitioners seek to bring their awareness in direct association with the Divine, whether that is Jesus, Allah, or God. The practice of contemplation focuses on a particular prayer or passage from a religious or spiritual scripture, such as the Bible, Torah, Koran, Dhammapada, or Bhagavad Gita. The reading is repeated in an ever-deepening relationship with the intention and meaning of the words. Ideally, one becomes unified with the divine through the contemplation of sacred passages.

In the Carmelite tradition, contemplation is a "wordless prayer, a deep communion with the Triune God."[89] Eknath Easwaran has written extensively on "passage meditation," in which he guides the student to read and contemplate a prayer or paragraph of their choosing, which they memorize to concentrate deeply on the meaning and purpose of the words. In the Judaic tradition, contemplation involves introspection, repetition of divine names, and concentration on ethical or mystical ideas, leading to *devekut*, or cleaving to God.

In my own practice, there have been times when I have used contemplative techniques with significant results. From a spiritual perspective, contemplation has a powerful effect on our ability to connect with a higher power.

Meditation, however, is separated from contemplation by the techniques employed and the ultimate purpose. Where one seeks to commune or cleave, the other seeks to help us experience the calm presence of self-energy, which does not cling, attach, or grasp. Instead, meditation frees us from a desired outcome by training us to just *be*.

Meditation and Mindfulness

The terms *meditation* and *mindfulness* have become inextricably linked. However, there is a marked distinction between the two. Meditation is an actual *practice*, whether sitting, standing, or walking; mindfulness is a *state* of awareness.

We can be mindful while driving, speaking with another person, or standing in the grocery line. We meditate while seated on a cushion or in a chair; our conscious state of awareness is engaged in the practice of meditation.

There is mindfulness with a capital "M" and a small "m." According to Joe Loizzo, capital "M" *Mindfulness* has come to be referred to as "a contemplative practice that serves as basic meditation training in most Buddhist teaching traditions."[90]

Lowercase "m" *mindfulness* maintains its original meaning as a mental tool that strengthens and controls our attention. Achieving this is a process that I liken to strengthening our muscles with weights. We don't begin with a fifty-pound dumbbell; we start with five-pound weights and work our way up. So, too, with meditation. The "muscle" of attention needs to be trained so our minds can settle into what is referred to as "sustainable calm." This means that we are aware of and sense a pervasive calm throughout our being that stays with us as we strengthen it for longer periods of time. From minutes to hours and from a day to weeks, the long-term effects of mindfulness and meditation can infuse our lives in dramatically positive ways.

The origins of the term "mindfulness" can be traced to an Englishman stationed in Sri Lanka during the late nineteenth century who was responsible for arbitrating ecclesiastical or religious disputes between Buddhists.[91] Learning Pali, the ancient language of Vedic scriptures, he created the word "mindfulness" as a translation for the Buddhist principle "*sati*," which means "retention" or the "lucid awareness of bodily and mental phenomena" in which one "remembers to observe."

In 1994, Jon Kabat-Zinn published *Wherever You Go, There You Are: Mindfulness Meditation in Everyday Life*. It was one of the first guides written on meditation for a non-Buddhist or layperson. Zinn defines mindfulness as "awareness that arises through paying attention, on purpose, in the present moment, nonjudgmentally."[92] He also noted, "People think of meditation as some kind of special activity, but this is not exactly correct. Meditation is simplicity itself.... It is about stopping and being present, that is all."[93]

Kabat-Zinn believed the word "meditation" would too easily evoke the religious connotations of Hinduism and Buddhism, thus alienating those who would most benefit from the practice.[94] Creating a more pleasing definition that would appeal to more people, mindfulness became a ubiquitous term in the realms of self-help, wellness, positive thinking, vision boards, and a dizzying array of psychotherapeutic approaches. In 2014, the cover of *TIME* magazine hailed a new era: "The Mindful Revolution: The Science of Finding Focus in a Stressed-Out, Multitasking Culture."

Eight years later, the "revolution" has become a norm for sports teams, executive leadership retreats, the one-percenters, Olympiads, Wall Street executives, and news anchors like Dan Harris, who had a nationally televised panic attack during a broadcast. As a direct result, he sought help, which led him to write his book, *10% Happier: How I Tamed the Voice in My Head, Reduced Stress Without Losing My Edge, and Found Self-Help That Actually Works—A True Story*. It chronicles his journey with finding meditation and brings it to national attention.

Along the way, scientists took note, and a different kind of revolution began. With advanced brain scanning technology, researchers could peer into the depths of our lobes and watch, in real time, how meditation as a practice and mindfulness as an awareness altered the gray matter in our brains. The result is an exponential body of knowledge that has informed all manner of health workers: nurse practitioners, cardiologists, stress specialists, gerontologists, and addictionologists. Why? Because meditation, or mindfulness techniques, helps to reset the brain and has been shown to aid in the process of neuroplasticity, as well as positively changing the shape and function of many brain parts.

Stopping Thoughts

There is a misperception about meditation that you must "stop your thoughts." In fact, in the vipassana tradition (also known as insight meditation), being *aware* of your thoughts as they arise is the first step to achieving a calm and balanced state of being. When we observe our reactions to thoughts, we begin to "notice" what happens to our mind, moment to moment. As we practice discernment, our minds begin to relinquish their attachment to thinking and thoughts. This gives rise to a deeper understanding of the inner workings of our psyches. As Mark Waldman says, meditation is a "practice where all you do is neutrally watch your feelings and thoughts flow through your mind."[95]

Insight meditation teaches us to focus on our breath and use it as an anchor, a grounding for what might otherwise be a discursive or distracted mind. When we follow the breath as it enters the nostrils and fills the lungs and place our awareness on the exhale as it leaves the body through the nostrils, it creates a focal point for our awareness. As thoughts enter our mind, we label them "thinking" and return our attention to our breath. We are not pushing the thoughts away or trying to stop them—that is impossible. The mind thinks, and the constant scanning that is part of our brain function does not and will not ever stop. However, we tell our brains that we are safe by attending to our breath. This repeated practice sends reinforcing signals throughout our brain, which asserts that it is okay to sit and "be" with ourselves.

Daniel Siegel, MD, notes that "being aware of what is happening as it happens without being swept up by preestablished mental activities like judgments or ideas, memories or emotions" is the core of meditation practices.[96] He explains that the more we connect with the sensations of our body and breath, the more the "discursive thunder of the storms of thought quiets down."[97]

Thus, we don't need to stop our thoughts. They will calm down by themselves through the practice of meditation.

Distractions

In 2018, research presented to the American Psychiatric Association asserted, "Our digital lives may be making us more distracted, distant and drained."[98] In an article I wrote for *Social Work Today* that same year, I noted that there were 3.3 billion global internet users, representing 46.4 percent of the world's population. Of those, an estimated 30 percent fell squarely into the category of having an "impulse control disorder" with their use of technology.

Our culture has accepted and, in many ways, reinforced the tsunami wave of distractions that crash upon us twenty-four seven: emails, spam, text messages, alerts, friend requests, event invitations, Facebook, LinkedIn, Instagram, TikTok, Snapchat, WhatsApp, streaming news platforms "breaking" every hour, and the relentless "rabbit holes" that advertisers and search optimization engines have developed based on our clicks, to take us off track, sometimes for hours.

How often do we find ourselves in the whirlwind of life?

How often do we notice that we are so busy *doing* that we haven't given ourselves a chance to experience *being*?

How often do we tell ourselves that stopping doing is not an option?

We're too busy to stop!

As Gabor Mate says, people are "desperately seeking an escape from themselves" and will go to any length to seek out distractions to "obliterate the present."[99] This is particularly true of those of us who've used alcohol or drugs to escape the pain of abuse, trauma, or personal suffering that blankets our consciousness.

The genius behind online technology is that very astute developers have understood B.F. Skinner's stimulus-response experiments with pigeons and translated it to human behavior; pleasurable activities such as shopping online or playing a game are programmed in such a way as to stimulate and entice our brains to return to whatever application we are using based on the success or failure of our previous interaction. This is known as a "variable ratio reinforcement schedule," through which technology provides numerous layers of unpredictable rewards to users with no particular end (think Candy Crush, Angry Birds, etc.).[100] It keeps us coming back. The point is that these distractions have become so ingrained in the fabric of our society that even when we take a break, we feel the need to continue to stimulate our brains and nervous systems, and not necessarily in a positive way.

Let's go back to the person convinced they can't meditate. "It's too hard," "My thoughts race," and "I can't sit still." This might be you. But what if I suggest that instead of "meditating," you just sit quietly for *one minute* and look out the window at a street scene or birds in trees or squirrels cavorting on the lawn? What if I suggested that you bring your attention to your breath while you do that? If you can look around for *one minute* and bring your attention to your breath—you have just meditated.

Mark Waldman shares a poignant story in his coauthored book with Andrew Newburg, MD, *How Enlightenment Changes Your Brain*. Describing a conversation in which Dr. Newburg shared his mystical experiences, Waldman expressed that he could not imagine enjoying such a blissful state given that he has experienced "chronic self-doubt" throughout his life. But a memory emerged of a day when he was staring out his office window, "gazing mindlessly"; at that moment, he recalls that he was suddenly, "and for no reason that I could identify, filled with inner peace . . . . and everything felt connected to everything else."[101] That moment led to a lifetime pursuit of knowledge that would alter the course of his life and career forever. Our brains default to the negative. Our minds easily recall bad memories, hurtful words, stinging criticisms, and nasty exchanges. Like a needle stuck in a scratched record, the negativity bias returns over and over, relentlessly. Stopping ourselves from getting swept up in distractions, even for a moment, allows the brain to begin to discard negative inclinations and rewire to a positive perspective.

We "attend" to where we are in the present. When we focus on what is happening right now, the pathways in our brain begin to change. The more we pull ourselves away from distractions, the more those pathways rewire. A well-known phrase in neuroscience states,

"Neurons that fire together, wire together."[102] This means that the more we attend to what is happening *right now*, the more we rewire the direction of neurons. Meditation, among many practices, helps to create new pathways in the brain, reinforced through repetition. Simply put, the more you stop and smell the roses, the more your brain will create positivity and calmness.

While I was working in the Department of Defense, people would come into my office all day long with various requests, inquiries, etc. The phone rang nonstop. I worked with four computer monitors and was considered a whiz at multitasking. Crucially, I kept a small meditation bell on my desk. It consisted of a metal tube, eight inches in length, attached to a wooden block, with a small mallet to tap the metal tube, creating the sound of a bell ringing.

In a constrained environment such as the DoD, it was "out there," but for me, it was vital.

Almost every person who came into my office asked what "that" was, pointing to the bell with overt skepticism. I answered, "It's a mindfulness bell." The next question was always, "Huh?" So, I would pull out the mallet and tap the top of the metal tube, which elicited a delicate sound, resonating in waves, until it faded to silence. The military staff and senior officials looked cynical, if not bemused, when they first heard it. I was new, and obviously, I was weird. As I put the mallet away, I explained, "It reminds me to stop, take a breath, and bring my attention to the present moment." "Hmm" or "I see" would be the parting words. But something interesting happened over the early months in that job: men and women in uniform, lifetime government workers, contractors, and even the director of my division would come into my office and say to me, "Hey, can you ring that bell?" I would do so, and they would close their eyes and listen to the sound. I always got a "thank you, I needed that" before they left my office. Over the years, it became a "thing"—if folks got stressed, they were directed to my office, where they could sit down and ring the bell by themselves. No matter what I was doing, I would join them in closing my eyes, stopping the busyness, and taking in that much-needed moment of serenity.

Meditation Practice

The types, styles, and schools of meditation available today know no bounds. What any one person chooses is up to their personal taste and needs. Some people gravitate toward the Japanese schools of Zen, Vipassana, or "Thai Forest" Theravada Buddhism. Many people are interested in Tibetan schools and the Dalai Lama's techniques. There is focused meditation, loving-kindness meditation, movement, mantra, and transcendental meditation. There are secular and non-secular schools of meditation, and there are scientifically based techniques that are not associated with traditional approaches.

I tell my clients that no matter which path they choose, they should stick with it for a minimum of forty days before determining whether a particular approach works for them. I point out that Buddha sat under the bodhi tree for forty days before he achieved enlightenment, and Jesus was in the desert for the same time to overcome the devil's temptation. There are other examples, such as Moses on Mount Sinai, where he received the Ten Commandments, and Noah and the Ark in the deluge for forty days. In Islam, the Quran states, "He who purifies his faith for Allah for forty days, Allah will flow the springs of wisdom from his heart to his tongue."[103] So, throughout the world's religions and throughout time, there seems to be something magical about the idea of forty days.

A minimum of ten minutes of meditation can change your brain and mind. Studies from MIT, Harvard, Bingham University, UCLA, and Swarthmore, to name a few, have determined that ten minutes a day of mindfulness meditation improves executive attention, memory, and emotional regulation.[104] This short amount of time every day also increases our levels of compassion, gratitude, and kindness.

Meditation is one of the most profound spiritual practices we can engage in. When I teach meditation, I instruct that we close our eyes and focus on inhaling air entering our nostrils with lungs expanding and breathing out with lungs contracting—while bringing awareness to our body: the scalp, face, jaw, neck, shoulders, arms, torso, pelvis, thighs, knees, calves, and feet. Known as a body scan, we check in with any tension we might be holding in muscles, joints, or ligaments. If we notice our jaw clenched, we soften the area and allow it to relax. Once the body scan is completed, the technique is to breathe in and out regularly. If thoughts arise, label them "thinking" and bring the attention back to the breath. We can tell ourselves to "settle in and settle down" as a cue to enter our inner world and allow the external world of distractions and concerns to fade and become more distant.

In therapy sessions, I guide clients through a meditation to bring focus on the Self as defined by the IFS model. I ask clients to bring their attention to the heart center and notice the calm, clear, and centered place within. Taking long, slow breaths, I continue to guide them toward the qualities of their Self-energy: curiosity, clarity, connection, calm, creativity, compassion, courage, and confidence. I've found that clients almost instantly become less anxious and less stressed, with a marked difference showing in their facial features. This is particularly notable in the cases of depressed clients' whose faces are drawn and looking fatigued when they begin. Inevitably, by the end of the meditation practice, a softness is visible around the mouth and eyes, with a gentle smile appearing at the corner of their lips. What is remarkable is that these shifts in physical appearances soon become lasting changes.

Anxiety is reduced and turned into calm. Depression gives way to a recurring sense of peace. With consistent spiritual practices, and meditation being one of its core facets, the challenges clients faced prior to therapy become more manageable and, in many cases, dissolve. This is manifested in the light in their eyes, the sound of laughter replacing tears, the stories they tell of insight, increased awareness of the patterns of behavior, and willingness to do something different for a new result.

We call this phenomenon *altered traits*. Daniel Goleman, PhD, and Richard Davidson, PhD, describe it this way: "... at the start of contemplative practice, little or nothing seems to change in us. After continued practice, we notice some changes in our way of being, but they come and go. Finally, as practice stabilizes, the changes are constant and enduring, with no fluctuations. They are altered traits."[105]

Whether a beginner or an adept practitioner, the benefits of meditation have been replicated in tens of thousands of studies. The results are consistent; whether the meditation practice extends as few as six to eight hours total, more than 100 hours total, or to three-year retreats where yogis meditate for up to fourteen hours a day—the result is the same.

After months of consistent practice, brain scans show changes in the amygdala, our internal alarm bell region that sends signals of fight or flight. The amygdala has a reduced stress reactivity after eight weeks of mindfulness-based practice. Compassion increases in as little as two weeks. The anterior cingulate cortex, or activity center for empathy, shows strengthened connections in the same amount of time.[106] As Goleman points out, this is evidence of a "state morphing into a trait," although it will not last without continued, *consistent* daily practice.

Which One?

There are tens of dozens of books written on meditation. I've read just about all of them, and the recurring thought I've had while writing this chapter is, *What can I add that hasn't already been said?* The honest answer is this: I can't add anything new. All the knowledge, techniques, and wisdom are already available to you.

But I can tell you this: you will benefit in profound ways if you create your path in meditation and find what works best for you.

- Find a teacher who you resonate with.
- Find techniques that you connect with.
- Read books on the subject.
- Find an author whom you feel speaks directly to you. (There may be one; there may be many.)
- Join a meditation group or attend Twelve Step meditation groups.
- Go to Recovery 2.0, where meditation instruction is ample.
- Look up the schedule at Kripalu Center in Massachusetts.
- Go to the Omega Center in upstate New York's website and find retreats that interest you.
- Check out the Garrison Center in the Hudson Valley, New York.
- Shambhala in Colorado offers weeklong and weekend meditation retreats high in the Rockies at Red Feather Lakes.

If you are feeling brave, try a silent retreat. This can be found at a meditation center, a Christian retreat, or a monastery where laypersons are welcome to participate in programs. Not speaking for several days is a penetrating experience. I have been on several of these and discovered so much about myself that I didn't know before, allowing me to do some profound personal healing. On my second silent retreat, which lasted ten days, I discovered that despite evidence to the contrary, I am a bona fide introvert!

My experience, strength, and hope are this: *practice*. Practice every day. Commit yourself to that daily practice as if your life depends on it—because it does. Your recovery, sobriety, and path to healing rely on it. The healing of your brain depends on it. Your brain's neuroplasticity depends on using meditation techniques to rewire the neurons, quiet the mental chatter of your mind, and alter your traits. Your soul depends on it.

Mindfulness Moment

Take an honest assessment of how much time you spend every day on social media, surfing the internet, or online shopping. (Most phones have a calculation of your daily screen time in the settings.)

What do you gain from time spent on social media?

What do you lose from your time spent on social media?

What could you be doing instead?

What do you tell yourself about the time you spend on the internet? Is it true?

Would you consider actively engaging in reducing your screen time by 50 percent? Or 60?

What would it be like to spend an entire day without checking any social media, text messages, emails, playing games, etc.?

> Are you willing to try it and see what happens?

> What's the best that could happen?

What lengths are you willing to go to for your recovery?

Are you ready to commit, be disciplined, dedicate yourself, and become devoted to recovery?

If you are resisting, what is the concern, fear, or reluctance?

What changes in your daily routine could support spiritual practices such as meditation?

If meditation seems too daunting, could you spend fifteen minutes every day journaling?

Do you get lost in your thoughts when you meditate? Are you aware this is happening?

Are you able to redirect your attention to your breath when it happens?

CHAPTER NINE

Prayer & Mantra

"The function of prayer is not to influence God, but rather to change the nature of the one who prays."[107]
—Søren Kierkegaard

"A prayer can be a silent meditation or a full chorus of chanting. In some traditions, people sit and pray, in others they lie prostrate, kneel, stand, or even dance. Some people pray regularly with devout faith, others pray only as a last-minute plea for help"
—Thich Nhat Hahn

"Prayer is not asking. It is a longing of the soul. It is daily admission of one's weakness. It is better in prayer to have a heart without words than words without a heart."
—Mahatma Gandhi

Prayer

There's an old adage that says, "Meditation is listening *to* God, and prayer is speaking *with* God." We could also say that while meditation is receiving or accepting something *from* our higher power, prayer is reaching *out* to our higher power. Either way, prayer is an essential tool in recovery and in living a spiritual life. It is no coincidence that prayer forms the basis of the Eleventh Step in the Twelve Step program: "Sought through prayer and meditation to improve our conscious contact with God, *as we understood Him,* praying only for knowledge of His will for us and the power to carry that out."[108]

From a spiritual perspective, prayer can be a profound activity that connects us more deeply to our recovery path. Think of prayer as an invocation that can establish a rapport with your higher power through deliberate communication. It helps us to be "shown all through the day what our next step is to be, that we be given whatever we need to take care of such problems."[109] Prayer centers us and brings us to the center at the same time.

The root origin for the word prayer is from the Medieval Latin, *precari*, to entreat, or to petition, to ask earnestly. Some definitions include the word "beg," but theologians would take issue with this concept as it distorts the pure intention of prayer. According to the St. Paul Center, prayer is the means by which a relationship with God, or a higher power, is built. The invitation is not to pray once a week in church or even once a day. Instead, to "pray without ceasing."[110] Much like the sacred words of a mantra, prayer can be used consistently to maintain our connection to a higher power. I think of it as an ongoing conversation with my higher power. In between my words, there are silences to which I listen. This is particularly powerful when walking, weeding, raking the autumn leaves, washing dishes, or any other daily task.

- There are a million kinds of prayers.
- There are foxhole prayers: "Please get me out of this; don't let me die."
- There are prayers for others: "Please heal them, make them better."
- Prayers that bargain: "I swear if you help me now, I'll never drink again."

- Prayers that supplicate: "Please make me an instrument..."
- Prayers that celebrate: "Thank you for the blessings..."

There are Christian, Judaic, Muslim, Hindu, Sikh, Native American, and Buddhist prayers. There are even atheistic and agnostic prayers. It seems that our human race has been praying since the dawn of time. We've been looking up and out and calling upon whatever exists in the cosmos to affect us. The effort has always been to reach out to that "thing" above or around us that is in control and have it work *with* us instead of *against* us. In the earliest days, we may have prayed for safety from storms or rain for crops. Invocations by early man were made for healing from sickness or helping a loved one transition into death.

Today, we seem to have more control over our ability to survive, prosper, and procreate. But we continue to pray as a means of managing the many things beyond our control: cancer, death, plane crashes, natural disasters, viruses, mental illness, and so much more that can bring us to our knees. In sickness and in health, we pray for intervention for ourselves and others. When we get what we seek, we say our prayers are answered and exclaim that our higher power "heard" our prayers. When we fail to get the outcome we desire, we say prayers are unanswered, and we ask why God turned his back on us. The eternal question arises. What is the purpose of prayer? Why pray?

C.S. Lewis speaks of prayer not as magic or "our advice offered to God" but rather as "trying to get into touch with God." Rabbi Abraham Twersky writes that the purpose of prayer is "peace of mind. It is a way to turn our needs and drives over to a Supreme Being, and thereby, lighten our own burden." Prayer, then, is the vehicle that brings us closer to what we believe God to be. Or a higher power. Or nature. Or the Buddha. Call it what you will, prayer is the activity that helps us to connect with a deeper inner knowing, a sacredness, the presence of the universe.

There is nothing wrong with engaging in prayer like a child

begging for a toy. "Please let me win the multimillion-dollar Power Ball!" But this falls short of the intention of prayer. Instead of asking God to do *our* will, it is recommended that we do our *higher power's* will. By praying with humility and surrender, we can create a different relationship to our higher power.

Pray to Who?

There are words in prayer that name an entity whom we believe is listening: God, Allah, Krishna, Yahweh, Buddha, Jesus, Siva, Mother Mary, Mother Earth . . . the list is long. For some of us, this is a powerful way to connect back to the most sacred part of ourselves.

For others, these names do not provide connection. Perhaps we are not oriented to their associated faiths or belief systems. The agnostics and atheists I've worked with have initially expressed resistance to prayer, or what they believe prayer to be. Many say that prayer is religious or directed to a "god" they categorically reject. But if an atheist client is open to a conversation about prayer, I am willing to discuss it. However, if they reject it outright, I accept their position wholeheartedly. It does not change the work we might do together in recovery.

A beautiful quote from *Anne of Green Gables* resonates with me: "Why must people kneel down to pray? If I really wanted to pray I'll tell you what I'd do. I'd go out into a great big field all alone or in the deep, deep woods, and I'd look up into the sky—up—up—up—into that lovely blue sky that looks as if there was no end to its blueness. And then I'd just feel a prayer."[111]

In other words, prayer does not have to be *to* anyone or anything. It can just be a connection with ourselves and the innermost Self. For Buddhists, there is no differentiation between ourselves and an external "god." Buddhism views the action of prayer as a connection to the collective consciousness or the "one mind." Prayer can create energy, emit energy, and be a vehicle to receive energy. To feel a prayer is to experience the powerful existence of an "all-that-is," beyond definition and restriction.

How to Pray?

As Anne points out in the quote above, we don't need to kneel—although we, by all means, can. Some might prostrate themselves as people of certain faiths do. The point is that we can pray anywhere, anytime, either by ourselves or collectively. We can pray while walking in nature or weeding our garden. We can pray while folding laundry or washing dishes. We can pray while driving.

If we memorize the Serenity Prayer, we can say it to ourselves any time of the day or night. We might prefer to pray in a more formal way by sitting quietly in the early morning or evening hours to recite the Lord's Prayer or the Prayer of St. Francis of Assisi.[112]

We can pray silently. We can pray aloud. We can whisper our prayers. We can include a closing prayer after a meditation session. We can begin our yoga practice with a prayer.

In other words, the way of prayer is unlimited, just as there are an unlimited number of pathways to spiritual healing. There is no right way. There is no wrong way. There can only be *your* way. Any path that supports you is the perfect one for you.

What Prayers to Use?

Those of us raised in traditional religious realms were given prayers at an early age. In the Episcopal Church, the Book of Common Prayer is used; in the Catholic church, it may be the Liturgy of the Hours. In Judaism, it is the Siddur, in Hinduism, the Vedas or Upanishads, and in Islam, the Salat. In Alcoholics Anonymous, the Serenity Prayer forms the basis of nondenominational prayer: "Grant me the serenity to accept the things I cannot change, the courage to change the things I can, and the wisdom to know the difference."[113]

Twelve Step meetings may begin with the Lord's Prayer as an invocation to a higher power or to give thanks for the hour spent in the community. There is no requirement to participate in the recitation of the prayer, but many have found that there is a connection that occurs when a room full of people, mostly strangers, holds hands as they stand in a circle and pray. Andrew Newburg, MD, found that "prayer permanently strengthen(s) neural functioning in specific parts of the brain that are involved with lowering anxiety and depression, enhancing social awareness and empathy, and improving cognitive and intellectual functioning."[114]

Well-known prayers mentioned in the Big Book as well as those written by Eknath Easwaran, include the *Prayer of St. Francis of Assisi*, St. Paul's *Epistle on Love*, and Thomas A Kempis' *Imitation of Christ*. The Big Book also includes a prayer of surrender known as the Third step and Seventh step prayers:

> "God, I offer myself to Thee
> To build with me and to do with me as Thou wilt.
> Relieve me of the bondage of self, that I may better do Thy will.
> Take away my difficulties, that victory over them may bear witness to those I would help of Thy Power, Thy Love, and Thy Way of Life.
> May I do Thy will always."[115]

> "My Creator, I am now willing that You should have all of me, good and bad.
> I pray that You now remove from me every single defect of character which stands in the way of my usefulness to you and my fellows.
> Grant me strength, as I go out from here, to do Your bidding.
> Amen"[116]

Agnostics or atheists may take exception to some of the recitation of prayers in Twelve Step meetings. As I explain to clients, there is no rule or requirement that states you must participate in this activity. My advice is to either leave before the closing prayer or join hands with group members but not participate in the recitation. Experiencing the connection of a roomful of people assembled for a unified purpose—recovery—can be, in and of itself, a prayer.

There are many nonreligious prayers invoking gratitude, thanks, and healing. The prayer of James Whitcomb Riley, *Thanksgiving*, is a perfect example: *"Let us be thankful for the loyal hand, That love held out in welcome to our own, When love and only love could understand, The need of touches we had never known."*[117]

Or this from poet Joanna Fuchs:

> *"May you be well.*
> *May you be cleansed and purified*
> *Of all that isn't health.*
> *May every cell in your body*
> *Wake up and fight.*
> *May the powerful light of healing*
> *Move into every part of you.*
> *May you return to being purely you.*
> *May you be well."*[118]

Finally, in the Buddhist tradition, *The Four Immeasurables* prayer is recited to generate compassion for the suffering of others. This prayer is also said to cultivate loving kindness, empathetic joy, and equanimity. It opens the heart and deepens our relationship to ourselves, others, and the world. Used as part of a meditative practice, it is said to empower the mind. Used as a stand-alone prayer that may be recited anytime, anywhere, it is a powerful tool that can bring us into the present moment and help us to focus on others instead of ourselves:

> "May all sentient beings have happiness and the causes of happiness.
> May all sentient beings be free from suffering and the causes of suffering.
> *May all sentient beings have joy and the cause of joy.*
> *May all sentient beings remain in great equanimity, free from attachment and aversion.*"[119]

Indigenous People:

Indigenous people have venerated the natural elements as part of their traditions handed down through generations. Traditional beliefs centered on the earth that brought forth food, the sun and rain that nourished the earth, the winds that carried communication and the souls of beings, and the moon and stars that guided time and the cycles of nature. In the American Indian tradition, Navajo, Cherokee, and Lakota tribes are well-known for their prayers, which are often used in lieu of secular petitions.

> "Oh, Great Spirit,
> Whose voice I hear in the winds
> and whose breath gives life to all the world.
> Hear me! I need your strength and wisdom.
> Let me walk in beauty, and make my eyes
> ever hold the red and purple sunset.
> Make my hands respect the things you have made
> and my ears sharp to hear your voice.
> Make me wise so that I may understand
> the things you have taught my people.
> Let me learn the lessons you have hidden
> in every leaf and rock.

Help me remain calm and strong in the
face of all that comes towards me.
Help me find compassion without
empathy overwhelming me.
I seek strength, not to be greater than my brother,
but to fight my greatest enemy: myself.
Make me always ready to come to you
with clean hands and straight eyes.
So when life fades, as the fading sunset,
my spirit may come to you without shame."
—Great Spirit Prayer of Lakota Sioux Chief Yellow Lark, 1887[120]

"Treat the earth well.
It was not given to you by your parents,
it was loaned to you by your children.
We do not inherit the Earth from our Ancestors,
we borrow it from our Children."
—Ute Prayer[121]

Writing Our Prayers

Several years ago, during a very dark winter morning, I sat in front of my notebook, staring at a blank page with a blank mind. I felt uninspired and unmotivated. A permeation of *blah* had settled into me. Noticing it, I said out loud, "May this be lifted." I waited a few seconds, then added, "Amen." From that day on, for a period of over two years, I wrote personal prayers almost every morning. Some were short, like the first one. Some were longer. Some appealed to challenges I was facing; many appealed to the healing of others. There were prayers that repeated themselves, prayers that were gentle and humble, and prayers that were forceful and certain.

Each day, as I picked up the pen to place it on the notebook paper, a stillness came over me, and from that inner calm rose a soft and melodic voice deep within my mind. Each prayer began with "may" or "dear God" as if I was writing a letter to my Higher Power or invoking the energy from above. The writing seemed to flow from somewhere in my unconscious. My prayers set the tone for my day and invariably helped me during a challenging moment or prompted me to feel deep gratitude in a moment of grace. Here are some examples:

Prayer #1:
"May today be light-filled.
May I remain aware of my intentions.
May I hold my silence and respond instead of reacting.
May I breathe consciously throughout the day as I accomplish tasks.
May I remind myself of all that I am grateful for.

A short prayer:
May the day unfold and reveal the truth of all that is.
May the light shine forth from within and touch all those I meet.

Prayer #2:
May today bring the calm of long, slow breaths.
May my thoughts turn to kindness and compassion.
May there be acceptance and understanding, knowing that everything is temporary and will change again.
All that is required by me today is to be present to whatever arises.

Whether you are spiritual, religious, agnostic, or atheist, writing your own prayers is a powerful exercise for creating a connection to your Self-energy and, by extension, the energy of what exists outside of all of us. Whatever your perception may be of a higher power, try writing out your thoughts, hopes, dreams, desires, challenges, fears, or concerns in an invocation or prayer. You may find the process brings you a calm, centeredness that lasts throughout the day.

The Power of Prayer

Time and again, we hear stories about the power of prayer. Prayers answered, prayers heard, the miracle of prayers. It is easy to be skeptical of these outcomes, particularly if we are quantum physicists, and many in science or medicine have been examining prayer in various ways.

In her book, *The Awakened Brain*, Lisa Miller, PhD, writes about the power of *awakened attention* as a critical aspect of spiritual awareness. She reports numerous studies that suggest when we consciously engage in spiritual practices such as "chanting, prayer, creative expression, meditation . . ."[122] there are significant positive benefits on those parts of the brain where anxiety, depression, or negative affect take place. The direct result, she writes, is that when we quiet ourselves, we prepare our brain for spiritual awareness, which opens us to "noticing and making meaning in ways that support our growth and healing."[123]

Gnosticism, a prominent heretical movement of the second-century Christian church, defines prayer as energy. Its ideas emphasize "personal spiritual knowledge" and the concept that our inner being or "God within" contains our awakened consciousness. Neuroscientists Mario Beauregard and Denyse O'Leary devoted decades to researching the effects of spiritual and mystical experiences, including prayer, on the brain. Their findings support the ideas of Gnosticism centuries ago, due in part to today's advanced scanning technology. The results of brain scans performed on individuals who engaged in spiritual practices repeatedly showed lower scores on adverse mental health questionnaires and higher scores on the scales of well-being. Referred to as "psychospiritual transformation," the indicators include "changes in thoughts, emotions, attitudes, core beliefs about the Self and the world, and behaviors."[124]

Research professor of psychology and psychiatry Richard J. Davidson, PhD, and psychologist Daniel Goleman, PhD, echo these results in their studies of meditation. Our personality *traits* can change over time when we have a consistent practice involving meditation. Davidson and Goleman state, "What gets practiced gets improved." By extension, the deeper our practice of prayer, the more the practice improves. By deeper, I mean going within at a heartfelt level of having a relationship with the Self and our concept of a higher power. Doing so improves our connection to the positive traits available to us through neural rewiring.

Lisa Miller, PhD, has adeptly associated spiritual awakening with the area of physics known as quantum theory, noting that "waves underlie all of reality—that at a fundamental level, everything behaves like waves of energy"[125] and before anything is an actual "thing," it is a wave. Thoughts, ideas, and intentions are all waves of energy. What brings them to reality is our attention. Through observation, reality is created. This is important because this branch of science asserts that nothing is separate; everything is part of an inseparable whole. Prayer begins as a wave of energy, and as we place our attention on whatever we wish to call our higher power, it becomes a part of our collective consciousness.

Why is this important? Because it shows that science and medicine are finally acknowledging and honoring ancient principles. Larry Dossey, MD, has written extensively on this subject and is at the forefront of bridging the gap between science and spirituality. He talks about prayer as an attitude of the heart "and implies infinitude in space and time," with "shared qualities with the Divine – 'the Divine within' – since infinitude, omnipresence, and eternity are qualities that we have attributed also to the Absolute."[126] Each morning, he prays for his patients and himself as a means of bringing spiritual healing to his medical practice.

In 2004, I faced a major emergency surgery. My doctors did not know what they would find, but they were certain it wasn't going to be good. I had an excellent relationship with each of them, and they were well aware that my life was informed by my spirituality. I did not know some other members of the surgical team who introduced themselves at the time of the operation. The kindness and concern in their eyes were palpable. I thanked each of them for being there.

I remember being wheeled on a gurney down long hallways as overhead lights flashed above me. It was a classic hospital scene that I found surreal. The pre-op sedative was beginning to flow through my body. We entered the cold, sterile, green-walled room where it seemed as if at least a dozen people in masks were assembled. I doubt it was that many, but I had this sense that the room was too small to hold everyone.

The anesthetist was about to place the mask on my face. I raised my hands and asked him to stop. I half sat up, looked at my doctors, and said, "Last month, I met the Dalai Lama, who gave me a life blessing. I am going to hold that blessing as a prayer for this surgery to be a success. Can I ask you; would you hold in your minds the gift each one of you has been given to heal? Please focus on the light within you that has brought you to this moment. No matter what happens, I know we are all in this together."

There was dead silence. I think everyone was a bit stunned—perhaps they had not had a patient make such a request. Each person was looking at me intently. For a moment, I thought the sedatives had made my speech slurred or unintelligible. My lead doctor leaned toward me and said, "Kimberley, thank you for bringing prayer to us this morning. We're going to take the best care of you." It was the last thing I remember before I slipped into the depths of a nether sphere.

Later, many days later, I would come to find out that during a seven-and-a-half-hour surgery, things had gone wrong. The team had "staged" the entire area of my abdomen, which means they scraped cells off all the major organs for biopsies, leaving them exposed, which is standard procedure. They were sewing me up when the results of the tissue sample from my uterus came back via telemetry. Positive. Stage 3 cancer.

According to the lead surgeon, they immediately realized they needed to perform a complete hysterectomy and opened me back up to begin the procedure. However, what should have been a routine removal became a panic when the organ burst open in my abdominal cavity, exposing my entire system to the potential of spreading cancer throughout my body. She told me that after a few choice words were uttered, a calm seemed to descend on the entire team as they proceeded to do everything they could to ensure that the cells would be flushed out with multiple liters of saline lavage. Later, as they were taking off their scrubs, she reported to me that one of the doctors said to her, "Did you notice what happened in there?" to which she replied, "I noticed that every one of us seemed to have been touched by something, for which I have no explanation." One of the nurses apparently said, "Well, docs, that would be God that you felt in there. Pure and simple." My surgeon told me she didn't disagree, nor did the others.

Mother Theresa said, "Everything starts with prayer. Love to pray—feel the need to pray often during the day and take the trouble to pray. If you want to pray better, you must pray more. The more you pray the easier it becomes. Perfect prayer does not consist of many words but in the fervor of the desire which raises the heart to Jesus."[127] If that is true, and I believe it is, then in 2004, my life was spared because all of us in that operating room put ourselves in the hands of God, whether we knew it or not.

They say meditation is food for the mind, and prayer is food for the soul. In my work with clients and my personal work, prayer is an important spiritual practice that we should try to engage in as much as possible.

May we support each other in what we do.
May we serve each other in our practice.

May our practice inform our daily lives.
And in our daily lives, may we bring grace and mercy to those we meet.
Amen

Mantra

"Mantras are passwords that transform the mundane into the sacred."

—Deva Premal

"We meditate so that our minds can be sharp and alert. We chant mantras so that our souls may be ignited like candles. We walk in the light of this beauty."

—Harbhajan Singh, Yogi Bhajan

I first discovered mantras during my initial training in yoga at the Stanford University workshop in the late 1960s. After being taught yoga postures, we were guided through twenty minutes of meditation. A bell rang, and one of the facilitators had us repeat the following words:

"Om Asatoma sad Gamaya
Tamasoma Jyotir gamaya
Mrityor ma Amritam gamaya"[4]

The recitation became melodic as the words were repeated over and over. Someone tapped on a small hand drum, while someone else strummed a guitar. A tune emerged, and soon, the entire room sang the words with some brave voices harmonizing, the notes rising to the upper rafters of the Spanish Mission hall. I looked around and

---

[4] For all mantra references, see appendix 2.

saw broad smiles on joyful faces and bodies swaying. I was swaying to the rhythm, too. I felt infused with a connection to myself, to others, and to what I would come to know as my version of a higher power. While I didn't know the meaning of the words at the time, there was a sweetness to them and the melody. The repetition drew me into something I couldn't name but somehow *knew*.

I would come back to this mantra and many others years later in the first year of my recovery from alcoholism. That is not to say I forgot them or discarded them. They were stored in my memory and emerged from time to time in the most unlikely moments and places. In Morocco, for instance, I sat on the roof and softly sang the parts of mantras I remembered while drinking wine and contemplating what my life would be going forward. The mantras soothed my immediate unknowns, but had I not been drinking, I believe there would have been a deeper effect on my situation and the decisions I made going forward. It is possible I would have listened more closely to that still voice within.

The hurricane that scared me out of the ocean was another time when mantra helped me to move from one mental state to another. Akumal, a young man whose name I shall never forget, had taught me how to navigate a 120-foot yacht as the captain lay sick in his cabin and the entire crew was similarly impaired. He and I sat together in the wheelhouse, rocked up and down by the turbulent sea, and as we made our way through deadly waves, Akumal sang softly under his breath. Bracing myself against the navigation desk, I turned to him and asked what he was singing. In a beautiful lilting voice well-known to Sri Lankans, he smiled and replied that it was "just a little something" he learned as a young boy. "Akumal, that little something—I know it. I know it really well!" He looked surprised, and I began to sing the Sanskrit words to the Moola mantra prayer.

> "*Om Sat chit Ananda Para-brahma*
> *Purushothama Paramatta*

Sri Bhagavati Sametha
Sri Bhagavati Namaha.
Hari Om Tat Sat
Hari Om Tat Sat
Hari Om Tat Sat
Hari Om Tat Sat"

A broad beam of a smile crossed his face. His soft song became a loud declaration against the angry ocean, invoking God for protection and freedom from suffering. Together, we chanted over and over. Time became irrelevant. The mantra seemed to lift our boat over the waves with grace and bolstered us to survive the tumultuous hurricane.

What Is a Mantra?

According to Eknath Easwaran, a mantra is a "powerful spiritual formula," which, when repeated, "has the capacity to transform consciousness."[128] He adds that there is no magic to this formula. Just practice. Using a mantra enables us to call up "what is best and deepest in ourselves."[129] While the word *mantra* has a Sanskrit derivation, recitations exist in every world religion, from Catholicism to Judaism, and are found in practices of all indigenous people. It can be one word, a phrase, or many verses.

The Sanskrit definition of mantra is derived from "man" for mind and "tra" for vehicle. When a mantra is repeated silently during meditation, it becomes a "vehicle of the mind" or "instrument of the mind,"[130] which grounds our otherwise chattering inner dialogue. It's not that we want to *stop* our thoughts; we want to be able to train them to settle down and sail the calmer waters of our interior landscape.

Taken together with the focus on the breath, using a mantra has a powerful effect on our nervous system. Andrew Newburg and Mark Waldman conducted extensive research on the impact of spiritual practices on the body and brain. The result was a fascinating book entitled *How Enlightenment Changes Your Brain.* They conducted MRI scans on subjects while they engaged in spiritual practices from many different faiths. These included Pentecostals speaking in tongues, Sufis practicing Dhikr, and Hasidic Jews davening. The scans showed a marked reduction in activity in the emotional centers of the limbic system and the frontal lobe. Simply put, when we focus our awareness on a spiritual practice such as using a mantra, our common default of negativity bias softens at the edges, and a pervading calm infuses our being. The distractions that otherwise stimulate anxiety, apprehension, and the sensation of being overwhelmed settle down. Using a mantra (or any spiritual practice) calms the sympathetic nervous system, which generally floods the body with the neurochemical epinephrine and the hormone adrenaline. In scientific terms, the calming effect results from the parasympathetic nervous system, releasing acetylcholine and the hormone dopamine into the brain.

Mantras are rooted in the ancient scriptures of India and range from the well-known and perhaps overused "Om" to more complicated and lengthy recitations like "Japji," which consists of thirty-eight stanzas. Mantras can stand alone as a prayer but are also used in "mantra yoga" or "mantra meditation." Some refer to mantra meditation as *japa* because a string of beads is used to track the number of times you recite a mantra. There are 108 beads on a japa for one "round" of recitation. These mantras can be recited silently, out loud, or chanted to rhythms or music.

Transcendental Meditation(TM) has been the best-known mantra meditation technique since the days of the Beatles. Traditional schools of mantra yoga require that a mantra be given by a teacher to a student. These come in the form of a sacred word given secretly and are never to be shared or told to others. TM continues the tradition to this day, using a personalized mantra given by a seasoned teacher to each student, much in the tradition of guru to acolyte. It is a special ritual that "initiates" the student and creates a sacred bond with their teacher.

Many people choose not to receive a formal mantra from a teacher. They may be interested in using a mantra for broader purposes. For this reason, mantras have been made widely available in many formats, both for recitation and/or chanting. In addition to the mantras mentioned here, appendix 2 contains dozens of mantras to choose from.

Mantra is found in many religions and spiritual traditions. From Christian to Judaic faiths, Greek Orthodoxy to Islam, and Buddhism to the impersonal or agnostic, they resonate at every level because they are a call to our higher Self. Whether that encompasses the notion of God or nature with a "capital N," the purpose comes down to connection. Focusing on word patterns or single syllables results in producing positive "mental tracks."[131] We will look at the neurological benefits shortly, but suffice it to say that anything positive that we take into our system will result in an overall benefit.

As noted, the most well-known mantra is "Om." The instruction is to pronounce it as "au-mm" with a long exhale breath on the "au" and the remaining breath on the short "mm." The vibration is felt in the chest as the word and sound blend.

Close your eyes for a moment. Take a long, slow inhale. At the top of the breath, open your mouth only slightly to form an "O" shape on your lips. Allowing the breath to release from your lungs slowly, sound the "au" on almost the entire exhale. In the last seconds of the exhale, your lips close, and the "mm" sound is made. If you do this for a few minutes, adjusting to the pattern of your breath and the vibration of the sound in your chest, you will find a calm settling within you. This is the mantra in action.

Mantra Chant

Another form of mantra application is to chant or sing the words to a set tune or rhythm. These consist of a set of words, single verses, or lengthy odes composed of dozens of stanzas. The difference between a chant and a song is the intention and repetition brought to our awareness. Because these mantras have meaning, when we chant them with added rhythms and tunes, they come alive—and are vibrant and resonant in our voices.

From Sanskrit to Gurmukhi, hundreds of mantra chants are available to choose from. In Christianity, we can choose to listen to recordings of Gregorian and Benedictine monks and nuns singing in Latin. The hymnal found in most Christian churches contains hundreds of hymns and Psalms. The Judaic tradition also offers many chants from liturgy to choose from.

Many teachers recommend that we choose *one* mantra and incorporate it into our lives, so it becomes a deep part of our spiritual fabric. We recite or chant it every day, listen to it being performed by any one of dozens of modern-day artists, or use it mindfully while engaging in everyday tasks. My favorite is to chant while driving. It's hard to get worked up about how other drivers misbehave when I'm singing or humming sacred words that contain positive vibrations.

In the '60s and '70s, there was a lot of hype around mantras. The mystical and transformative claims about mantra yoga seemed wildly excessive as they went far beyond the promise of a blissed-out state. However, when neuroscientists and psychologists at the University of California Los Angeles conducted brain scans of individuals who chanted for ten minutes, they found that the stress hormones adrenaline and cortisol were significantly reduced, with effects lasting up to forty-eight hours after each session.[132] It turns out that the blissed-out claims were not so far-fetched after all.

In 2018, James Hartzell, PhD, conducted MRI scans on Thai monks who had chanted Sanskrit mantras from childhood or young adulthood. Some of these recitations took six hours to complete, all from memory. Hartzell found that the hippocampi or memory centers of these monks were markedly more prominent than those in normal brains, which indicated greater strength in facilitating memory and storage capacity. Further, the monks had more gray matter than those who did not engage in chanting. Hartzell's research supports the assertion that among the many benefits of mantra recitation or chanting are greater memory and an improved power of concentration.[133]

What to Recite, What to Chant?

If you are new to the idea of a mantra or chanting, the most important thing I can share is to start slowly and be consistent. Learning something new takes time. Make a commitment to use a mantra during meditation, yoga, or breath practices. Perhaps you have chosen "*har*," a one-word mantra that calls to the higher power, which translated directly means "creative infinity." You can repeat this word to an external beat, such as a hand drum, your breath, or an internal rhythm. There are wonderful recordings of this chant in the resources section of this book.

One mantra that has been researched extensively by neuroscientists is the Kirtan Kriya "sat ta na ma," which translates to "truth is my essence." This mantra is recited while touching the tips of your fingers on each syllable. "Sa" is thumb and forefinger, "ta" is thumb and middle finger, "na" is thumb and ring finger, and finally, "ma" is thumb and little finger. You can recite this mantra silently or aloud to yourself while in meditation, using the four syllables for a four-beat rhythm. The instruction is to engage in this practice using your fingers for at least five minutes, preferably ten.

Newburg and Waldman conducted MRI scans of individuals who used this mantra as a regular part of their spiritual practice and found that activity in the frontal and parietal lobes of the brain was significantly decreased, indicating a reduction in anxiety and fear. Other researchers, as we've noted, have found that spiritual or religious chanting induces a calming effect and reduces negative thinking.[134] Areas of the brain associated with positivity, emotional regulation, modulation, and memory were all positively impacted by chanting.

If reciting or chanting Sanskrit or Gurmukhi phrases is not comfortable for you, by all means, turn to a Christian hymnal and use any one of the hundreds of beautiful examples found there. I personally have memorized dozens of hymns and Psalms that inspire me and offer a deep connection to the divine. Gregorian or Benedictine chants are another example of moving musical incantations. Sung in Latin and originating hundreds of years ago, they have enjoyed a resurgence over the years with many new arrangements recorded in high-quality sound. Any music platform, such as Spotify or Amazon, carries dozens of artists to choose from.

Step Eleven of the Twelve Steps of Alcoholics Anonymous states that we "Sought through prayer and meditation to improve our conscious contact with God *as we understood Him*, praying only for knowledge of His will for us and the power to carry that out." That step reaffirms what I hope this chapter has conclusively shown you: that these spiritual practices are some of the most important we can use daily. They connect us to both the inner and outer worlds of a higher knowing and bring us closer to a reverence for the sacred. It also allows us to listen—to the still voice within that is sometimes a whisper and occasionally clear as a bell.

Mindfulness Moment—Prayer

What role, if any, does prayer have in your life?

If none, how could you perceive prayer differently?

>As a means of connecting to your own inner knowing?

>As a means of connecting to the natural order of our beings?

Are there any prayers that speak to you that you could memorize?

What would it be like to write your own prayers? Have you tried?

If you are interested in writing your own, try writing a prayer every day for forty days and see what unfolds.

Mindfulness Moment—Mantra or Chant

Create a playlist of sacred music to listen to during the day.

Memorize one mantra or hymn and sing it daily for forty days. (Notice what changes occur.)

Drive in your car listening to sacred music. Notice the calming effect!

Play sacred music around your children and notice the shift in their energies.

> Instead of watching the news, put on some sacred music and read a book, do a jigsaw puzzle, draw, do yoga, paint, or . . . the list goes on.

CHAPTER TEN

Body Recovery

"The body says what words cannot."
—Martha Graham

". . . many of our most important exchanges occur simply through the 'unspoken voice' of our body's expressions in the dance of life."
—Peter Levine

"Take care of your body. It's the only place you have to live."
—Jim Rohn

Attending to our physical health in recovery is more than necessary—it's vital. Each of us is inclined to forget the toll alcohol or drugs have exacted on our bodies; we tend to focus on their impact on our brains, minds, and personalities. But our body is the home that houses our existence. We must never take it for granted. Instead, we must explore ways to nurture our bodies and treat them like the temple they are. Because our physical form contains the very spirit of our life, getting in touch with our bodies—the flesh, tissue, organs, muscles, and sinew of our being—is a spiritual practice. Awareness of what we put in our body and how we treat and regard it can begin a powerful healing path.

So many of my clients tell me that they hate their bodies, and by extension, they hate themselves. They have a distorted body image and a disconnected intrapersonal relationship. As they begin to experience healing on their path of recovery, detoxing from substances, working a program, and connecting spiritually in all areas of their lives, the lens of their self-perception reveals a sharper focus. Self-criticism or self-loathing begins to be replaced by acceptance—of who they are and how they look.

When trauma freezes us physically, we tend to be disconnected from the neck down; we use substances to numb whatever sensation arises in our bodies that might have an emotion or a feeling attached to it. The sadness from a memory of loss, the rage toward an abuser, the regret of our actions, paths taken or left behind. All of us experience some emotional memory; for some, these are too much to bear as they elicit a physical response—panic, trembling, difficulty breathing, or rapid heartbeat. Those stored physical sensations may be numbed with drugs and alcohol, but substances cannot erase the actual effects of the trauma itself. A healing process that includes attention to the body is vital to our overall well-being in recovery.

The courage to turn our attention toward our physical body is one that inevitably arises during the process of spiritual healing. At some point, we desire to create a deeper relationship with our interior world. To connect to the vital life force in every cell of our being. Call it the Self, Ātman, or the Tao; we become open to exploring, feeling, sensing, and discovering a new relationship with our physical form. Body recovery through movement, nutrition, and attention to health concerns enables us to experience our whole being with greater appreciation, acceptance, and love.

I have realized that the path of recovery indeed involves the holy trinity of our existence: body, mind, *and* soul. I decided early in my career that as an addiction specialist, I would bring body awareness to my clients both in and out of sessions. During the first year of my private practice, I began using yoga during client sessions in my office. Some clients were experiencing chronic lower back pain or constant neck and shoulder tension, and some had been diagnosed with crippling conditions such as fibromyalgia. Combining breath practices with gentle hatha and trauma-informed yoga, we worked through emotional blocks that had become trapped in the body over time. Slowly, the healing began.

A lifetime of body knowledge has come into play in my client's work. Years of dance training, studies in kinesiology, Rolfing, Reiki, and my dedication to yoga all came together as I developed my approach to helping others overcome addiction. Over the past decade, that knowledge has become even more refined thanks to the work of leaders in the field, such as Gabor Mate and Bessel van der Kolk.

Somatic Therapy

Engaging in physical movement helps us connect to more than just our muscles. There is an entire field focused on the "soma" or body—ranging from Feldenkrais to yoga and everything in between. The former is a method of exercise therapy consisting of gentle movements that help individuals connect to the range of motion in their joints, muscles, tendons, and ligaments. Bringing attention to these single body parts helps to "reorganize connections between the brain and body," which improves movement and affects emotional regulation.[135]

Developed by Dr. Moshe Feldenkrais in the 1960s after he suffered a knee injury, the physicist, nuclear researcher, engineer, and avid sports player began to apply his knowledge to create a new "understanding of human function," resulting in this method.[136] The technique has been used with dancers, athletes, older adults, children, and individuals with chronic health conditions such as autism, fibromyalgia, and Parkinson's.

Dr. Feldenkrais said that how we move has to do with how we perceive ourselves, which is reflected in our physical tensions and muscle constrictions. His method is intended to increase sensitivity to our bodies, enabling us to move more comfortably and efficiently. By extension, that allows us to experience the body more confidently.

Somatic therapy is enjoying a resurgence from its initial development in the nineteenth century by Pierre Janet, who focused on the bodily experiences of dissociation and acute traumatic memory.

At a time when Sigmund Freud's theories of the psyche were the groundbreaking ideas of the day, Pierre Janet's work was almost in complete opposition. He theorized that the mind processes traumatic experiences so that memories, remembered or forgotten, are "stored" in the body. Specifically, he believed that trauma is held in our muscles and skeletal structure. One example is rigid and chronically tight muscles. We see it in people with their shoulders hunched or raised to their ears. The awkward or uncoordinated physical movement that looks robotic is another example that is sometimes referred to as "character armor" and can be easily recognizable in the posture of, for example, many military personnel and government officials.

Janet's work would form the basis of Bessel van der Kolk's research and groundbreaking book, *The Body Keeps the Score.* Van der Kolk's contribution to the importance of understanding the causes and subsequent effects of trauma on the body, mind, and spirit has reshaped how psychotherapy is taught and practiced.

In the 1970s, psychotherapist Peter A. Levine developed a model called "somatic experiencing," which was influenced by his observations of the animal kingdom and his own experience with trauma. In his books, *Waking the Tiger* and *In an Unspoken Voice,* Levine illuminates how humans become trapped in their stress responses by "freezing" both physically and emotionally. Chronic trauma gives rise to symptoms of feeling numb, depressed, angry, or trapped and hopeless. For millions of individuals who experience these states of being, the most easily accessible neutralizer is alcohol, with a close second to drugs. Desperately seeking an escape from ourselves fuels the seemingly endless cycle of pain. We numb out in order to not feel and then feel numb due to the emotions caused by pain too great to face.

Countless research studies point to the predisposition of illness when trauma goes untreated. Experiencing emotional, physical, or mental wounding that is not processed or healed remains tightly bound in our musculoskeletal structure and down to our DNA. The discovery of telomeres, minute sheathlike structures that protect our chromosomes, by Nobel Prize winner Dr. Elizabeth Blackburn in 2009 forever altered our understanding of how chronic stressors such as trauma can affect our health and lifespan. Diseases such as rheumatoid arthritis and asthma are correlated to "chronic psychological stress . . . which impacts immune cell function and may accelerate aging."[137] The psychological factors of stress, abuse, and trauma, to name but a few, are the same factors that contribute to alcoholism, substance abuse, and many other types of addiction. It also relates to extreme reactionary behaviors such as disassociation, self-harming, and personality disorders.

In my experience with clients who come to me for help with acute trauma or anxiety, inevitably, there is a correlated physical challenge: arthritis, pinched nerves, degenerative disc disease, asthma, and immune or autoimmune conditions. Almost to a one, these physical manifestations began at some level within the time frame of their trauma. One woman came to me for panic attacks. She could not fathom why these had plagued her for so many decades and had come to a point where they were getting worse, more frequent, and debilitating. The additional factor of being an active alcoholic and finding that what used to be the panacea for her anxiety was now exacerbating it was even more confounding to her.

When she arrived at my office, she called for help as she tried to open the door. Her hands were crippled with rheumatoid arthritis. Unable to turn knobs, lift her arms above waist height, or raise her legs to insert them into her jeans, her physical restrictions were on equal par with her emotional pain. It was not until we began to furl back the layers of sexual and emotional abuse that had taken place in her life that we were able to address the physical issues she struggled with. When we did, my client found that her response to so much of what had happened when she was young was to "cringe" and "contract." Turning in on herself like a turtle pulling into its shell, she had created a motionless physical condition to deal with past harms and avoid potential future ones.

Using IFS therapy and trauma-informed yoga, we began a healing journey that was remarkable to witness. Approximately six to eight months into our work together, the door opened, and she almost bounced into my office. With a massive smile, she announced, "Ta-da!" and raised both arms above her head. The tears of joy that suddenly came to my eyes rose from a profound, compassionate connection. She had worked so hard, so diligently, experiencing steps forward and backward on her way to one breakthrough after another. She was finally able to experience herself in her body with an ease she had not known for most of her life.

Again and again, trauma experts and researchers point to the inevitable physical "contraction" that occurs when our psychological experiences collide with our body in response to trauma. We lose our connection to ourselves and our *Self*, the core of our spiritual identity.

Ayurveda

Ayurveda is a science of health and medicine native to India that dates back thousands of years. It is a multifaceted approach to wellness that comprehensively addresses body, mind, and spirit. This approach is based on the five elements: earth, fire, water, and air or ether. These elements comprise the three "humors" of the body: *Vata* dosha, *Pitta* dosha, and *Kapha* dosha. These humors are responsible for the physiological functioning of the blood, bones, tissues, muscles, and all other aspects of our physical constitution. Knowledge of our constitution helps us understand our stress reactions and make wiser decisions about diet and lifestyle.

Ayurveda offers simple daily and seasonal routines that create a strong foundation of balance for the body-mind system. It also offers a profound detoxification process (Pancha Karma) that can re-establish chemical, metabolic, and hormonal balance in our physiological system. This much-needed physical repair is often overlooked. It can provide the support needed to end dependence on medication support for basic body functions like proper digestion, elimination, and sleep.

Knowing which dosha you are aligned with is an important step to understanding the difference between being dry, light, and subtle (Vata) or heavy, oily, and soft (Kapha). Identifying your dosha helps to inform what foods to avoid, what practices to engage in to support your dosha, and how to avoid imbalance or disease.

The body of knowledge for Ayurveda is vast. Durga Leela, author of *Yoga of Recovery: Integrating Yoga and Ayurveda with Modern Recovery Tools for Addiction*, is one of the most respected authors and teachers of this approach to recovery. Her application of Ayurveda to healing addiction is highly researched, detailed, and filled with practical day-to-day tools and techniques.

If addiction treatment centers were to incorporate Ayurvedic principles in their detox and wellness approaches, they might be surprised to find how rapidly the physical trauma caused by alcohol and drugs could be healed. They could give clients invaluable tools by which to live life after treatment and offset the risks of being caught in the vicious cycle of the overuse of sugar, nicotine, and fast or processed foods.

Yogic Spiritual Recovery

Yoga can be a profound spiritual practice. I have watched it transform from traditional Indian philosophy and way of life to a modern physical and mental health approach. From the early days of Paramahansa Yogananda to the New Age era of Ram Das, Kripalu, Esalen, and Spirit Rock Center, yoga remained a steadfast form of the original teachings brought to America by Swami Vivekananda. One didn't just "do" yoga; one *lived* it. The body of practice included a comprehensive understanding of the *Yoga Sutras of Patanjali*, embracing the *yamas* and *niyamas*, relinquishing meat, alcohol, tobacco, and mind-altering substances, and lastly, opting for a celibate life unless married.

Somewhere along the line, the sutras were dropped because they were "too difficult to understand," the Yamas and Niyamas were "outdated," and the only thing that had any importance was the physical practice of asanas. Even those became distorted as the focus in yoga studios across the country became a rigorous physical practice that could replace cardio classes at a gym and eventually morphed into the absurd: wine yoga, goat yoga, dog yoga, paddleboard yoga, beer yoga, nude yoga, aerial yoga, cannabis yoga.

The good news is that these fads have been just that. Lately, we are seeing a resurgence of the original intention of yoga: as a philosophy, an ethic, a way of life, and a physical practice that brings the body toward health, strength, and longevity.

Yoga as a spiritual recovery was my mainstay for years and is still my heartfelt love. Many clients seek the yogic path based on testimonies from others and a keen interest. However, what is seen on social media or in a studio can be impossible poses for a beginner. Tight hamstrings, challenged core muscles, and shoulder and arm weakness can deflate someone before they even begin. My admonition to *any* beginner is to refrain from engaging in classes or online sessions beyond the *beginner* level. Start slow!

There are three main approaches to physical yoga practice: hatha, the most traditional and slower of the yogic schools; Vinyasa, a modern adaptation of hatha with more rapid transitions between poses; and Kundalini, known as the yoga of awakening, which uses "kriyā" to aid in spiritual development.

Whichever yogic path you choose, the daily practice of meditation, breathing exercises, and physical body engagement should be the mainstay of your practice.

When I work with clients to create a daily spiritual practice for recovery, I always suggest certain rituals to begin—lighting a candle or a stick of incense with attention and reverence and setting an intention or reciting the "Set Aside Prayer" is also a wonderful ritual:

God, please help me set aside everything I think I know about You, everything I think I know about myself, everything I think I know about others, and everything I think I know about my own recovery, so I may have an open mind and a new experience with these things and come to know You better. Please help me see the truth. Amen.

You'll also need a solid yoga mat of five millimeters or more to give you support and cushioning and a comfortable, affordable meditation cushion that is neither too soft nor too hard.

Choosing to meditate or engage in yoga practices first is a personal preference. There will be days when your body asks you to move before sitting quietly and days when sitting first feels right and natural. I suggest ten or twenty minutes of meditation and fifteen to twenty minutes of yoga practice for beginners.

I discovered the Sun Salutation prayer years ago and have used it as a template for my yoga practice. It is not essential, but I've found it helpful, and you might want to try it.

The instruction is to inhale before each movement while reciting the Sanskrit and exhale during the exercise. Inhale on "om mitraya namah," arch backward as you exhale, and then inhale on "om ravaye namah." Exhale as you fold over the legs, continuing through the entire Sun Salutation, using your breath as a fulcrum for the movements. Breath informs the body, and engaging intentionally in this way affects areas of the brain associated with memory and mental clarity. It is not a requirement to recite the Sanskrit prayers related to the Sun Salutation, but if you are feeling adventurous, try it and see if there is a difference between the two approaches.

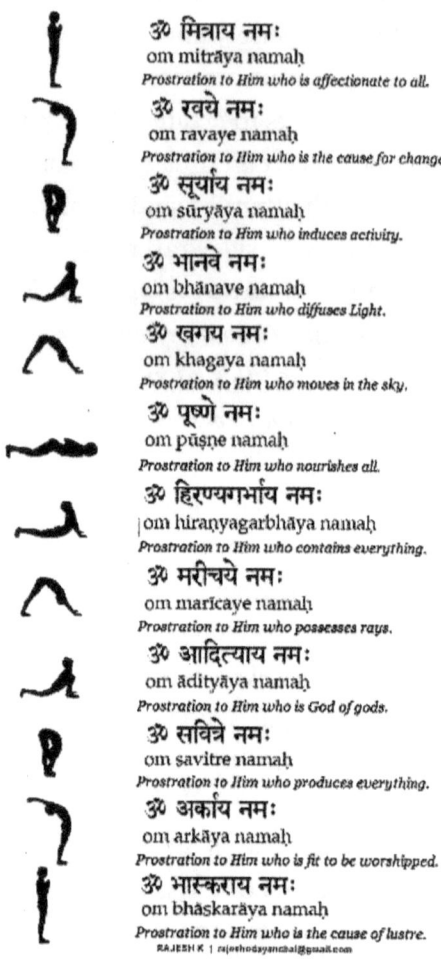

Figure 3 Sun Salutation Prayers[138]

If you are more inclined to practice Kundalini yoga, there are outstanding resources on YouTube and the internet. The first place I recommend is to go to Tommy Rosen's YouTube channel and watch his "Morning Sadhana—Breakfast of Champions" kriya set. You will be challenged in the best sense of the word and feel enlivened after twenty minutes of this daily routine.

Kia Miller has beautiful Kundalini videos that lead students through an unlimited variety of kriyas on YouTube. The 3HO (Happy Healthy Holy Organization) is the go-to website for Kundalini yoga and a virtual encyclopedia of kriyas, mantras, community, study, recipes, and much more. Websites such as Gaia, Yoga Journal, or Glo offer abundant Kundalini guidance.

Individuals such as Guru Singh have public and member-driven websites; Guru Prem (Tommy Rosen's teacher) has a YouTube channel that engages beginners and advanced practitioners alike. His wife, Simran Kaur, a noted Kundalini practitioner, has a channel dedicated to her teachings.

Hatha, Vinyasa, or Kundalini practices will allow you to experience body-changing and life-altering results. Neurologically, the brain is being healed through kriya, pose, or flow, with each movement targeting specific energy centers in the body. Fibers, tissue, fasciae, joints, muscles, sinew, and cartilage are all given a deep massage. The breath guides each moment of practice toward ultimate neuroplasticity in the brain. By using spiritual techniques for recovery, you will be altering the negativity bias and mapping new mental health pathways. That's a vast, stunning benefit from something as simple and basic as "exercise"!

Gaga Movement

Imagine being able to move your body so that you don't have to know "steps" or "sequences" and don't have to be limber, flexible, or have any particular body shape. Imagine being able to move just by following cues; no matter how you follow them, there is no wrong way of moving. What if you could move your body with freedom, connection, and passion? What if you could also find your "groove"?

In March 2022, I discovered Gaga movement language. This was initially created for professional dancers by Ohad Naharin, the creative director of the Batsheva Dance Company. Based in Tel Aviv,

Israel, it is a highly regarded company that Naharin has brought to the forefront of contemporary dance.

His movement system, Gaga, is both an approach and a tool. He created it partly to heal from his painful back injuries and as a more accurate means to communicate his choreographic visions to company dancers.

As with so many dancers pushing their bodies' limits to excruciating extremes, Naharin suffered a severe back injury. He found himself unable to move, much less dance. His left leg became partially paralyzed, and he sought numerous "therapies" to assist in his healing process. Among these were Pilates, Tai Chi, and his knowledge of Feldenkrais, which he had learned from his mother.[139] Over the course of months of healing, Naharin began to "research" how to best incorporate the wisdom of learned movement with the innate intelligence of his own body. Thus, Gaga came into being. Naharin taught his dancers what he had developed for himself and soon found that positive changes were taking place in how they moved their bodies, let go of emotional restrictions, and appeared to connect more authentically to their artistic expression.

After several years of watching how the resident dancers were improving their bodies, minds, and spirits, staff members of Batsheva Dance Company asked Naharin if he could adapt the language to "people." In response, Naharin created "Gaga/people," and in just a few years, this method of movement has taken its rightful place in the somatic field.

Gaga is at once an awareness and a presence. It requires paying attention, sometimes at a cellular level, to what the body is sensing and how it moves. At the same time, it is about connecting to our inner world of imagination, pleasure, and personal joy. It is a methodology almost the opposite of yoga, without "form" or specific "routine." Unlike ballet, modern, jazz, or other movement styles, there are no steps to learn or footwork to master. This is all about *you* and *your* body and *your* experience.

A Gaga class is approximately thirty to forty-five minutes long, and participants move through the entire class without stopping. The approach to movement consists of "layers" of cues for movement. The teacher may suggest "find curves" in your body or "waves" and then bring your attention to everything from your fingertips to your toes. Naharin promotes the belief that we can become efficient in our body movements while at the same time accessing the "explosive power" that lies within every one of us.[140] The result is a sense of complete freedom in movement and an inner release of emotional constraint or self-consciousness.

Gaga/people is online every day (http://www.gagapeople.com/en/ongoing-classes/), streaming from teachers' living rooms or dance studios worldwide. You can take a class at 4 a.m. from an instructor in Australia or a 6 p.m. class from one in Tel Aviv. Live courses are easily found at dance centers if you live in a major city such as New York, Paris, Berlin, and London. My personal experience with Gaga has been life-changing. My body is moving more freely, with less "holding back" from the fear of looking foolish, and the physical strength I am gaining is translating into increased energy and focus. I have brought the techniques into therapy sessions with clients who report immediate physical relaxation and softening of long-held body tension.

Tools and Techniques

Sometimes, we need an easy, short, and effective tool during our busy lives. While long and intense practices for our body recovery are lovely and highly effective, only some have the time or resources to join a somatic therapy class or afford a therapeutic specialist in body healing. Finding a yoga class that fits our schedule and abilities can also be challenging.

The following practices are spiritually based, can be practiced in the comfort of your home or hotel room, and are highly effective at reducing stress and bringing body and mind to the center.

The Body Scan

In the yogic tradition, *Savasana* or "corpse pose" is used for deep relaxation and energy restoration at the end of a class. It is also called "yoga nidra" or yogic sleep because of the profound physical and emotional state of calm generated. The mind and the senses are awake; however, the depth of muscular and skeletal relaxation mirrors the sleeping state. It is not unusual to fall asleep during Savasana!

Jon Kabat-Zinn refers to the practice as "the body scan," an appropriate term for the process. We begin at the top of our head and scan our entire body for tension in our muscles, joints, ligaments, and tendons, down to cellular awareness. At the same time, we bring our attention to the thoughts, feelings, and emotions that may be present. We use the breath as a vehicle for the entire practice, which activates the parasympathetic or calming nervous system. After twenty, thirty, or even sixty minutes of this practice, the sense of tranquility and physical well-being is so powerful that it will have you coming back as often as you can.

There are many videos, YouTubes, audios, and documents to support this practice on your own. The following is one I created for my yoga classes and can be found on my YouTube channel.

Savasana—Yoga Nidra—Body Scan

- Begin by lying on your yoga mat, with a blanket underneath your body and one over your body. The purpose is to have support beneath you for your skeletal structure and to keep your body temperature comfortable.
- Focus on your inhale through your nostrils. Long, slow inhale, filling your lungs with oxygen, and long, slow exhale from your nostrils, releasing toxins and anything that does not serve you from your body.
- Bring your attention to the crown of your head. Bring your

awareness to any tension that may be present on your scalp. See if you can allow the muscles of your scalp to soften. Relax.

- Bring attention to your forehead and soften the muscles that contract into a frown. Move your attention to your eyes, cheekbones, lips, and chin, softening and relaxing each set of muscles as you go.
- Move your awareness to your neck and intentionally soften the muscles around your lower jaw, throat, and back of the neck.
- Move your awareness to your clavicle and the breath to your shoulder tips. Relax any tension in this area of your body and notice any attending thoughts or emotions that might arise as you do so. We hold an enormous amount of stress in this part of our body; focusing and allowing the muscle structure to soften will help release pent-up energy.
- Now bring your attention to your chest: rib cage, bronchia, lungs, and the thoracic area around the spine. Take a few long, slow inhalations through the nose here and connect to your breathing. Relax.
- The stomach and gut region are primary stress holders. See if you can begin to soften the muscles of your abdomen and then go deeper inside to soften the muscular structure that protects your organs. Go deeper and see if you can visualize your upper digestive tract, your gastrointestinal pathway, and your colon relaxing, softening, and easing from the tension it may have been holding.
- Bring awareness to your pelvic region—lower intestines, bowel, bladder, and reproductive system. Soften the muscles around your pelvic area, hips, and glutes. Relax the muscles held in a sitting position for hours on end. Relax the deeper tendons and ligaments in the pelvic region.
- Move your awareness to your thighs and the robust muscle structure of the quadriceps. Allow these muscles to soften

and relax. Behind them are ligaments and hamstrings. Allow them to let go of the tension they hold throughout the day, sitting, walking, and carrying your body to and fro.

- Breathe into your knees, kneecaps, and tendons behind the knees. Soften the tendons, ligaments, and muscles.
- Bring awareness to your calves and shins, relaxing and softening the muscles, tendons, and ligaments that support you all day.
- Now bring your attention to your ankles and let them relax completely. Begin to soften the muscles in each foot and focus on each toe, intentionally relaxing the muscles one by one.
- Focus on the soles of your feet. Sweep the entire area that carries you each day through your life, and intentionally relax the muscles and tendons.
- Your body should be fully relaxed by now. Focus on your breath as it comes in and out of your nostrils.
- Rest here as long as you like.

It is not unusual to fall asleep during Savasana. Permit yourself to do so, and you will wake up refreshed—as if you had eight hours of sleep!

The Five Tibetans

This powerful and energetic series of movements for body healing was introduced to the US in 1939 by Peter Kedler in his book *The Five Rites of Rejuvenation*. The practice of "the Five Tibetans," as it has become known, has become very popular in the healing arts as one approach to health, well-being, and overall physical strength. The best book I have found to date that describes the exercises clearly and concisely is by Christopher S. Kilham, *The Five Tibetans*.

The sequence consists of five easy asanas repeated twenty-one times each and performed daily. As author Kilham explains, building up to twenty-one repetitions may take time but is worth the effort. Each "rite," as they are called, engages particular areas of the body, as well as the energy pathways that run from the base of our spine to the top of our head. In between are the seven "chakras," or nerve centers and glands that exist from the bottom of the spine to our crown.

Practicing this simple sequence allows energy to flow more smoothly through the pathways and stimulate the chakras through a gradual detoxification process. Over time, health, vitality, focus, and strength increase, with benefits to the body, mind, and spirit.

The first rite consists of turning clockwise with arms spread out to the sides, fingers together, and palms facing down. Turn slowly at first! Over time, you can increase your speed, but until your inner ear has adjusted to the motion, my best advice is to take this very slowly.

After repeating the turn twenty-one times, stand with your legs apart and take deep breaths through your nose. In this exercise, exhale through the mouth while forming your lips into the shape of an "O."

The remaining poses or rites are all performed on a yoga mat. Core energy is engaged in rite two when lifting legs and the head simultaneously. Rite three helps to open the chest area, tighten the glutes and quads, and strengthen balance. Go slowly with rite four. The shoulders and upper arms may not be strong enough to lift your body, so take your time. Rite five will be familiar to anyone who has done yoga as this is the classic Downward Dog.

Figure 4 The Five Tibetans[141]

The Shake

Peter Levine writes extensively about the effects of trauma on our bodies, particularly the adverse effects of not allowing our bodies to shake when we experience something physically or emotionally challenging. According to Levine, animals engage in this activity naturally: watch any dog, cat, horse, or other animal shake themselves after a variety of activities. The shake helps them to recenter themselves and readjust their nervous system.

In our human world, the shaking reaction is perceived as part of "being in shock" and needing to be repressed or stopped. It is a widespread practice to be tranquilized after surgery when the body begins to engage in tremors and shaking naturally. As a result, the body cannot release the stressor of what it experienced under anesthesia (being cut open, having body parts removed); subsequent trauma reactions post-surgery are not uncommon as the more the body tries to shake off what happened, the more medications are prescribed.

Engaging in deliberate shaking of our body resets the nervous system and releases minor, built-up stressors that are stored in our muscles over time. While this practice dates back to historical yoga traditions, David Berceli, PhD, developed a therapeutic approach to trauma called "neurogenic tremoring."[142] Berceli created exercises to aid in the trauma recovery process, including the controlled act of letting go through shaking.

Shaking is also found in Gaga movement. One of the cues is to begin shaking our fingers, hands, wrists, arms, and shoulders. The echo of shaking the arms and shoulders is then brought to the upper chest, neck, and head. The shake moves to our lower torso, waist, hips, pelvis, legs, knees, ankles, and feet until the whole body is shaking. In Gaga, the instruction is to allow the shake to overtake our body as if it is in a state of chaos.

Similarly, Berceli's instructions to his patients are to allow the shake to take over entirely to let go of stress and anxiety. This process is a primitive mechanism that resets our muscles and skeletal structure from a "frozen" state of trauma into more fluid body awareness. I have found that when I engage in the shake, pent-up stress is released, frustration diminishes or disappears, and I become calmer, centered, and connected to myself.

You can find an excellent example of the shake on YouTube by Deva Premal and Miten[143] and on my YouTube channel.

Body Recovery—Intake

Go to any Twelve Step meeting virtually anywhere in the world, and you will find two staples: coffee and sugar. Endless cups of caffeine are provided to newcomers and old-timers alike, with heaps of sugar poured in. Powdered milk products like Cremora are available as a milk substitute and contain a lot of sugar. At anniversary celebrations, attendees bring plates of cookies, donuts, pastries, brownies, a celebration cake, and other delectable items for one and all to share, even though sugar, like alcohol and drugs, is highly addictive and detrimental to bodily healing.

Establishing a healthy relationship with our bodies includes detoxifying and learning beneficial nutrition and physical movement approaches. Treatment facilities now focus on this as part of their programs, but the struggle can be arduous for any sober person. We can give up alcohol and drugs. But giving up cigarettes and sugar and engaging in physical health often seem an insurmountable goal. I know; I've been there.

Nicotine

When I got sober in 1994, I smoked a pack of cigarettes daily. After quitting alcohol, I attended at least one Twelve Step meeting a day, sometimes two, and they were all smoking meetings. Part of my service work was to clean out the ashtrays. By the time I pursued a doctorate, I was up to almost two packs daily. The dissertation process had me sometimes dipping into a third pack late at night.

I started coughing in August of 1998. A particularly nasty cough started to produce dark phlegm. This scared me so much that I immediately pledged to stop smoking. I tried everything from rubber bands on my wrists to chewing nicotine gum, using filters, eating raw carrots and celery by the bagful, and a stint at quitting cold turkey, which lasted three days.

Torture is an understatement.

But something began to happen as I went through this process of trying to stop one of the worst and most tenacious addictions known to humanity. The smell of smoke started to bother me. I noticed it on everything and began washing, cleaning, steaming, and doing anything else I could to remove it. I stopped smoking in my apartment. I stopped smoking in my car. Despite this, I still couldn't quit.

I met someone at a meeting who told me they had successfully quit through hypnosis. I got the phone number but resisted calling because the cost ($450) was prohibitive for a starving student like me. Then one day, as I was about to light up, it occurred to me that the cost of cigarettes was only going to get more expensive, and I was shelling out a swift $1.50 per pack, which was pricey in those days. I calculated that I was paying almost $100 monthly for this habit. That stopped me in my tracks. In four months or so, I would "earn" back the cost of hypnosis. So, I booked an appointment.

I walked in a smoker and walked out a nonsmoker. For three weeks. Then one day, I hit a brick wall of emotion that stopped me and brought on a severe panic attack. Back I went to the hypnotist, who spent over an hour with me in a deep state of relaxation, taking me all the way back to the point in time when I had made a conscious decision to smoke.

Suddenly, I was ten years old, looking at the adults in my life who were not helpful. As I observed the insanity around me, my young self was convinced that if I smoked cigarettes, I would have *control*. That awareness alone allowed the hypnotist and I to undo a very specific subconscious decision and replace it with an understanding that the opposite was true. Smoking had controlled me for decades. I walked out as a nonsmoker in November 1998 and have never smoked a cigarette again.

If you are currently smoking cigarettes or vaping, try as best as possible to commit to quitting. I recommend the American Lung Association website, any smoking cessation program, or hiring a hypnotherapist to stop. It's not easy—but freedom from smoking truly liberates. Bypassing the insistent urges will take time, effort, and commitment. Breath practices help with cravings: particularly the nadi shadona and the sitali breaths. Doing these regularly throughout the day will help your parasympathetic nervous system to remain engaged, offsetting the fight-flight effect of cravings. Chewing crunchy foods like carrots, celery, nuts, apples, or sugarless candy can also help, as well as chewing sugarless gum. Nicotine patches and gum are options, but they transmit the same chemical into your system, making quitting more challenging.

I would also not recommend trying to quit nicotine concurrently with quitting alcohol or substances. This may be way too much for your system to handle. Instead, try cutting down and substituting crunchy foods or gum. The first year of sobriety is tough on the body, mind, and spirit. Be gentle with yourself!

Sugar

Sugar as an addiction is something I have struggled with off and on for the better part of my life. Despite being thin, sugar has wreaked havoc on my body, more so as I have aged. Because ingesting sugar replicates dopamine surges in the brain, it acts as a panacea for anxiety or depression.

For many, sugar is a pacifier. The sweetness on our tastebuds elicits a reaction to "feel-good" chemicals that attach to our brain reward center and carry signals across our nervous system that tell it to "soothe." These chemicals are created in the pituitary gland, which then relays to the hypothalamus, which sits below the pituitary gland. The most important thing to know is that when the endocrine system is activated by sugar, the hypothalamus creates oxytocin, a neurochemical that manages certain aspects of human behavior. It is called the "love hormone" because it is associated with feelings of love, tenderness, and bonding.[144]

It is no surprise that when the detox process is in full swing, we gravitate toward sugar in the form of chocolates, candies, ice cream, cupcakes, muffins, cakes, and puddings, to name a few. Doing so gives us a feeling of comfort as we experience the unpleasant sensations of withdrawal. Sugar can also relieve the sensations in the body and repeated self-talk that arises from our emotional discomfort of not having a soothing substance like alcohol to lessen the impact. We may not be fully aware, but the immediate pull toward a calming substance like sugar is almost automatic.

There is much research on the association between childhood trauma and sugar addiction. Trauma can cause a rise in cortisol, a stress hormone that can raise blood sugar levels. This leads to sugar cravings that have us consuming more significant amounts of sugar than our bodies can handle. As a result, adult diabetes and hyperglycemia are two conditions that can develop over time, as is the effect of never quite feeling "full." It takes a lot of sugar to assuage emotional and physical triggers. Even then, the body dissociates from its normal functioning and sends the wrong signals to our brain's reward center. Instead of receiving the appropriate attachment, nurturing, or love from our caregivers, we seek a substance replicating the dopamine high of comfort.

I had an alarming example of this in my life, which caused me to not only give up sugar for long periods but also to look into extensive research on the subject. This occurred years ago when I was in an internship for my clinical substance abuse license at an intensive outpatient program (IOP). I had a particularly officious supervisor who disapproved of my suggestions to bring meditation techniques to clients to calm their post-acute withdrawal symptoms. She overheard me suggest a book to a client and called me into her office, where she gave me a severe dressing-down that left me trembling. Before a long drive home, I stopped at the grocery store to pick up several items. Then I trolled the candy aisle. Since we were low on chocolate, and almond clusters were on sale, I thought that I might as well buy more than one pound. I filled a bag with almost three pounds. As I pulled out of the parking lot, I reached for the bag of chocolates, took one out, and popped it into my mouth. The rest of the thirty-mile drive was a blur. I mainly was ruminating about the supervisor admonishing me, which recalled my father constantly berating me during my summer visits with him. He found fault with me from top to toe: my New York accent, the way I wore my hair, the books I wanted to read, the music I loved, or how I set the table or made my bed.

I pulled up to our house and unloaded the car. It was late; I was exhausted and emotionally drained. Milk, butter, and lettuce went into the fridge. I was too tired to deal with the dry goods and left them on the counter, opting instead to crawl into bed and curl up into a ball. The following day, I was putting away the shopping and couldn't find the chocolates. The plastic bag that contained them was empty—and thinking they had fallen out in the car, I checked the front seat. Bits of chocolate were all over the driver's seat, on the floor mat, and sprinkled over the console. I had eaten nearly three pounds of almond clusters and had done so in a dissociative state while reliving my past trauma triggered by the dress-down from my supervisor. I had no recollection of putting any pieces in my mouth after the first one, much less chewing and swallowing them.

This horrifying event woke me up to the harsh reality that I had been using sugar for decades to soothe, comfort, and avoid physical feelings of emotional trauma. Taking a Twelve Step approach to my sugar addiction, I remained sugar-free for over two years. A relapse set me back for a month or two, but I returned to a sugar-free diet for several years after that. It has been an up-and-down journey, with shorter and shorter relapses as time passes. Today, my resolve to abstain from sugar is stronger than the pull to consume it. In addition, by engaging almost daily in body movement and awareness, I have become far more adept at recognizing my triggers and the connection between the desire for emotional soothing and the physical call for sugar.

Overall Nutrition

Fresh fruits, salads, lean meats, legumes, and vegetables. This was how I was raised, and it is perhaps why today, in my late sixties, I have excellent cholesterol levels, virtually no body fat, normal to low blood pressure, and an excellent heart rate. I was blessed to have had the "Mediterranean diet" as a part of my life from the early age of two, and except for a few years in my teens when I experienced five pesky pounds that were hard to drop, my body weight has remained pretty much on the slender side to this day.

Today, terms like "eating clean," "gluten-free," "carb-free," "keto," and "intermittent fasting," to name a few, are, in my opinion, fads. I do not adhere to "diets" because, in so many cases, they do not align with our lifestyles and often do more harm than good. Diets can be a one-way setup for failure. When we use a mindful and healthy approach to what we take into our bodies to fuel and sustain them, we achieve a much better balance.

My recommendation to all my clients who ask me about nutrition is simple: avoid fast-food restaurants or take-out *at all costs*; avoid red meat as much as you can or eliminate it completely. Avoid or significantly reduce carbohydrate-filled foods such as potatoes, bread, cookies, cakes, muffins, and sugary foods such as candy or ice cream as much as you can, if not eliminate them entirely.

When we perceive our body to be the temple it is, we begin to have a very different relationship to it than merely this "thing" that moves us through our lives. We start to realize that it houses more than just bones and gristle. Our soul lives here, our compassion and our love. Most importantly, this is where our *Self* lives. And in the overused words of Shakespeare, "to thine own self be true."

Mindfulness Moment

What are you doing daily to attend to your body?

Could you devote ten to fifteen minutes daily to some movement?

What do your eating habits look like?

How much fast food, precooked meals, sugar, or carbs are you eating daily?

>Take an honest inventory.

Would you be willing to begin to make incremental changes in your diet to feel better, sleep better, and function better?

Do you smoke or vape nicotine?

Have you thought of giving it up?

>What would you be willing to do to make that commitment?

CHAPTER ELEVEN
Living the Spiritual Life

"Spirituality in its broadest sense remains humankind's only salvation."

—Rabbi Abraham J. Twersky

"We are not human beings having a spiritual experience. We are spiritual beings having a human experience."

—Pierre Teilhard de Chardin

"Your sacred space is where you can find yourself over and over again."

—Joseph Campbell

When we are in the throes of addiction, our world is narrow, restricted, and limited. We experience indescribable emotional pain. It cries out to be numbed, and we heed its call. We may not have lost our jobs or our home, but we suffer a relentless roller coaster of waking up in a fog, swearing to do it differently, and succumbing again and again.

We are brutal with ourselves and, many times, with others. If we lose jobs, we face the financial hell zone of never having enough, or we spend much-needed money to stave off our internal demons or accept dreary, low-paying jobs to ensure a roof over our heads.

Some of us end up homeless. Not all of us make it. Many die from overdoses, cirrhosis, alcoholic dementia, or suicide. Those of us who survive this debilitating and incapacitating disease are true miracles. We have been spared. And we are given another chance at life.

The spiritual path of recovery gives us hope. The Twelve Steps of Alcoholics Anonymous assure us that we will experience a new freedom in our lives and happiness that gives us the understanding of peace. No matter how far to the bottom we have gone, we are shown the ways in which our stories and subsequent victory from the addictive processes can help others.

Our regrets, self-pity, and sense of uselessness will subside as our perceptions and perspectives on life change. Our fears begin to melt. We realize that we are being carried by a power far greater than ourselves. It is what some choose to call God. That same sense of hope is provided as well by other forms of recovery, such as Refuge Recovery, Yoga and the Twelve Steps, or Christian Recovery. There are so many paths to freedom. You simply need to choose the one that suits you best.

The grace of sobriety is that it allows us to live a life we could not have imagined while drinking or drugging. If, while sipping on my third or fourth cocktail, I fantasized that, one day, I would realize my dreams, the reality was that if I continued to drink, this could never have become a reality. I was disheveled and broken inside, without any credentials or ability to go any further than a low-income job that barely covered my living expenses. I was undisciplined, unable to finish anything I had started. I bounced from jobs and careers like a jack-in-the-box, always looking for the silver bullet around the corner. My relationships were fractured and unstable. My two failed marriages attested to that.

Today, I hold degrees, licenses, and certificates that show I can finish what I start but also that I have developed the wherewithal to apply myself to a broad swath of specialties that support my career trajectory. Twenty-three years ago, I met the man to whom I am still married, and together, we have created a life beyond our wildest dreams. We built a house, we bought land, and we rescued dogs. We grew as a couple in love and life. I created a private practice that has thrived for almost a decade, and amid it, I started programs that support recovering people and wrote this book. None of this could have been accomplished without my sobriety.

I was born to express myself through movement. At a young age, I showed great promise for a career as a dancer, and my parents were encouraged to nurture my passion for ballet or any other form of movement expression. While I never achieved the dream of being a principal dancer and performing worldwide, I trained with some of the most outstanding teachers and dancers in the business and got close, very close. Now, over forty years later, at sixty-eight, I have come full circle with the opportunity to dance again through Gaga movement language—not to perform but to rediscover and revel in my passion for movement. I could not have experienced this without my sobriety.

Today, I am free of shame and from the self-imposed prison of the mind and body-numbing agents that took me to the lowest depths imaginable.

The spiritual life is the only one I want to live. It is my hope that you will appreciate the benefits and joy this life brings and want it as well.

Alcoholics and drug addicts commonly experience fear, anxiety, sadness, agitation, unease, and fright. Some of us can handle these better than others, but the truth is our vulnerability becomes the object of an addictive process that robs us, severing us from our families, society, and ourselves. The spiritual path does not require us to believe in "God" or a deity who sits in judgment. The spiritual path is simply about rising above our egos and committing ourselves to "serve something greater than our immediate desires."[145]

Holocaust survivor and psychiatrist Victor Frankl points out that giving up hope is at the heart of early death. Men in concentration camps would become sick, commit suicide, or lose the will to live and become the target of execution by their captors. The meaning of life, and the search for that meaning, is to find tasks that go beyond the narrow limits of ourselves. Serving the greater good and helping others who suffer are tasks that give our lives a purpose and fulfill our destiny.

In living a spiritual life, every day, I connect with my higher power. Every day, I engage in prayer, contemplation, meditation, movement of my body, and creative expression. Throughout the day, I bring my awareness to my breath and, by extension, to this physical form and how I am holding it and experiencing it. Every day, I try to engage in intentional acts of compassion.

My life is spent helping others to heal and embrace a spiritual path. Those who have journeyed on this path are sober and thriving and have remarkable stories to tell. They, too, relate miraculous experiences.

My experience as a therapist has convinced me that unburdening our internal system and protective parts of the wounds carried throughout our lives is essential. It is also critical to rewire our brains to reframe our experiences and help our healing process. Alcohol and drugs have taken their toll on our neurons and the millions of connectors that intersect with crucial areas there. Spiritual practices help us to restructure much of that damage; therapy enables us to heal within and relearn appropriate responses and behaviors.

Each day brings a new revelation from those I work with as they discover the spiritual path to healing. One client recently told me that she was experiencing a new relationship with her daughter. This came about when she finally became clear about boundaries and limits and what she was and was not willing to tolerate. These insights came from a place of clarity, compassion, courage, and confidence, attributes she had had no access to when drinking. And though nothing was discussed or mentioned between them, it was as if some intelligent force had shifted the entire dynamic between mother and daughter. Their relationship began to heal.

Another client had spent years struggling with self-esteem issues and childhood trauma. The work we did focused on unburdening the wounds of her past and encouraging her to fully accept and embrace the integral core of who she was and is. In one session, the tears pouring down her face were not ones of sadness but prompted by the joy that, for the first time in her life, she could say with confidence that she loves who she is—a beautiful, creative, passionate soul.

Most of my clients have benefited enormously from choosing a spiritual path of healing. Some have gone on to become monks, some have dedicated their lives to healing others, and more than I can count remain sober even years after leaving therapy. As they step into new lives, they pursue their dreams and realize their goals. They marry and have children. They become who they were always meant to be. They become the highest version of themselves.

Spiritual work helps us reclaim our true nature and undo the intrinsic belief of humanity: that we are separate beings from each other and everything around us. The concept of separation is at the root of so much suffering. The Buddha and Jesus addressed this idea as part of their core teachings. It is an ageless truth that we are not *apart from*, but rather, we are *a part of* the human experience, whether in joy or suffering.

We are truly spiritual beings having a human experience. Every one of us is divine. Behaviors such as addiction or violence will overturn reason. But these are actions, not the core of who you are. Inside you is *all* of heaven. Inside your heart center is the entire universe, without end. An unlimited resource available to you always. I believe that God resides in every single individual and speaks in soft whispers to us all. I believe that God is within and without. No matter how low we have gone, the actions we engaged in at that time do not reflect who we truly are.

Committing to living a spiritual life takes three simple things: deciding you want something different, being disciplined about working toward it, and then being devoted to keeping it. It begins with a first step, whether it be taking ten minutes to focus on your breath each morning, meditating on a cushion regularly, praying, reciting mantras, or energizing your body through movement.

The spiritual life provides a daily reprieve from the demons of our past, the traumas that haunted us, and the nightmares that shook us awake at night. It is a path to recovery that we create for ourselves and walk with grace and dignity. When we take the spiritual path, we awaken. Noted psychologist Lisa Miller, PhD, remarked, "The awakened brain is our seat of perception for the transcendent and immanent. It's our internal point-wave function that alerts us to the felt guiding presence and the sacredness in daily life."[146]

To *Rise in Recovery* is to soar beyond the limitations that alcohol or drugs certainly guarantee. To *Rise in Recovery* is to live a life that sparkles with hope, authenticity, joy, and an unbridled sense of freedom. To *Rise in Recovery* means trusting that the universe has your back while you do the next right thing.

> *May you claim your birthright as a human*
> *and live the spiritual life that is available to you.*
> *May you live your best life in the embrace of God.*
> *May you be sober and free today and every day.*

ACKNOWLEDGMENTS

A book of this breadth does not write itself. I have drawn on decades, if not centuries, of knowledge to guide me through this topic. Every author cited in the references and bibliography has informed me in more ways than I can count through hours of page-turning, note-taking, and synthesizing. I am in debt to every learned scientist, theorist, practitioner, and groundbreaker in this field who has been my inspiration. Thank you.

Following a series of seemingly random coincidences, I was connected to my initial editor, Elizabeth Kaye. Little did I realize that she would not only guide me on the journey to completing this manuscript but also make me a better writer. Thank you, Elizabeth, for your steady hand. You not only gave me the confidence but the courage to speak my truth throughout these pages.

On January 27, 2000, at 2:15 p.m., I met the man who would become my husband a year later. I owe my life to you, Don. Your love, guidance, and support have made me the person I have become over the past twenty-four years. None of my accomplishments would have happened without your encouragement, honesty, and constant reminders that I had it in me to do anything I set out to do. After all, "You knew that."

To Tommy Rosen, my teacher and mentor, I am forever grateful to you for bringing your wisdom and vision to the field of recovery. Thank you for the heartfelt conversations, the encouragement, and your belief in me that this work could unfold. You have changed the way we view addiction and have created a new paradigm for recovery—"the path of discovery." You have given us a path of spirituality that is life-transforming. Thank you for paving the way to healing for all of us!

To Dick Schwartz for creating and bringing forth the IFS model to the world. Your courage, perseverance, and humility are an inspiration. Working with you and learning through you has changed my life, my career, and helped me to help others heal. You are truly a light in this world that is a beacon of hope for our present and our future.

To Cece Sykes, Chris Ratte, Gwen Hurd, Pam Krause, and every IFS trainer I have studied under, worked as a PA with, or had the honor to get to know – thank you from the bottom of my heart for everything you have given me. I hold it with reverence and deep gratitude.

To Lisa and Sophie, thank you for your patience while I talked your ears off about my processes. Sophie, writing and getting published concurrently has been a grace and a blessing to share with you, particularly as *you* are the writer in the family!

To my publisher, John Koehler, my deepest gratitude to you for giving me a chance to see this book through to a reality. Your trust in me has been one of the greatest gifts I have received in this process. Thank you for creating a space for writers like me to have the opportunity to be published. Your humor, kindred spirit, and professionalism are an inspiration.

To my editor at Koehler, Miranda Dillon, your steady hand and eye for detail have raised my bar to yet another level. From APA to CMOS is no easy leap! Thank you for your patience and your kindness.

To my designer, Lauren Sheldon, thank you for putting into three dimensions that which I could only see within my mind's eye.

Last, but never least, to every client I have ever worked with, thank you. It has been an honor and a privilege to share your journey. I have learned from each and every one of you. The challenges you have brought into sessions have inspired me to research more, train further, and elevate my skills to be of greater service to you. Your trust in me has never been taken for granted. If I have erred along the way, it is because I am human.

APPENDIX 1

Daily Spiritual Practices

Throughout this book, I have offered suggestions of how you can create your own daily spiritual practice to support your healing path of recovery. Many clients ask me for specific suggestions to help them get their commitment underway. The following are ideas only. Get creative and use what works best for you. A forty-day discipline will take you on a remarkable journey!

Daily Practice #1: Ten minutes

Ten minutes of simple breath awareness (inhale four, hold two, exhale six) while sitting still with your eyes closed. Also known as meditating.

Daily Practice #2: Ten minutes

Two minutes of simple breath awareness (inhale four, hold two, exhale six).

Eight minutes of meditation.

Daily Practice #3: Ten minutes

Ten minutes of movement (yoga sun salutations, qigong, or five Tibetans) while focusing on your breath in a mindful state.

Daily Practice #4: Fifteen-twenty minutes

Three minutes of simple breath awareness (inhale four, hold two, exhale six).

Three minutes of spiritual reading (see bibliography).

Five minutes of journaling with prayer, mantra, or chanting. Write your own prayer or use a favorite upon which to reflect.

Five-seven minutes of movement (yoga sun salutations, qigong, five Tibetans, walking, etc.).

Daily Practice #5: Fifteen-twenty minutes

Ten-twelve minutes of movement with breath (yoga sun salutations, qigong, five Tibetans, walking, etc.).

Three-five minutes of spiritual reading.

Five-ten minutes of journaling with prayer, mantra, or chanting.

Daily Practice #6: Forty minutes

Three minutes of Nadi Shadona.

Ten minutes meditation—close with a prayer, mantra, or chanting.

Ten-twelve minutes of journaling.

Five minutes of spiritual reading (see bibliography).

Ten minutes of movement (yoga sun salutations, qigong, five Tibetans, walking, etc.).

Daily Practice #7: Forty-sixty minutes

Five-ten minutes of breath practice.

Ten-fifteen minutes of meditation—close with a prayer, mantra, or chanting.

Ten-fifteen minutes of journaling.

Fifteen-twenty minutes of movement (yoga sun salutations, qigong, five Tibetans).

Daily Practice #8: Sixty minutes—Great for Weekends

Twenty minutes Tommy Rosen Morning Challenge (located on R20.com or YouTube).

Twenty minutes of journaling with prayer, mantra, or chanting.

Fifteen minutes of spiritual reading.

Five-ten minutes of meditation

Daily Practice #9: Thirty-forty minutes

Fifteen minutes of spiritual reading.

Ten minutes of meditation.

Ten minutes of journaling.

Daily Practice #10: Thirty-forty minutes

Twenty minutes walking outside in nature.

Five-ten minutes of spiritual reading.

Ten minutes of journaling.

Daily Practice #11: Twenty-thirty minutes

Fifteen minutes outside using simple breath awareness (inhale four, hold two, exhale six) while meditating.

Five-fifteen minutes of journaling with prayer, mantra, or chanting.

Daily Practice #12: Two-hour retreat immersion—great for weekends

Five minutes of simple breath awareness (inhale four, hold two, exhale six).

Five minutes of Nadi Shadona.

Five minutes of Breath of Fire.

Twenty-thirty minutes of meditation.

Five minutes of prayer, mantra, chanting.

Ten-twenty minutes of spiritual reading.

Ten-thirty minutes of journaling.

Forty minutes of yoga, Kundalini, qigong, or any engaged somatic movement.

APPENDIX 2

Mantras and their Translations

Mantra is the use of sound to affect consciousness; *man* means mind and *trang* means wave or projection. Every mantra produces a unique sound and vibration that, when recited, can stimulate various areas of the brain, bringing about positive results that include relaxation, clarity, and natural healing. Through the "waves" of sound, the mind is brought to a "natural" calm, centered, and connected state.

There are hundreds of mantras to choose from, each with its own intention and purpose. I have shared my personal favorites, as well as "foundational" mantras that form the core of a spiritual practice. The linked source of each mantra is given, but there are literally dozens of different artists who play these mantras, so I encourage you to explore and find those that suit you best.

Listen to these while walking your dog, cleaning the house, and sitting quietly in the evening looking at the stars. Anywhere. Anytime. May you experience a deeper calm and a more profound connection to "divine" energy.

SHANTI MANTRA [147]

This Sanskrit Mantra is recited for its ability to create a serene environment, in particular, to calm the mind and create inner peace. Often, the sound vibrations created by chanting the syllables are more important to creating this peace than any meaning ascribed to the words. A beautiful rendition by Deva Premal can be found on Spotify, Amazon Music, or iTunes.

Om Asatoma sad Gamaya

Tamasoma Jyotir gamaya

Mrityor mā Amritam gamaya

From ignorance, lead me to truth;

From darkness, lead me to light;

From death, lead me to immortality.

Alternate Translation:

Lead me from the unreal to the real

Lead from the darkness to the light

Lead me from death to immortality

Let there be peace, peace, and peacefulness.

AAD GURAY NAMEH [148]

This mantra is part of the *Sukhmani Sahib*, a hymn written at the turn of the seventeenth century by the Sikh guru Arjan Dev. It is part of the Sikh scripture, *Sri Guru Granth Sahib*. It is recited for protection.

Aad Guray Nameh,

Jugaad Guray Nameh,

Sat Guray Nameh,

Siri Guroo Dayvay Nameh.

I bow to the Primal Wisdom.

I bow to the Wisdom through the Ages.

I bow to the True Wisdom.

I bow to the great, unseen Wisdom.

AAD SACH [149]

This mantra helps to balance the hemispheres of the brain, break through negative blocks, and connect you to your Higher Self.

Aad Sach

Jugaad Sach

Hai Bhee Sach

Nanak Hosee Bhee Sach.

True in the beginning,

true throughout the ages,

true even now,

Nanak, truth shall ever be.

MOOLA MANTRA PRAYER [150]

This mantra evokes the living God, asking for protection and freedom from all sorrow and suffering. Whenever you chant the Moola mantra, even without knowing the meaning of it, that itself carries power. But when you know the meaning and chant with that feeling in your heart, then the energy that flows from your heart is even more powerful.

Om Sat Chit Ananda Parabrahma

Purushothama Paramatma

Sri Bhagavati Sametha

Sri Bhagavate Namaha

Hari Om Tat Sat

Hari Om Tat Sat

Hari Om Tat Sat

Hari Om Tat Sat

Oh, Divine Force, Spirit of All Creation, Highest Personality,

Divine Presence manifests in every living being.

Supreme Soul manifested as the Divine Mother and as the Divine Father.

I bow in deepest reverence.

I bow in deepest reverence.

I bow in deepest reverence.

I bow in deepest reverence.

MAY THE LONG-TIME SUNSHINE . . . [151]

May the long-time sun, shine upon you

All love surround you,

And the pure light within you,

Guide your way on.

HUMEE HUM[152]

This mantra is recited for the heart center, which represents the bridge between heaven and earth.

Humee Hum

Brahm Hum

Humee Hum

Brahm Hum

We are We. We are God.

HAR[153]

This mantra translates to "God as the Creative Infinity" while supporting our co-creation with the Divine. Thomas Barquee has created an especially beautiful rendition.

Har, har, har, har...

Creative Infinity.

BIJA MANTRA OF SARASWATI[154]

The beautiful call-and-response by Krishna Das on YouTube is one of my favorites of this mantra. Saraswati is the goddess of education, music, and creativity. The Sanskrit root "saras" translates to "that which is fluid." Saraswati is said to bring order out of chaos.

Om

Ayee

Saraswati

Namaya Om

Salutations to Goddess Saraswati!

GREEN TARA MANTRA[155]

The Green Tara mantra is often used to overcome physical, mental, emotional or relational blockages. Its origins are in Tibetan Buddhism.

Om Taare

Tuutaare Ture

Soha.

I prostrate to the Liberator, Mother of all the Victorious Ones.

RA MA DA SA:[156]

My favorite rendition of this mantra is by Mirabai Ceiba. The YouTube video is a beautiful production from this talented duo.

Ra Ma Da Sa

Sa Se So Hung

Sun, Moon, Earth, Infinity: All-that-is in infinity, I am Thee.

PEACE MANTRA[157]

Tina Turner performed a beautiful rendition of this mantra, which is a call to find our inner peace in the midst of unsettling world events.

Sarveśām Svastir Bhavatu

Sarveśām Shāntir Bhavatu

Sarveśām Pūrnam Bhavatu

Sarveśām Mangalam Bhavatu

May there be happiness in all,

May there be peace in all,

May there be completeness in all,

May there be success in all.

THE HEART SUTRA MANTRA[158]

This mantra focuses on the groundlessness of our existence, and recitation gives us protection against negativity.

Gate, Gate, Paragate, Para Sam gate Bodhi svaha

Gate, Gate, Paragate, Para Sam gate Bodhi svaha

Gate, Gate, Paragate, Para Sam gate Bodhisvaha.

Bodhi Svaha

> Gone from suffering to the liberation of suffering.
>
> Gone from forgetfulness to mindfulness.
>
> Gone from duality into non-duality.
>
> Gone all the way to the other shore.
>
> Oh, the light inside! Welcome!

ADI SHAKTI[159]

This is a devotional mantra which invokes the feminine and creative energies of the universe and our consciousness.

Adi Shakti, Adi Shakti, Adi Shakti, Namo Namo

Sarab Shakti, Sarab Shakti, Sarab Shakti, Namo Namo

Pritham Bhagvati, Pritham Bhagvati, Pritham Bhagvati, Namo Namo

Kundalini Mata Shakti, Mata Shakti, Namo Namo

I bow to the primal power,

I bow to the all-encompassing power,

I bow to the creative power at the beginning,

I bow to the divine mother of all peace.

OM NAMO[160]

Known as the Adi Mantra, this mantra connects each and every one to the other. It is also known as the golden chain. In Kundalini, the Golden Chain refers to the energetic link that exists between a teacher, their teacher, their teacher's teacher, and so on back into history. By chanting this mantra, we remind ourselves that we are our own greatest teacher.

Om namo,

Guru Dev, namo.

I bow to the All-That-Is.

I bow to the Divine Wisdom within myself.

SO HUM[161]

The yogic mantra "so hum" is not only a reflection of the sound of the breath but also carries a contemplative meaning: "I am that" (*so* = "I am" and *hum* = "that"). Here, "that" refers to all of creation, the one breathing us all. This contemplation meditation is an opportunity to focus "thinking mind" on the mystery of being and to reflect upon the interdependent nature of all phenomena revealed by the sages and confirmed by contemporary physics.

So Hum

I am that, and that is what I am.

SA TA NA MA[162]

Sa Ta Na Ma is translated to: SA: Infinity, TA: Life, NA: Death, MA: Rebirth.

It is used to shed the old you and become the who you were meant to be—your true self.

Using this mantra with the mudra of touching your fingertips on each syllable, helps to calm the physical system and increase serotonin production.

Sa, Ta, Na, Ma

MAHA MRYTANJAYA MANTRA[163]

This is also known as the Tryambakam Mantra. It is offered to the ancient Hindu deity Shiva. It is believed to help overcome illness and disease and nourish those who recite it with renewed energy and clarity.

Om Tryambakam Yajamahe

Sugandhim Pushtivardhanam

Urvarukamiva Bandhanam

Mrityor Mukshiya Maamritat(e)

I worship that fragrant Shiva of three eyes, the one who nourishes all living entities.

> May he help us severe our bondage with samsara by making us realize that we are never separated from our immortal nature.

MEDICINE BUDDHA MANTRA[164]

This is the Tibetan Buddhist mantra to one of the manifestations of the Buddha, known as the Bhaisajyaguru, or healer who cures suffering. This YouTube video was taped in 2008 when His Holiness the Dalai Lama gave the Medicine Buddha Empowerment to an audience in New Delhi, India (https://www.youtube.com/watch?v=y7YfVfmzOIs).

Tayata

Om Bekanze

Bekanze

Maha BeKanze

Radza Samudgate Soha

May the many sentient beings who are sick, be freed from sickness soon.

And may all the sicknesses of beings never arise again.

JAP JI MANTRA (Japji Sahib)[165]

Ek ong kaar sat naam

kartaa purakh nirbha-o nirvair

akaal moorat ajoonee saibhang

gur prasaad. Jap.

Aad sach jugaad sach hai bhee sach

Naanak hosee bhee sach.

One Universal Creator God,

the Name is Truth,

Creative Being personified,

no fear, no hatred,

image of the Undying,

beyond birth, self-existent,

by Guru's Grace.

Chant and meditate!

True in the primal beginning,

True throughout the ages,

True here and now,

O Nanak, forever and ever True.

24ᵗʰ Pauri Thunderbolt Mantra[166]

Ant na sifatee kehnn na ant.

Ant na karnnai daynn na ant.

Ant na vaykhann sunnann na ant.

Ant na jaapai ki-aa man mant.

Ant na jaapai keetaa aakaar.

Ant na jaapai paaraavaar.

Ant kaarann kaytay bilalaa-eh.

Taa kay ant na paa-ay jaa-eh.

Ayho ant na jaannai ko-ei.

Bahutaa kehee-ai bahutaa ho-ei.

Vaddaa saahib oochaa thaa-o.

Oochay oopar oochaa naa-o.

Ayvadd oochaa hovai ko-ei.

Tis oochay kau jaannai so-ei.

Jayvadd aap jaannai aap aap.

Naanak nadaree karmee daat.

Endless are His praises, endless are those who speak them.

Endless are His actions, endless are His gifts.

Endless is His vision, endless is His hearing.

His limits cannot be perceived.

What is the mystery of His Mind?

The limits of the created universe cannot be perceived.

Its limits here and beyond cannot be perceived.

Many struggle to know His limits, but His limits cannot be found.

No one can know these limits.

The more you say about them, the more there still remains to be said.

Great is the Master, High is His heavenly home.

Highest of the High, above all is His Name.

Only one as great and as high as God can know His lofty and exalted state.

Only He Himself is that great.

He Himself knows Himself.

O Nanak, by His Glance of Grace, He bestows His Blessings.

Dance of Ganesha[167]

Lord Ganesha is thought to bring prosperity, good luck and success. He is also thought to remove all obstacles to our true path. It is said that chanting this mantra brings clarity to our lives and our activities.

Om gam ganapataye namaha

Om gam ganapataye namaha

Om gam ganapatayei namaha

Om gam ganapatayei namaha

Salutations to the Lord Ganesha, may your power remove obstacles to success.

APPENDIX 3

Prayers (Unedited)

The Lord's Prayer (Traditional)[168]

Our Father, who art in heaven,

Hallowed by Thy name.

Thy kingdom come, Thy will be done,

On earth as it is in heaven.

Give us this day our daily bread, and forgive us our trespasses,

As we forgive those who trespass again us.

Lead us this day not to temptation,

But deliver us from evil.

For Thine is the kingdom, the power and the glory.

For ever and ever,

Amen.

The Lord's Prayer in Aramaic[169]

Abwûn d'bwaschmâja Nethkâdasch schmach

Têtê malkuthach.

Nehwê tzevjânach aikâna d'bwaschmâja af b'arha.

Hawvlân lachma d'sûnkanân jaomâna.

Waschboklân chaubên wachtahên aikâna daf chnân schwoken l'chaijabên.

Wela tachlân l'nesjuna

ela patzân min bischa.

Metol dilachie malkutha wahaila wateschbuchta l'ahlâm almîn.

Amên.

"Oh Thou, from whom the breath of life comes, who fills all realms of sound, light and vibration.

May Your light be experienced in my utmost holiest.

Your Heavenly Domain approaches.

Let Your will come true - in the universe (all that vibrates) just as on earth (that is material and dense).

Give us wisdom (understanding, assistance) for our daily need,

detach the fetters of faults that bind us, (karma) like we let go the guilt of others.

Let us not be lost in superficial things (materialism, common temptations),

but let us be freed from that what keeps us off from our true purpose.

From You comes the all-working will, the lively strength to act, the song that beautifies all and renews itself from age to age.

Sealed in trust, faith and truth.

(I confirm with my entire being)"

Amen

The Prayer of St. Francis of Assisi[170]

Lord, make me an instrument of Your peace;

Where there is hatred, let me sow love;

Where there is injury, pardon;

Where there is error, the truth;

Where there is doubt, the faith;

Where there is despair, hope;

Where there is darkness, light;

And where there is sadness, joy.

O Divine Master, Grant that I may not so much seek

To be consoled, as to console;

To be understood, as to understand;

To be loved as to love.

For it is in giving that we receive;

It is in pardoning that we are pardoned;

And it is in dying that we are born to eternal life.

Universal Prayer (Tommy Rosen)[171]

Great Spirit—

Put me in the places you want me to be,

With the people you want me to be with,

Doing the things you want me to do.

Thank you for the joys and challenges of my life.

I accept myself completely.

Amen.

St. Theresa's Prayer[172]

May today there be peace within.

May you trust your highest power that you are exactly where you are meant to be.

May you not forget the infinite possibilities that are born of faith.

May you use those gifts that you have received and pass on the love that has been given to you.

May you be content knowing you are a child of God. Let his presence settle into your bones, and allow your soul the freedom to sing, dance, praise, and love.

It is there for each and every one of you.

Miguel Ruiz, The Four Agreements: A Practical Guide to Personal Freedom[173]

Prayer for Love

"Thank You, Creator of the Universe for the gift of Life you have given me,

Thank You for giving me everything that I have ever needed,

Thank You for the opportunity to experience this beautiful body and this wonderful mind,

Thank You for living inside me with all Your Love and Your pure and boundless Spirit,

with Your warm and radiating Light.

Thank You for using my words, for using my eyes, for using my heart to share your love wherever I go.

I love You just the way you are and because I am your creation, I love myself just the way I am.

Help me to keep the Love and the Peace in my Heart and to make that Love a new way of life, that I may live in Love the rest of my life.

Amen."

Sioux American Indian Prayer[174]

"O our Father, the Sky, hear us

and make us strong.

O our Mother, the Earth, hear us

and give us support.

O Spirit of the East,

send us your Wisdom.

O Spirit of the South,

may we tread your path.

O Spirit of the West,

may we always be ready for the long journey.

O Spirit of the North, purify us

with your cleansing winds."

The Four Things that Matter Most—
Ira Byock, MD[175]

"Please forgive me.

I forgive you.

Thank you.

I love you."

I Will Drink Thy Joy—Paramahamsa Yogananda[176]

I will drink vitality from the golden fountains of sunshine;

I will drink peace from the silver fountain of mooned nights;

I will drink Thy power from the mighty cup of the wind;

I will drink Thy consciousness as joy and bliss from all the little cups of my thoughts.

Universal Prayer—Paramahamsa Yogananda[177]

May thy love shine forever on the sanctuary of my devotion, and

May I be able to awaken Thy love in all hearts.

Lalla—Kashmiri Woman Mystic, 14th century[178]

Flowers, sesame-seed, bowls of fresh water, a tuft of kusha grass,

all this altar paraphernalia is not needed

by someone who takes the teacher's words in

and honestly lives them.

Full of longing in meditation,

one sinks into a joy that is free of any impulse to act,

and will never enter a human birth again.

Traditional Jewish Prayer[179]

"How wonderful, O Lord, are the works of your hands!

The heavens declare Your glory,

the arch of the sky displays Your handiwork

In Your love You have given us the power

to behold the beauty of Your world

robed in all its splendor.

The sun and the stars, the valleys and the hills,

the rivers and the lakes all disclose Your presence.

The roaring breakers of the sea tell of Your awesome might,

the beast of the field and the birds of the air

bespeak Your wondrous will.

In Your goodness You have made us able to hear

the music of the world.

The voices of the loved ones

reveal to us that You are in our midst.

A divine voice sings through all creation."

Traditional Jewish Prayer Before Meals[180]

Baruch ata Adonai

Eloheinu Melech ha'olam

hamotzi lehem min ha'aretz.

Blessed is the Oneness that makes us holy and brings forth bread from the earth.

Illuminata—Marianne Williamson[181]

Dear God,

Thank you for this new day, its beauty and its light.

Thank you for my chance to begin again.

Free me from the limitations of yesterday, today may I be reborn.

May I become more fully a reflection of Your radiance.

Give me strength and compassion and courage and wisdom.

Show me the light in myself and others.

May I recognize the good that is available everywhere.

May I be, this day, and instrument of love and healing.

Lead me to gentle pastures.

Give me deep peace that I might serve You most deeply.

Amen.

Serenity Prayer[182]

Grant me the serenity to accept the things I cannot change;

the courage to change the things I can,

and the wisdom to know the difference.

Earth Teach Me[183]

Earth teach me quiet ~ as the grasses are still with new light.

Earth teach me suffering ~ as old stones suffer with memory.

Earth teach me humility ~ as blossoms are humble with beginning.

Earth teach me caring ~ as mothers nurture their young.

Earth teach me courage ~ as the tree that stands alone.

Earth teach me limitation ~ as the ant that crawls on the ground.

Earth teach me freedom ~ as the eagle that soars in the sky.

Earth teach me acceptance ~ as the leaves that die each fall.

Earth teach me renewal ~ as the seed that rises in the spring.

Earth teach me to forget myself ~ as melted snow forgets its life.

Earth teach me to remember kindness ~ as dry fields weep with rain.

The Passing of Time—Dr. Lila Fahlman[184]

"In The Name Of Allah, Most Gracious, Most Merciful

By the passing of time

Surely one is in a state of loss

Except those who have faith

And perform righteous deeds.

And those who enjoin upon one another

Abiding by the truth,

Enjoin upon one another steadfastness."

Kimberley's Prayers

#1

May Light continue to shine in my life.

May I be slow to react and quick to respond with love, understanding and compassion.

May this day be focused on the positive.

May I listen more and speak less.

May I accomplish what I set out to do.

May today unfold with ease.

May I accept what is given to me today with grace.

#2

May today be Light-filled.

May today I remain aware of my intentions;

To hold silence, to hold response instead of reaction, to breathe consciously throughout the day as I accomplish tasks.

May I remind myself of all that I am grateful for.

#3

May the Divine always be present in my life.

May I always be aligned with the Divine.

#4

Thank you, God for all that you have brought to me.

Thank you for the joys and the pain.

Direct me to where I need to be, and what you would have me do.

#5

Dear God,

Direct me to the right path—the right way;

And the best way to accomplish your will.

If I resist, send me a sign to remember the direction You have set before me.

If I forget, send me a message that will wake me up to Your presence.

Amen

#6

Dear God,

Let me be a unicorn in a field of horses.

Let me surrender the burdens that have held me back from my authenticity.

Let me join in the Divine Light of joy.

Let me relinquish my fear of judgment, my shame, and my self-consciousness.

Let me be in complete alignment with the freedom of expressing my true self.

Amen

The Set Aside Prayer

God, please set aside everything that I think I know about myself and others;

My unmanageability, my judgments, my opinions,

for an open mind and a new experience of You and myself.

Amen

—Source Unknown

APPENDIX 4

Resources

By no means complete, these resources are meant to guide you on your own journey of spiritual healing. I am familiar with every listing here and have either purchased, visited, or used the services of each entity. As with anything, this is intended for discovery and broadening horizons.

May this support your journey.

Meditation Apps:

Aura

> https://www.aurahealth.io/
>
> This is my favorite app to date. The options are plentiful, ranging from meditation and breathwork to affirmations and sleep programs. You can find sound bathing, prayers, life coaching, and podcasts. There is an annual fee of $60 for Aura, but it is well worth it if you use it every day.

Calm

> https://www.calm.com
>
> I continue to use Calm for sleep, and I really like the programs for mental focus and attention. You can get a

seven-day free trial, and then it's $69.99 per year. They also have a lifetime billing for $399.99.

Headspace

https://www.headspace.com/

This is a very popular app offering many types and kinds of meditation and mindfulness. In addition, they have a very good section on sleep with excellent supporting materials like breathing, music, and sleep casts. Subscriptions begin with fourteen days free and $69.99 a year, or seven days free and $12.99 per month.

Insight Timer

https://insighttimer.com

This well-known app features some top-ranking teachers, including Russell Brand, Lama Rod Owens, and Matthieu Ricard. The app features live events, ranging from relationship issues to accessible yoga. The staff offers their "picks," which range from Tara Brach to Dr. Justin Ross. Sleep programs are also featured, as well as calming music and children's programs.

UCLA Mindful

https://www.uclahealth.org/programs/marc/free-programming-resources/ucla-mindful-app

The UCLA Mindful Awareness Research Center has

dedicated years to research on mindfulness, stress-related health conditions, anxiety, depression, and overall well-being. This app offers introductory meditation instruction, podcasts, and informational videos. This is a free app.

Breethe

https://breethe.com

This is a fairly new app that offers hypnotherapy, stories, music, and options for a healthier life.

Meditation guidance and nature sounds for sleep are also offered. The app is offered for a fourteen-day free trial and then $12.99 per month. It is customizable for your personal needs and situations in life.

The Mindfulness App

https://www.themindfulnessapp.com/

This app is beautiful in its simplicity, focused specifically on mindfulness and meditation. The teachers are some of the best in the world, including Daniel Siegel, Eckhart Tolle, Kristin Neff, and Mark Williams.

Buddhify

https://buddhify.com/

This is a unique app that offers mindfulness-on-the-go that can be practiced anytime, anywhere. You can choose from a variety of options, from taking a work break to traveling. This is a family-run business that is entirely self-funded. As a result, there is no monthly fee or up-charging. Instead, you pay a $30 annual flat fee.

The Breathing App

https://breathingapp.com/

Focused solely on breathing and breathwork, the beauty of this app is that it concentrates on one thing and does it very well. If you just want to work on your breathing techniques, this is a great app to have. You can download this for Android or IOS for $3.99.

Sattva—Meditation

https://sattva.life/

For those who lean more toward a yogic approach, this app offers guided meditations, mantras, chants, and playlists. It also includes teachings of *mudras*—hand gestures that are incorporated with chanting and meditation. The app offers a lifetime subscription for $199 without a monthly subscription option.

Ten Percent Happier

https://www.tenpercent.com/

When ABC anchor Dan Harris had a panic attack on air, he turned to meditation as a means to de-stress and eventually ended his career as a journalist to focus on *Ten Percent Happier*, his book, podcast, and app. Membership begins with a seven-day free trial, with an $8.33 per month or annual $99.99 fee. This app offers many different resources, including The Dalai Lama's Guide to Happiness course.

Yoga:

Yoga International

https://yogainternational.com/

The premier yoga resource, YI, offers an extensive array of yoga classes, meditation instruction, breath, and pranayama. In addition, there are featured courses on topics ranging from trauma awareness to prenatal yoga, as well as Ayurveda. The teachers at YI are well-known personalities such as Cyndi Lee, Rod Stryker, and Shanna Small. A free seven-day trial is available with membership at $19.99 per month or $169 per year.

Glo Yoga

https://www.glo.com/

Glo Yoga is also a long-standing online resource with a myriad of different yoga offerings. From yoga conditioning to Tao Yin yoga and from classes such as "when you're feeling stiff" to "everyday essentials," there is plenty at Glo Yoga for beginners to advanced students.

MyYogaTeacher

https://www.myyogateacher.com/

This is a yoga app that allows you to practice yoga from your home or hotel room. With over 100 yoga teachers presenting, you can choose from one-on-one or group sessions, sign up for workshops, or do a yoga teacher training. The membership plan ranges from unlimited group classes for $49 per month to one one-on-one session per month, in addition to unlimited participation for $89 per month.

Gaia

https://www.gaia.com/yoga

Gaia is one of the top yoga resources on the internet, with a rich and diverse offering. Not only can you access yoga practices, learn meditation, and develop a morning ritual, but you can also watch inspirational documentaries and access an endless array of informational articles. With a library of thousands of offerings, Gaia has made a significant overall impact on health and well-being.

Yogaworks

https://yogaworks.com/

Vinyasa, yin, and restorative yoga are offered on this site, along with Iyengar, Pilates, and YogaWorks' own style of yoga. Take live classes, access a library of offerings, or take teacher training. They offer a fourteen-day free trial with full sign up.

Alo Moves

https://www.alomoves.com/

Alo Moves is the brainchild of Dylan Werner, author of *Illuminated Breath*. He created a platform where teachers from around the world could teach in real time from anywhere in the world. In addition to a full array of yoga knowledge, the site has expanded to include barre, fitness, mindfulness, and nutrition. On-demand classes, series, or topic driven. Yoga is also offered in Spanish. At $20 per month, this is a rich site with extensive content.

Kia Miller

https://www.youtube.com/@KiaMiller Kia Miller is the founder of *Radiant Body Yoga* and the wife of Tommy Rosen. Kia teaches on Glo Yoga and has her own YouTube channel. She is masterful, accessible, compassionate, and one of the top twenty teachers in the US. She has numerous event offerings throughout the year, including intensive yoga teacher training. For a deep dive into Kundalini yoga, Kia will bring a wide range of knowledge to your experiences.

Candles, Incense, and Oils:

Uma Oils and Candles

https://www.umaoils.com

I discovered Uma Oils and Candles quite a few years ago and became a dedicated fan. You can purchase direct from their website, as well as from Nieman Marcus or Saks Fifth Avenue. Uma is also available on Amazon. The smells are clean, and the products are all based on Ayurvedic principles. Try *Pure Calm* or *Equinox* to fill your room with peace and tranquility.

The White Company

https://www.thewhitecompany.com

Founded in London and now with a presence across the US, the theme of this company aligns with its name. Affordable and beautifully packaged in white, the fragrances from The White Company are true to their descriptions. They are also refreshing and long-lasting. Excellent value with price ranges between $15 for fragrance oil, $44 for diffusers, and $24, $39, and $44 for candles of varying sizes.

Voyage et Cie

https://wwwvoyageetcie.com

This is where *haute* scent meets *haute classe*. When you breathe in the scent of any of Voyage et Cie's products, you will be transported to the Bois de Boulogne, the Tuileries, or any other Parisian parc famous for its whimsy and beauty. Also featured are a range of citrus, floral, wood, and herbal scents. While it is pricey, the value is that you only have to burn a candle for a short while before your entire room is infused with scent.

Maison Louis Marie

https://maisonlouismarie.com/

This company has a history dating back to 1792 and was brought forward to the 2000s by a descendant of the original family. All the products are botanically based; these luxury candles and oils create a beautiful aromatherapeutic environment in your home. Environmentally conscious as well as reasonably priced, with candles in the $38 range.

Mrs. Meyer's Clean Day

https://www.mrsmeyers.com/

For those of us who are not in the market to pay a high price for our in-home scents, I have found that Mrs. Meyer's candles are as reliable as their household products. Soy-based candles with a twenty-five-hour burn time, Mrs. Meyer's are high value for an average of $10.99.

Nag Champa

https://www.nagchampa.com/

Nag Champa is a fragrance used in Indian incense with a distinctive temple smell. Created by combining sandalwood and champak or frangipani, this is the most familiar smell in many temples, yoga studios, or meditation halls. I began using this scent back in the 1970s and have never used anything else. While I may occasionally try a sample of another type or kind, it never matches the purity and specific call to meditate or do yoga. *Nag Champa* is also available on Amazon in various sizes and price points. This site offers soap, oil, incense, and solid perfumes, among many other products. I have found them to be highly reliable over the years.

Yoga Supplies:

Yoga Direct

https://www.yogadirect.com

This yoga resource has been my go-to for supplies as their prices are very reasonable, and product lines are superior. Yoga mats, blocks, blankets, bolsters, clothing, and a wide array of props are available here.

Everyday Yoga

https://www.everydayyoga.com/

Reasonably priced with great sales, Everyday stocks mats, props, clothing, and home and wellness supplies. From oil diffusers, crystals, and windchimes to candles, you will find a rich trove of resources here.

Yoga Warehouse

https://theyogawarehouse.com

This is a wholesale resource for anyone purchasing supplies for a studio, personal training, or fitness center. This means you will not be able to buy one mat or one bolster but rather meet a minimum purchase requirement. The product line is superior, as is the customer service and delivery time.

Yoga Accessories

https://yogaaccessories.com

Very reasonably priced, with a wide array of supplies for yoga, Pilates, barre, and fitness needs, Yoga Accessories also offers custom printing with a minimum number. The quality of products is good, and the customer service and delivery time are also reliable.

Spiritual, Religious, and Nondenominational Retreat Centers:

Kripalu Center

https://kripalu.org/

Kripalu has a rich history as a yoga center, and today encompasses all aspects of yoga, Ayurvedic, and holistic wellness. Located on beautiful acreage in Western Massachusetts, with many updated renovations and a new wing to the original Jesuit monastery, this retreat center offers a rich array of options for beginners to advanced students, and from a long-weekend unwind to weeklong immersions.

Omega Institute

https://www.eomega.org/

Omega is another health and wellness center that has a rich history as a nonprofit educational center known to be at the forefront of holistic studies. Located in the Hudson Valley with some of the best food I have ever eaten, the accommodations are simple, clean, and reasonably priced, with programs that range from a long weekend to weeklong.

Ghost Ranch

https://www.ghostranch.org/

Located in Abiquiu, New Mexico, this retreat center is set in the desert landscape made famous by Georgia O'Keefe. A Presbyterian-affiliated retreat center offers self-led and guided programs. With over 150 workshops and offerings on 21,000 acres of open space, the lodging is advertised as simple and clean.

The Garrison Institute

https://www.garrisoninstitute.org/

Located in Garrison, New York, the mission of the institute is to apply insights from science and wisdom of contemplation to address social and environmental challenges. In-person retreats range from *Compassionate Leadership* to *Contemplative-Based Resilience*, and virtual offerings include a daily meditation session, as well as the *Fellowship Forum* series.

Isabella Freedman Retreat Center

https://adamah.org/retreat-centers/isabella-freedman/

This center offers kosher, pluralistic retreats in the Connecticut Berkshires focused on Jewish holidays, meditation, yoga, music, and farm-to-table food. There are programs for adults and children alike, ranging from the Adamah learning farm to wellness retreats and everything in between.

Abbey of Gethsemani

https://monks.org/

This Trappist monastery offers retreats to guests of all faiths. This is the place where Thomas Merton lived from 1941 until his death in 1968. With 1,500 acres of nature trails, participants can immerse themselves in a monastic environment that includes silent retreats, contemplative prayer, and attending the monastic schedule throughout the day.

Yogaville

https://www.yogaville.org/

Swami Satchidananda founded this ashram and retreat in Virginia as a place where physical, spiritual, devotional, intellectual, ethical, karmic, and mantra yoga could be learned and practiced. In addition to numerous retreat offerings, Yogaville offers 200- and 300-hour yoga teacher training and an 800-hour Integral Yoga Therapy certificate. Whether you wish to visit for a weekend or an immersive silent retreat, this is one of the most authentic yoga centers in the US.

BIBLIOGRAPHY

Alexander, William. *Ordinary Recovery: Mindfulness, Addiction, and the Path of Lifelong Sobriety.* Boston: Shambhala, 1997.

Amen, Daniel. *Unchain Your Brain: 10 Steps to Breaking the Addictions that Steal your Life* California: Mind Works Press, 2005.

Anderson Frank, Martha Sweezy, and Richard Schwartz. *Internal Family Systems Skills Training Manual: Trauma-Informed Treatment for Anxiety, Depression, PTSD and Substance Abuse.* Eau Claire: PESI Publishing and Media, 2017.

Ashley-Farrand, Thomas. *Healing Mantras: Using Sound Affirmations for Personal Power, Creativity, and Healing.* New York: Ballantine Wellspring, 1999.

Aslan, Reza. *God: A Human History.* New York: Random House, 2017.

Beattie, Melody. *Codependent No More.* Minnesota: Hazelden Publishing, 1992.

Beattie, Melody. *Codependent No More: Workbook.* Minnesota: Hazelden Publishing, 2011.

Beattie, Melody. *Codependent's Guide to the Twelve Steps.* New York: Simon & Schuster, 1990.

Beattie, Melody. *Make Miracles in 40 Days.* (New York: Simon & Schuster, 2010.

Badenoch, Bonnie. *Being a Brain-Wise Therapist: A Practical Guide to Interpersonal Neurobiology.* New York: W.W. Norton & Company, 2008.

Beauregard, Mario, and Denyse O'Leary. *The Spiritual Brain: A Neuroscientist's Case for the Existence of the Soul,* New York: Harper One, Harper Collins, 2008.

Bien, Thomas, and Beverly Bien. *Mindful Recovery: The Spiritual Path to Healing from Addiction.* Hoboken: Wiley Publishing, 2008.

Bien, Thomas. *Mindful Therapy: A Guide for Therapists and Helping Professions.* Boston: Wisdom Publications, 2006.

Blandon, Lee. *The Science of Spirituality: Integrating Science, Psychology, Philosophy, Spirituality and Religion.* Coppell: Evolving Souls, 2007.

Bowen, Sarah, and Chawla Neha, and Alan Marlatt. *Mindfulness-Based Relapse Prevention for Addictive Behaviors: A Clinician's Guide.* New York: Guilford Press, 2011.

Brach, Tara. *Radical Acceptance.* New York: Bantam Books, 2003.

Brach, Tara. *True Refuge.* New York: Bantam Books, 2010.

Brown, Richard, and Patricia Gerbarg. *The Healing Power of the Breath: Simple Techniques to Reduce Stress and Anxiety, Enhance Concentration, and Balance Your Emotions.* Boulder: Shambhala, 2012.

Cameron, Julia. *Answered Prayers: Love Letters from the Divine.* New York: Tarcher Press, 2004.

Cameron, Julia. *Blessings: Prayers and Declarations for a Heartfelt Life.* New York: Tarcher, 2012.

Cameron, Julia. *The Artist's Way.* New York: Tarcher, 1992.

Cameron, Julia. *Transitions: Prayers and Declarations for a Changing LIfe.* New York: Tarcher, 2010.

Carreira, Jeff. *The Spiritual Implications of Quantum Physics: Reflections on the Nature of Science, Reality and Paradigm Shifts.* Philadelphia: Emergence Education, 2023.

Dalai Lama, and Desmond Tutu. *The Book of Joy: Lasting Happiness in a Changing World.* New York: Avery, 2016.

Das, Lama Surya. *Awakening the Buddha Within: Eight Steps to Enlightenment.* New York: Broadway, 1997.

Das, Lama Surya. *Awakening to the Sacred: Creating a Spiritual Life from Scratch.* New York: Broadway, 1999.

Das, Lama Surya. *Letting Go of the Person You Used to Be: Lessons on Change, Loss, and Spiritual Transformation.* New York: Broadway Books, 2003.

Dowrick, Stephanie. *Intimacy and Solitude: Balancing Closeness and Independence.* New York: Norton Publishing, 1991.

Duhigg, Charles. *The Power of Habit.* New York: Random House., 2012.

Duncan, Joan. *Commit to Sit: Tools for Cultivating a Meditation Practice.* Carlsbad: Hay House, 2000.

Easwaran, Eknath. *The Upanishads.* Tomales, CA: Nilgiri Press, 2007. Easwaran, Eknath. *The Bhagavad Gita.* Tomales, CA: Nilgiri Press, 2007. Easwaran, Eknath. *The Dhammapada.* Tomales, CA: Nilgiri Press, 2007.

Easwaran, Eknath. *Seeing with the Eyes of Love: A Commentary on a Text from The Imitation of Christ.* Tomales, CA: Nilgiri Press, 2007.

Easwaran, Eknath. *Love Never Faileth: Commentaries on Texts from St. Francis, St. Paul, St. Augustine & Mother Theresa.* Tomales, CA: Nilgiri Press, 2007.

Easwaran, Eknath. *Words to Live By: Daily Inspiration for Spiritual Living.* Tomales, CA: Nilgiri Press, 2007.

Easwaran, Eknath. *The Mantram Handbook: A Practical Guide to Choosing Your Mantram & Calming Your Mind.* Tomales, CA: Nilgiri Press, 2007.

Emerson, David, and Elizabeth Hopper. *Overcoming Trauma through Yoga: Reclaiming Your Body.* Berkley: North Atlantic Books, 2011.

Epstein, Mark. *Thoughts Without a Thinker: Psychotherapy from a Buddhist Perspective.* New York: Basic Books, 1995.

Erickson, Carlton. *The Science of Addiction: From Neurobiology to Treatment.* 2nd Edition.

New York: WW. Norton & Company, 2018.

Farhi, Donna. *Yoga Mind, Body & Spirit: A Return to Wholeness.* New York: St. Martin's Press, 2000.

Fralich, Terry. *The Five Core Skills of Mindfulness: A Direct Path to More Confidence, Joy and Love.* Eau Claire: PESI Publishing and Media, 2014.

Frankl, Victor. *Man's Search for Meaning.* Boston: Beacon Press, 1992.

Glass, Michelle. *Daily Parts Meditation Practice©: A Journey of Embodied Integration for Clients and Therapists.* Eugene: Listen3r, 2017.

Goddard, Dwight, ed. *A Buddhist Bible.* Boston: Beacon Press, 1970.

Goldstein, Joseph. *Mindfulness: A Practical Guide to Awakening.* Boulder: Sounds True, 2013.

Goleman, Daniel and Davidson, Richardson. *Altered Traits: Science Reveals How Meditation Changes Your Mind, Brain, and Body.* New York: Penguin Random House, 2017.

Griffin, Kevin. *One Breath at a Time.* Emmaus: Rodale Books, 1993.

Grisel, Judith. *Never Enough: The Neuroscience and Experience of Addiction.* New York: Doubleday, 2019.

Hanh, Thich Nhat. *The Energy of Prayer: How to Deepen Your Spiritual Practice.* Berkeley: Parallax Press, 2006.

Hahn, Thich Nhat. *Going Home: Jesus & Buddha as Brothers.* New York: Riverhead, 1999.

Hanh, Thich Nhat. *The Heart of the Buddha's Teaching: Transforming*

Suffering into Peace, Joy, and Liberation. New York: Harmony Books, 1999.

Hanh, Thich Nhat. *How to Sit.* Berkley: Parallax Press, 2014.

Hanh, Thich Nhat. *How to Fight.* Berkley: Parallax Press, 2017.

Hanh, Thich Nhat. *Peace is Every Step: The Path of Mindfulness in Everyday Life.* New York: Bantam Books, 1992.

Hanh, Thich Nhat. *Silence: The Power of Quiet in a World Full of Noise.* New York: Harper One, 2015.

Hansard, Christopher. (2004). *The Tibetan Art of Positive Thinking: Skillful Thought for Successful Living.* New York: Atria, 2003.

Hanson, Rick. *Buddha's Brain: The Practical Neuroscience of Happiness, Love and Wisdom.* Oakland: New Harbinger Publications, 2009.

Hanson, Rick. *Hardwiring Happiness: The New Brain Science of Contentment, Calm, and Confidence.* New York: Harmony, 2013.

Hanson, Rick. (2020). *Neurodharma: New Science, Ancient Wisdom, and Seven Practices of the Highest Happiness.* New York: Harmony, 2020.

Hanson, Rick. *Resilient: How to Grow an Unshakable Core of Calm, Strength, and Happiness.* New York: Harmony Books, 2018.

Harris, Sam. *Waking Up: Searching for Spirituality Without Religion.* London: Transworld Publishers, 2014.

Hay, Louise. *You Can Heal Your Life.* Carlsbad: Hay House, 1994.

Herron, Abigail, and Tim Brennan. *The American Society of Addiction Medicine Essential of Addiction Medicine, Third Edition.* Philadelphia: Wolters Kluwer, 2020.

Holmes, Tom, and Lauri Holmes. *Parts Work: An Illustrated Guide to Your Inner Life.*

Kalamazoo: Winged Heart Press, 2007.

Holmes, Tom. *Parts Work: A Path of the Heart: Healing Journeys Integrating IFS and Spirituality.* Kalamazoo: Winged Heart Press, 2022.

Iliff, Brenda. *A Woman's Guide to Recovery.* Center City: Hazelden Foundation, 2008.

Jay, Jeff, and Debra Jay. *Love First: A New Approach to Intervention for Alcoholism and Drug Addiction.* Center City: Hazelden Foundation, 2000.

Judith, Anodea. *Eastern Body, Western Mind: Psychology and the Chakra System as a Path to the Self.* Berkley: Celestial Arts, 2004.

Jung, Carl. *Synchronicity.* Princeton: Bollingen Series, 1973.

Kabat-Zinn, Jon. *Coming to Our Senses: Healing Ourselves and the World Through Mindfulness.* New York: Hyperion Books, 2005.

Kabat-Zinn, Jon. *Full Catastrophe Living: Using the Wisdom of Your Body and Mind to Face Stress, Pain, and Illness.* New York: Delta Trade Paperbacks, 1990.

Kabat-Zinn, Jon. *Wherever You Go, There You Are: Mindfulness Meditation in Everyday Life.* New York: Hyperion Books, 1994.

Kornfield, Jack. *A Path with Heart: A Guide Through the Perils and Promises of Spiritual Life.* New York: Bantam Books, 1993.

Kornfield, Jack. *After the Ecstasy, the Laundry: How the Heart Grows Wise on the Spiritual Path.* New York: Bantam Books, 2000.

Kornfield, Jack. *Bringing Home the Dharma: Awakening Right Where You Are.* Boston: Shambhala, 2011.

Kornfield, Jack. *The Wise Heart: A Guide to the Universal Teachings of Buddhist Psychology.* New York: Bantam Books, 2008.

Kornfield, J. (1997). *The Art of Forgiveness.* Bantam Books.

Kurtz, Ernest, and Katherine Ketcham. *The Spirituality of Imperfection: Storytelling and the Search for Meaning.* New York: Bantam Books, 2002.

Leela, Durga. *Yoga of Recovery: Integrating Yoga and Ayurveda with Modern Recovery Tools for Addiction.* London: Singing Dragon, 2022

Levine, Noah. *Refuge Recovery: A Buddhist Path to Recovering from Addiction.* New York: Harper One, 2014.

Levine, Stephen. *Guided Meditations, Explorations & Healings.* New York: Anchor Books, 1995.

Loizzo, Joe. *Sustainable Happiness: The Mind Science of Well-Being, Altruism, and Inspiration.* New York: Routledge, 2012.

Manejwala, Omar. *Craving: Why we Can't Seem to Get Enough.* Center City: Hazelden Publishing, 2013.

Mate, Gabor. *In the Realm of Hungry Ghosts: Close Encounters with Addiction.* Berkeley: North Atlantic Books, 2007.

Miller, Lisa. *The Oxford Handbook of Psychology and Spirituality.* Oxford: Oxford University Press, 2012.

Miller, Lisa. *The Awakened Brain: The New Science of Spirituality and our Quest for an Inspired Life.* New York, NY: Random House, 2021.

Miller, William, and Rollnick, Stephen. *Motivational Interviewing: Preparing People for Change, Second Edition.* New York: Guilford Press, 2002.

Mingyur, Yongey. *Joyful Wisdom: Embracing Change and Finding Freedom.* New York: Three Rivers Press, 2009.

Mingyur, Yongey. *The Joy of Living: Unlocking the Secret & Science of Happiness.* New York: Harmony Books, 2007.

Mooney, Al, and Arlene Eisenberg, and Howard Eisenberg. *The Recovery Book.* New York: Workman Publishing, 1992.

Nepo, Mark. *Finding Inner Courage.* New York: MJF Books, 2007.

Nepo, Mark. *The Book of Awakening: Having the Life You Want by Being Present to the Life You Have.* New York: Conari Press, 2011.

Nepo, Mark. *Seven Thousand Ways to Listen: Staying Close to What is Sacred.* New York: Atria Paperback, 2012.

Nestor, James. *Breath: The New Science of a Lost Art.* London: Penguin Random House, 2020.

Newberg, Andrew, and Mark Waldman. *How Enlightenment Changes Your Brain: The New Science of Transformation.* New York: Avery, 2016.

Newberg, Andrew, and Mark Waldman. *How God Changes Your Brain: Breakthrough Findings from a Leading Neuroscientist.* New York: Ballantine Books, 2009.

Newburg, Andrew, and David Halpern. *The Rabbi's Brain: Mystics, Moderns and the Science of Jewish Thinking.* New York: Turner Publishing, 2008.

Newberg, Andrew. *Neurotheology: How Science Can Enlighten Us About Spirituality.* New York: Columbia University Press, 2018.

Paulson, Genevieve. *Kundalini and the Chakras: Evolution in this Lifetime, A Practical Guide.* Woodbury: Llewellyn Publications, 1991.

Peck, Scott. *The Road Less Travelled & Beyond: Spiritual Growth in an Age of Anxiety.* New York: Simon & Schuster, 1997.

Peltz, Lawrence. *The Mindful Path to Addiction Recovery: A Practical Guide to Regaining Control Over Your Life.* Boston: Shambhala Publications, 2013.

Perry, Bruce, and Oprah Winfrey. *What Happened to You? Conversations on Trauma, Resilience, and Healing.* (New York: Flatiron Books, 2021).

Rinpoche, Sogyal. *The Tibetan Book of Living and Dying.* San Francisco: Harper Collins, 1994.

Rohr, Richard. *Breathing Under Water: Spirituality and the 12 Steps.* Cincinnati: Franciscan Media, 2011.

Rosen, Tommy. *Recovery 2.: Move Beyond Addiction and Upgrade your Life*. Carlsbad: Hay House, 2014.

Rushnell, Squire. *When God Winks at You: How God Speaks Directly to You Through the Power of Coincidence*. Nashville: W Publishing Group, 2006.

Sadhguru. *Inner Engineering: A Yogi's Guide to Joy*. New York: Spiegel & Grau, 2016.

Saradananda, Swami. (2009). *The Power of Breath: Yoga Breathing for Inner Balance, Health and Harmony*. London: Watkins, 2009.

Saraswati, Swami Niranjanananda. *Prana and Pranayama*. Bihar: Yoga Publications Trust, 2009.

Schaef, Anne Wilson. *Living in Process: Basic Truths for Living the Path of the Soul*. New York: Ballantine Wellspring, 1999.

Schwartz, Richard. *Greater than the Sum of our Parts*. Louisville: Sounds True Publishing, 2018.

Schwartz, Richard. *Internal Family Systems Therapy*. New York: Guilford Press, 1995.

Schwartz, Richard. *Internal Family Systems Therapy, Second Edition*. New York: Guilford Press, 2020.

Schwartz, Richard. *Introduction to Internal Family Systems Model*. Boston: Self Leadership Organization, 2001.

Schwartz, Richard, and Robert Falconer. *Many Minds, One Self: Evidence for a Radical Shift in Paradigm*. Oak Park: Trailheads Publications, 2017.

Schwartz, Richard. *No Bad Parts: Healing Trauma & Restoring Wholeness with the Internal Family Systems Model*. Boulder: Sounds True Publications, 2021.

Sheldrake, Rupert. *Science and Spiritual Practices: Transformative Experiences and Their Effects on Our Bodies, Brains, and Health*. Berkley: Counterpoint, 2017.

Siegel, Daniel. *Aware: The Science and Practice of Presence, the Groundbreaking Meditation Practice*. New York: Penguin Random House, 2018.

Siegel, Daniel. *Mind: A Journey to the Heart of Being Human*. New York: W.W. Norton & Company, 2017.

Siegel, Daniel. (2010). *The Mindful Therapist: A Clinician's Guide to Mindsight and Neural Integration*. New York: WW. Norton & Company.

Siegel, Daniel. *Mindsight: The New Science of Personal Transformation*. New York: Bantam Books, 2010.

Siegel, Daniel. *Pocket Guide to Interpersonal Neurobiology: An Integrative Handbook of the Mind*. New York: W. W. Norton & Company, 2012.

Singer, Michael. *The Untethered Soul: The Journey Beyond Yourself*. Oakland: New Harbinger, 2004.

Singer, Michael. *The Surrender Experiment: My Journey into Life's Perfection*. New York: Harmony Books, 2015.

Sing, Guru Prem. *Everyday Devotion: The Heart of Being*. Santa Cruz: Kundalini Research Institute, 2011.

Sperry, Len. *Spirituality in Clinical Practice: Incorporating the Spiritual Dimension in Psychotherapy and Counseling*. Philadelphia: Brunner-Routledge, 2001.

Stahl, Bob, and Elisha Goldstein. *A Mindfulness-Based Stress Reduction Workbook*. Oakland: New Harbinger Publications: 2010.

Suzuki, Shunryu. *Zen Mind, Beginner's Mind: Informal Talks on Zen Meditation and Practice*. Boston: Shambhala Publications, 1970.

Swami, Om. *The Ancient Science of Mantras: Wisdom of the Sages*. India: Black Lotus Press, 2017.

Swami, Om. *The Hidden Power of Gayatri Mantra: How to Realize Your Full Potential Through Daily Practice*. India: Black Lotus

Press, 2018.

Swami, Om. *Kundalini: An Untold Story.* India: Black Lotus Press, 2016.

Swami, Om. *Mind Full to Mindful: Zen Wisdom from a Monk's Bowl.* India: Black Lotus Press, 2018.

Tanakh: A New Translation of The Holy Scriptures According to the Traditional Hebrew Text. Philadelphia: The Jewish Publication Society, 1985.

Taylor, Steve. *Spiritual Science: Why Science Needs Spirituality to Make Sense of the World.* London: Watkins, 2018.

Thondup, Tulku. *The Healing Power of the Mind: Simple Meditation Exercises for Health, Well- Being, and Enlightenment.* Boston: Shambhala Publications, 1996.

Tigunait, Rajmani. *The Practice of the Yoga Sutra.* Honesdale: Himalayan Institute, 2017.

Tolle, Eckhart. *A New Earth: Awakening to Your Life's Purpose.* New York: Plume, 2005.

Tolle, Eckhart. *The Power of Now: A Guide to Spiritual Enlightenment.* Novato: New World Publishing, 1999.

Tolle, Eckhart. *Practicing the Power of Now: Essential Teaching s, Meditations, and Exercises from the Power of Now.* Novato: New World Publishing, 1999.

Twersky, Abraham. *A Formula for Proper Living.* Nashville: Jewish Lights Publishing, 2009

Twersky, Abraham. *Addictive Thinking: Understanding Self-Deception.* Center City: Hazelden Publishing, 1997.

Twersky, Abraham. *The Spiritual Self: Reflections on Recovery and God.* Center City: Hazelden Publishing, 2000.

Van der Kolk, Bessel. *The Body Keeps the Score: Brain, Mind, and*

Body in the Healing of Trauma. New York: Penguin Books, 2015.

Vaughn, Frances, and Walsh, Roger. *Gifts from a Course in Miracles*. New York: Tarcher / Putnam, 1995.

Wangyal, Tenzin. *Tibetan Sound Healing: Seven Guided Practices for Clearing Obstacles, Accessing Positive Qualities, and Uncovering Your Inherent Wisdom*. Boulder: Sounds True, 2006.

Warner, Dylan. *The Illuminated Breath*. Las Vegas: Victory Belt Publishing, 2021.

White, Ganga. *Yoga Beyond Belief: Insights to Awaken and Deepen Your Practice*. Berkley: North Atlantic Books, 2007.

Williamson, Marianne. *A Return to Love*. New York: Harper Collins, 1992.

Williamson, Marianne. *Illuminata: Thoughts, Prayers, Rites of Passage*. New York: Random House., 1994.

Wilson, Rainn. *Soul Book: Why We Need a Spiritual Revolution*. New York: Hachette, 2023.

Wolf, Laibl Rabbi. *Practical Kabbalah: A guide to Jewish Wisdom for Everyday Life*. New York: Three Rivers Press, 1999.

Woodruff, Paul. *Reverence: Renewing a Forgotten Virtue*. Oxford: Oxford University Press: 2014.

NOTES

Introduction

1. Richard Schwartz, *Introduction to Internal Family Systems, Second Edition.*(Boulder, CO: Sounds True Publications. 2023), p. 21.

Chapter One: Understanding Addiction

2. Gabor Mate, *In the Realm of Hungry Ghosts: Close Encounters with Addiction.* (Berkeley, CA: North Atlantic Books, 2010), 1.

3. Abraham Twersky, *Addictive Thinking: Understanding Self-Deception.* (Center City: Hazelden Publishing, 1990), 18.

4. William White, *Slaying the Dragon: The History of Addiction Treatment and Recovery in America.* (Normal: Chestnut Health Systems Publication, 1998), xiii.

5. Ibid, 96.

6. Ibid, 96.

7. Ibid, 97.

8. Bessel van der Kolk, *The Body Keeps the Score: Brain, Mind, and Body in the Healing of Trauma.* (New York: Penguin Books, 2014), 265.

9. Mate, *In the Realm of Hungry* Ghosts, 35.

10. *Ibid*, 37.

11. William Miller, and Stephen Rollnick, *Motivational interviewing. Preparing People for Change.* Second Edition. (New York: The Guilford Press, 2002).

Chapter Three: Foundations of Spirituality

12 Wikipedia. "Hinduism." Accessed 2023. https://en.wikipedia.org/wiki/Atman_(Hinduism)

13 Richard Schwartz, *Introduction to the Internal Family Systems Model, Second Edition.* (Boulder: Sounds True, 2023), 21.

14 The Holy Bible, King James Version, *Philippians, 4, v. 7* (Tennessee: Thomas Nelson Publishers, 1989), 983.

15 Richard Schwartz, *Introduction to the Internal Family Systems Model, Second Edition.* (Boulder: Sounds True, 2023), 30.

16 Eknath Easwaran, *The Upanishads.* (Tomales: Nilgiri Press, 2007), 121.

17 Lesley Brown, ed., *The New Shorter Oxford English Dictionary* (London: Clarendon Press, 1993), 2990.

18 Louise Delagran, "What is Spirituality?" University of Minnesota, accessed 2018, https://www.takingcharge.csh.umn.edu/what-spirituality

19 Harris Friedman, Stanley Krippner, Linda Riebel, and Chad Johnson. "Models of Spiritual Development," in *The Oxford Handbook of Psychology and Spirituality*, ed. Lisa Miller (Oxford: Oxford University Press, 2012), 208.

20 Wikipedia. "Spirituality," accessed 2023, https://en.wikipedia.org/wiki/Spirituality.

21 Bill Wilson, *The Big Book.* (New York City: Alcoholics Anonymous World Services, Inc., 1934), xx.

22 *Ibid*

23 Lionel Corbett and Murray Stein, "Contemporary Jungian Approaches to Spiritually Oriented Psychotherapy" In *Spiritually Oriented Psychotherapy* eds. Len Sperry and Edward Shafranske (Washington: American Psychological Association,

2005), 51–73 https://doi.org/10.1037/10886-003.

24 Bill Wilson. *The Big Book.* (New York City: Alcoholics Anonymous World Services, Inc., 1934), p. 570.

25 Lisa Miller, *The Awakened Brain: The New Science of Spirituality and our Quest for an Inspired Life.* (New York: Random House, 2021), 60.

26 *Ibid.* 61.

27 *Ibid.* 61-62.

28 *Ibid* 76.

29 *Ibid.* 92.

30 The Holy Bible, King James Version, *Philippians,* 4, v. 7 (Tennessee: Thomas Nelson Publishers, 1989).

31 Lisa Miller, *The Awakened Brain: The New Science of Spirituality and our Quest for an Inspired Life.* (New York: Random House, 2021) 62.

Chapter Four: Know Your Brain, Know Your Mind

32 Daniel Amen, in person communication, November 9, 2019.

33 Nora Volkow, *Drugs, Brains, and Behavior: The Science of Addiction.* (Bethesda: National Institute on Drug Abuse, 2020), 2. https://nida.nih.gov/publications/drugs-brains-behavior-science-addiction/preface

34 Rick Hanson, *Buddha's Brain: The Practical Neuroscience of Happiness, Love & Wisdom* (Oakland: New Harbinger Publications, Inc., 2009), 11.

35 Judith Grisel, *Never Enough: The Neuroscience and Experience of Addiction.* New York: Doubleday 2019), 30.

36 *Ibid*, 31.

37 Nora Volkow, *Drugs, Brains, and Behavior: The Science of Addiction*. (Bethesda: National Institute on Drug Abuse, 2020), 22. https://nida.nih.gov/publications/drugs-brains-behavior-science-addiction/treatment-recovery

38 Recovery Research Institute. https://www.recoveryanswers.org/recovery-101/brain-in-recovery/

39 Patrice Voss, Maryse Thomas, Miguel Cisneros-Franco, and Etienne de Villers-Sidani, "Dynamic Brains and the Changing Rules of Neuroplasticity: Implications for Learning and Recovery," *Frontiers of Psychology*, 8 (2017): 1657.

40 Rick Hanson, *Buddha's Brain: The Practical Neuroscience of Happiness, Love & Wisdom* (Oakland: New Harbinger Publications, Inc., 2009), 28.

41 Gabor Mate, *In the Realm of Hungry Ghosts: Close Encounters with Addiction*. (Berkeley, CA: North Atlantic Books, 2010), 363.

42 C. Edward Richards, "Complementarities in Physics and Psychology" in Oxford Handbook of Psychology, Lisa Miller, ed. (Oxford: Oxford University Press, 2012), 72.

43 Maria Mavrikaki, "Brain Plasticity in Drug Addiction: Burden and Benefit," Harvard Health Blog, last modified June 26, 2020, https://www.health.harvard.edu/blog/brain-plasticity-in-drug-addiction-burden-and-benefit-2020062620479

44 Kenneth Kendler, Charles Gardner, and Carol Prescott, "Religion, psychopathology, and substance use and abuse; a multimeasure, genetic-epidemiologic study," *American Journal of Psychiatry*, 154, no. 3 (March, 1997): 322-9.

45 *Ibid*, 326.

46 Miller, L. (2021). The Awakened Brain: The new science of spirituality and our quest for an inspired life. (New York: Random House, 2021), 58.

47 Mario Beauregard and Denyse O'Leary, *The Spiritual Brain: A Neuroscientist's Case for the Existence of the Soul* (New York: Harper Collins, 2008), 292.

Chapter Five: The Grounding of Spiritual Practice

48 Bill Wilson, *The Big Book*. (New York City: Alcoholics Anonymous World Services, Inc., 1934), 83.

49 Jon Kabat-Zinn, *Wherever You Go, There You Are*, (New York: Hyperion Press, 1994), 8.

50 Rabbi Mark Borovitz, *Finding Recovery and Yourself in Torah*, (Woodstock: Jewish Lights, 2016), xiii.

51 *Ibid, xiii.*

52 Gabor Mate, *In the Realm of Hungry Ghosts: Close Encounters with Addiction.* (Berkeley: North Atlantic Books, 2010), 36.

53 Bruce Perry and Oprah Winfrey, *What Happened to You? Conversations on Trauma, Resilience, and Healing.* (New York: Flatiron Books, 2021).

54 Dwight Goddard, ed., *A Buddhist Bible* (Boston: Beacon Press, 1938), 23.

55 *Ibid, 33.*

56 Donna Farhi, *Yoga Mind, Body & Spirit: A Return to Wholeness*, (New York: St. Martin's Press, 2000), 8-12.

57 *Ibid, 12-15.*

58 New Jewish Publication Society of America, *The 10 Commandments*, last modified 2024, https://the10commandments.info/version/tanakh-new-jps-1985/

59 Lesley Brown, ed., *The New Shorter Oxford English Dictionary* (London: Clarendon Press, 1993), 52.

60 "Saint Francis de Sales", Goodreads, last modified 2023, https://www.goodreads.com/quotes

61 Jon Kabat-Zinn, *Wherever You Go, There You Are: Mindfulness Meditation in Everyday Life*, (New York: Hyperion, 1994), 22.

62 Abrams, Douglas. (2016). *The Book of Joy: His Holiness the Dalai Lama and Archbishop Desmond Tutu: Lasting Happiness in a Changing World*, (New York: Avery Press, 2016), 199.

63 Sakyong Mipham, personal communication, Drala Mountain Center, Red Feather Lakes, Colorado, 2007.

64 *Ibid.*

65 Tommy Rosen, *Recovery 2.0: Move Beyond Addiction and Upgrade Your Life*, (Carlsbad: Hay House, 2014), 260.

66 Shunryu Suzuki Roshi, *Zen Mind, Beginners Mind: Informal Talks on Zen Meditation and Practice*, (Boulder: Shambhala, 2011), 1.

Chapter Seven: Breath is Your Life (Pranayama)

67 Sri Swami Satchidananda, *The Yoga Sutras of Patanjali*, (Yogaville: Integral Yoga Publications, 1978), 149.

68 "Lungs", Wikipedia, last modified on 25 March 2023, https://en.wikipedia.org/wiki/Lung

69 Tatsiana Matusevich, Lung Diagram, https://www.istockphoto.com/vector/lungs-anatomy-medical-educational-diagram-isolated-gm1849775350-551857626

70 Nestor, James, *Breath: The New Science of a Lost Art*, (New York: Penguin Random House, 2020), 56.

71 Swami Saradananda, *The Power of Breath: Yoga Breathing for Inner Balance, Health and Harmony*, (London: Watkins Media, 2009), 14.

72 Grace Bullock, "What focusing on your breath does to your brain" Greater Good Magazine, University of California, Berkeley, October 31, 2019, https://greatergood.berkeley.edu/article/item/what_focusing_on_the_breath_does_to_your_brain

73 Jose Herrero, Simon Khuvis, Erin Yeagle, Moran Cerft, and Ashesh Mehta, "Breathing above the brain stem: volitional control and attentional modulation in humans," *Journal of Neurophysiology*, 119, no. 1, (Winter 2018): 145-159.

74 Thich Nhat Hanh, *Peace is Every Step*, (Berkeley: Parallax Press, 1991), 8.

75 Rinku Garg, Varun Malhotra, Yogesh Tripathi, and Ritu Agarwal, "Effect of Left, Right and Alternate Nostril Breathing on Verbal and Spatial Memory," *Journal of Clinical and Diagnostic Research*, 10, no. 2 (February 2016): CC01-CC03 doi: 10.7860/JCDR/2016/12361.7197

76 Mike Perotta. "Controlling Your Mind by Controlling Your Breath," *Medium*, June 10, 2020, https://medium.com/swlh/neuroscience-of-breath-63c32604be22

77 *Ibid*

78 Scott Frothingham, "Benefits of Ujjayi Breathing and How to Do It," *Healthline*, December 17, 2019, https://www.healthline.com/health/fitness-exercise/ujjayi-breathing#benefits

79 *Ibid*

80 "Ujjayi Breath—Blessing or Curse?," Himalayan Institute, 2022 https://www.himalayanyogainstitute.com/ujjayi-breath-blessing-curse/

81 Warner, Dylan, *The Illuminated Breath: Transform Your Physical, Cognitive and Emotional Well-Being by Harnessing the Science of Ancient Yoga Breath Practices,* (Las Vegas: Victory Belt Publications, 2021), 148.

82 Dhaniwala, Naresh, "Pranayama and Breathing Exercises—Types and Its Role in Disease Prevention & Rehabilitation," *Journal of Evolution of Medical and Dental Sciences*, 9, no 44 (2020): 3325-3331

83 Swami Saradananda, *The Power of Breath: Yoga Breathing for Inner Balance, Health and Harmony*. (London: Watkins Media, 2009), 76-77.

84 *Ibid.*

85 Kia Miller, "Ego Eradicator, Breath of Fire Part 2" YouTube, 2019, https://www.youtube.com/watch?v=oFFZ1XzdVoA

Chapter Eight: Meditation, Mindfulness & Contemplation

86 Anuradha Baminiwatta, and Indrajith Solangaarachchi, "Trends and Developments in Mindfulness Research of 55 Years: Bibliometric Analysis of Publications Indexed in Web of Science," *Mindfulness*, 12, no. 2, (Spring 202): DOI:10.1007/s12671-021-01681-x https://www.researchgate.net/figure/Number-of-articles-relative-to-meditation-published-by-year_fig1_303595426

87 *Ibid*

88 Sandra Anderson, "Contemplation vs. Meditation: Defining the Difference," *Yoga International*, http://www.yogainternational.com/contemplation-vs-meditation-defining-the-difference/

89 Colombiere, Sister Mary, "Meditation and Contemplation: What is the Difference," The Carmelite Sisters of the Most Sacred Heart of Los Angeles. (n.d.) https://carmelitesistersocd.com/2013/meditation-contemplation/

90 Loizzo, Joe, *Sustainable Happiness: The Mind Science of Well-Bing, Altruism, and Inspiration*, (New York: Routledge, 2012), 38.

91 Virginia Heffernan, "The Muddied Meaning of 'Mindfulness." *New York Times Magazine*, (April 14, 2015), https://www.nytimes.com/2015/04/19/magazine/the-muddied-meaning-of-mindfulness.html

92 Jon Kabat-Zinn, *Wherever You Go, There You Are: Mindfulness Meditation in Everyday Life*, (New York: Hyperion, 1994), 4.

93 *Ibid* p.11

94 Virginia Heffernan, "The Muddied Meaning of 'Mindfulness." *New York Times Magazine*, (April 14, 2015), https://www.nytimes.com/2015/04/19/magazine/the-muddied-meaning-of-mindfulness.html

95 Andrew Newburg, and Mark Waldman, *How Enlightenment Changes Your Brain: The New Science of Transformation*, (New York: Avery Press, 2016), 190.

96 Daniel Siegel, *Mind: A Journey to the Heart of Being Human*, (New York: W.W. Norton & Co., 2017), 223.

97 *Ibid.*

98 Elizabeth Dunn, and Sara Konrath, "Dealing with Digital Distraction." *American Psychological Association*, Last updated: April 20, 2022. https://www.apa.org/news/press/releases/2018/08/digital-distraction

99 Gabor Mate, *The Myth of Normal: Trauma, Illness and Healing in a Toxic Culture*, (New York: Avery, 2022), 32.

100 Christina Gregory, "Internet addiction disorder: Signs, symptoms, diagnosis, and treatments for those who may be addicted to the web on their PC or smart phone," *PsyCom*, (2018, May 15), https://www.psycom.net/iadcriteria.html.

101 Andrew Newburg, Mark Waldman, *How Enlightenment Changes Your Brain: The New Science of Transformation*, (New York: Avery Press, 2016), 190.

102 Donald Hebb, 1949, originally coined this phrase in reference to how gratitude reinforces positive behavior. https://en.wikipedia.org/wiki/Donald_O._Hebb

103 Salam Islam. "Forty: What is the Significance of Number Forty in Islam?," February 10, 2021, Retrieved from: https://salamislam.com/articles/lifestyle/what-significance-number-forty-islam

104 Catherine Norris, Daniel Creem, Reuben Handler, and Hedy Kober, "Brief Mindfulness Meditation Improves Attention in Novices: Evidence from ERPs and Moderation by Neuroticism," *Frontiers in Human Neuroscience*, 12, no. 315 (August 06, 2018): https://doi.org/10.3389/fnhum.2018.00315

105 Goleman, Daniel, and Richard Davidson, *Altered Traits: Science Reveals How Meditation Changes Your Mind, Brain, and Body,* (New York: Avery, 2017), 275.

106 *Ibid.* p. 250-251

107 Soren Kierkegaard, *Upbuilding Discourses in Various Spirits*, Retrieved from: https://www.sorenkierkegaard.nl/quote-attribution/

Chapter Nine: Prayer & Mantra

Prayer

108 Bill Wilson, *The Big Book*, (New York: Alcoholics Anonymous World Services, 1939), 59.

109 *Ibid*, 87.

110 The Holy Bible, King James Version, I Thessalonians. 5:17 (Tennessee: Thomas Nelson Publishers, 1989), 990.

111 Lucy Maud Montgomery, *Anne of Green Gables,* (e-artnow, 2016), 46. https://www.e-artnow.org/ebooks/

112 For a collection of prayers, refer to Appendix Two: Prayers.

113 Wikipedia. "Serenity Prayer." Last modified November 8, 2023. https://en.wikipedia.org/wiki/Serenity_Prayer

114 Andrew Newburg, and Mark Waldman, *How God Changes Your Brain: Breakthrough findings from a leading neuroscientist*, (New York: Ballantine Books, 2009), 149-150.

115 Bill Wilson, *The Big Book*, (New York: Alcoholics Anonymous World Services, 1939), 63.

116 *Ibid*, 76.

117 James Whitcomb Riley, "Thanksgiving." https://poets.org/poem/thanksgiving-2

118 Joanna Fuchs, "May You Be Well." https://www.poemsource.com/about-us.html

119 Yongey Mingyur Rinpoche, *The Joy of Living: Unlocking the Secret & Science of Happiness*, (New York: Harmony Books, 2007), 252.

120 Lakota Sioux Chief Yellow Lark, "Great Spirit Prayer," Jesuit Resource Organization, (n.d.) https://www.xavier.edu/jesuitresource/online-resources/prayer-index/native-american

121 A Ute Prayer, (n.d.) https://www.sapphyr.net/natam/quotes-nativeamerican.htm

122 Lisa Miller, *The Awakened Brain: The New Science of Spirituality and our Quest for an Inspired Life*, (New York: Random House, 2021), 176.

123 *Ibid* p. 185

124 Mario Beauregard, and Denyse O'Leary, *The Spiritual Brain: A Neuroscientist's Case for the Existence of the Soul*, (New York: Harper One, 2007), 291.

125   Lisa Miller, *The Awakened Brain: The New Science of Spirituality and our Quest for an Inspired Life*, (New York: Random House, 2021), 99.

126   Larry Dossey, M.D. *Healing Words: The Power of Prayer and the Practice of Medicine*, (New York: Harper One, 1993), 6.

127   Mother Teresa, *The Joy in Loving*, (New York: Viking, 1996), 218.

Mantra

128   Easwaran, Eknath, *The Mantram Handbook: A Practical Guide to Choosing your Mantram and Calming your Mind*, (Tomales: Nilgiri Press, 1977), 12.

129   *Ibid, 12.*

130   Deepak Chopra. "What is a Mantra?" Last modified January 14, 2021. https://chopra.com/articles/what-is-a-mantra

131   Georg Feuerstein. "Overcoming Spiritual Darkness: The Practice of Japa." Yoga International Last modified November 2003, https://yogainternational.com/article/view/overcoming-spiritual-darkness-the-practice-of-japa/

132   Jocelyn García-Sesnich, Mauricio Flores, Marcela Ríos, and Jorge Aravena, "Longitudinal and Immediate Effect of Kundalini Yoga on Salivary Levels of Cortisol and Activity of Alpha-Amylase and Its Effect on Perceived Stress," *International Journal of Yoga*, 10, no. 2 (May—August. 2017): 73-80. https://pubmed.ncbi.nlm.nih.gov/28546677/

133   James Hartzell, "A Neuroscientist Explores the 'Sanskrit' Effect," *Scientific American*, (January 2, 2018), https://blogs.scientificamerican.com/observations/a-neuroscientist-explores-the-sanskrit-effect/

134   Junling Gao, Stavros Skouras, Hang Leung, Bonnie Wu, Huijun Wu, Chunqi Change, and Hin Sik, "Repetitive Religious Chanting

Invokes Positive Emotional Schema to Counterbalance Fear: A Multi-Modal Functional and Structural MRI Study," *Frontiers of Behavioral Neuroscience*, 14 (November 24, 2020), https://www.frontiersin.org/articles/10.3389/fnbeh.2020.548856/full

Chapter Ten: Body Recovery

135 Feldenkrais Method. (n.d.) https://feldenkrais.com/about-the-feldenkrais-method/

136 Moshe Feldenkrais(n.d.) https://feldenkrais.com/about-moshe-feldenkrais/

137 Gabor Mate, *The Myth of Normal: Trauma, Illness & Healing in a Toxic Culture*, (New York: Avery Books, 2022), 66.

138 Aseem Jain. Beej Mantra for Surya Namaskar (n.d.) https://premaseem.wordpress.com/2011/08/31/beej-mantra-for-surya-namaskar/

139 Ine Hogstad, "Finding Layers in the Gaga Movement Language", Nordic Master's Thesis, Norwegian University of Science and Technology, Faculty of Humanities, Department of Music, Dance studies, Autumn 2015.

140 Ohad Naharin. Personal communication. Orsolina 28, Italy. October 2023.

141 Life Events. https://www.lifeevents.org/blog/2018/8/21/five-tibetan-rites

142 David Berceli, Melanie Salmon, Robin Bonifas, and Nkem Ndefo, "Effects of Self-induced Unclassified Therapeutic Tremors on Quality of Life among Non-professional Caregivers: A Pilot Study," *Global Advances in Health Medicine* 3, no. 5, (September 2014): 45-48 doi: 10.7453/gahmj.2014.032

143 Deva Premal, and Miten, "Shaking Meditation," Deva

Premal and Miten Channel, https://www.youtube.com/watch?v=iMKuCOWcums

144 "Oxytocin," Wikipedia https://en.wikipedia.org/wiki/Oxytocin

145 *Ibid*, 415.

146 Miller, Lisa, *The Awakened Brain: The New Science of Spirituality and our Quest for an Inspired Life*, (New York: Random House, 2021), 242.

APPENDIX 2: Mantras and their Translations

147 Om Asatoma Sad Gamaya, "YouTube," https://www.youtube.com/watch?v=LvsWXdunOqs

148 Snatam Kaur, "Prem" Found on: https://www.youtube.com/watch?v=9WhoWDtBJrw

149 Aad Such, "3HO" https://www.3ho.org/meditation/masters-touch-meditation/

150 Deva Premal "Moola Mantra Prayer," https://www.youtube.com/watch?v=duY7QvySsUY

151 Snatam Kaur, "Grace," Long Time Sun lyrics © Songtrust Ave, Warner Chappell Music, Inc., https://genius.com/Snatam-kaur-long-time-sun-lyrics

152 Humee Hum, "3HO", https://www.3ho.org/mantra/humee-hum-brahm-hum/

153 "Har Meditation Practice, "3HO," https://www.3ho.org/meditation/har-meditation-for-prosperity/ Thomas Barquee, https://open.spotify.com/track/6V7BpOT2tTxeoCD73Bccb6

154 Saraswati, "YouTube," https://www.youtube.com/watch?v=DOPXmLc0fcs

155 Green Tara Mantra, "YouTube," https://www.youtube.com/watch?v=eBopONbgNpQ

156 Ra Ma Da Sa, "YouTube," https://www.youtube.com/watch?v=VzlZC1n9Qjc

157 Peace Mantra, "YouTube" https://www.youtube.com/watch?v=6XP-f7wPM0A

158 Heart Sutra Mantra, "YouTube," https://www.youtube.com/watch?v=GzCn0gwJw68

159 Adi Shakti, "YouTube," https://www.youtube.com/watch?v=s-xSEkeUou8

160 Om Namo, "YouTube," https://www.youtube.com/watch?v=s-xSEkeUou8

161 So Hum, "YouTube," https://www.youtube.com/watch?v=S0j4yTY_eGI

162 Sa Ta Na Ma, "You Tube," Nirinjan Kaur, https://www.youtube.com/watch?v=S0j4yTY_eGI

163 Maha Mrityunjaya Mantra, Rigved 7.59.12 https://resanskrit.com/blogs/blog-post/maha-mrityunjaya-mantra-in-sanskrit-with-meaning

164 Medicine Buddha Mantra, Found on: https://www.thinkrightme.com/the-meaning-of-tayata-om-mantra-and-its-benefits/

165 Snatam Kaur, *Meditation of the Soul: Jap Ji Daily Practice and Learning Tool*, (Purceville: Spirit Voyage, 2015).

166 *Ibid.*

167 Dance of Ganesha, "You Tube", Ajeet Kaur, https://www.youtube.com/watch?v=M033WB6T9pE

APPENDIX 3: Prayers

168 The Lord's Prayer, *The Church of England*, https://www.churchofengland.org/our-faith/what-we-believe/lords-prayer

169   The Lord's Prayer in Aramaic. *The Living Hour Podcast,* https://livinghour.org/lords-prayer/in-aramaic/

170   St. Francis of Assisi, *Prayer for Peace,* The Cathedral of Saint Thomas More, https://www.cathedralstm.org/about-our-catholic-faith/expressing-our-faith/treasury-catholic-prayers/prayer-st-francis-assisi-prayer-peace/

171   Tommy Rosen, *"Universal Prayer,"* Recovery 2.0, n.d. https://r20.com/

172   St. Theresa, Sisters of the Divine Savior, https://www.sistersofthedivinesavior.org/pray_archive/st-theresas-prayer/

173   Miguel Ruiz. *The Four Agreements: A Practical Guide to Personal Freedom.* San Rafael: Amber-Allen Publishing, 1997.

174   Sioux American Indian Prayer, World Prayers Organization, https://www.worldprayers.org/archive/prayers/invocations/o_our_father_the_sky.html

175   Ira Byock, *The Four Things That Matter Most,*(New York: Simon and Shuster,2014). https://irabyock.org/books/the-four-things-that-matter-most/

176   Paramahansa Yogananda, *Metaphysical Meditations,* (Los Angeles: Self Realization Fellowship, 1964), 5.

177   Ibid, p. 25

178   Lalla, World Prayers Organization, https://www.worldprayers.org/archive/prayers/meditations/flowers_sesame-seed_bowls.html

179   Chaim Stern, ed., *Gates of Prayer: The New Union Prayerbook for Weekdays, Sabbaths and Festivals,* (Chicago: CCAR Press, 1975), 651. https://www.thehebrewcafe.com/forum/showthread.php?tid=427

180   Prayer before meals, https://www.myjewishlearning.com/article/blessings-for-food-drink/

181 Marianne Williamson. *Illuminata: A Return to Prayer.* New York: Riverhead Books, 1994. P. 79.

182 Alcoholics Anonymous. *The Big Book.* New York: Alcoholics Anonymous World Services, 1976.

183 Native American Wisdom Quotes, "Pearls of Wisdom," https://www.sapphyr.net/natam/quotes-nativeamerican.htm

184 Lila Fahlman, *The Passing of Time,* found on: https://www.worldprayers.org/archive/prayers/celebrations/by_the_passing_of_time.html

www.ingramcontent.com/pod-product-compliance
Lightning Source LLC
LaVergne TN
LVHW041752060526
838201LV00046B/980